This book is dedicated to my wife Donna,
without whose patience, support, and encouragement
it would not have been possible.

COMPUTERS IN THE CLASSROOM . . . WHAT SHALL I DO?

GARLAND REFERENCE LIBRARY
OF SOCIAL SCIENCE
(VOL. 359)

COMPUTERS IN THE
CLASSROOM . . .
WHAT SHALL I DO?
A Guide

Walter Burke

GARLAND PUBLISHING, INC. • NEW YORK & LONDON
1986

Library of Congress Cataloging-in-Publication Data

Burke, Walter J.
 Computers in the classroom—what shall I do?

 (Garland reference library of social science;
vol. 359)
 Includes index.
 1. Computer-assisted instruction. 2. Microcomputers—
Purchasing. 3. Computer literacy. I. Title.
II. Series: Garland reference library of social
science; v. 359.
LB1028.5.B8733 1986   371.3'9445   86-4653
ISBN 0-8240-8921-9 (alk. paper)

Cover design by Renata Gomes

Printed on acid-free, 250-year-life paper
Manufactured in the United States of America

CONTENTS

ILLUSTRATIONS

FOREWORD

There are a number of books that have been written that offer rigorous analyses of the philosophical and psychological implications of using the computer with young children. There are many catalogues and reference books that provide descriptions and analyses of educational hardware and software. There are formidable amounts of volumes available describing in great detail how a computer functions.

This book combines all of these features in a manner that a newcomer to the computer field can easily comprehend. Given these diverse topics, organizing material into a comprehensive volume that has continuity was a challenge. I hope that readers will find that the content makes for interesting and informative reading. More important, I hope that this book will not be relegated to a shelf on a bookcase, but that it will be used as a tool to help teachers make informed decisions about how the computer can be most efficiently used to further and broaden the learning experiences provided for young children.

W.J. Burke

PREFACE

The impact that computers are having and will have on the education of present and future children is an all-encompassing subject that would require several volumes to do it justice. I chose to focus my attention on how computers can be used with young children from kindergarten through sixth grade because elementary, junior high, and high school classes have quite different sets of academic goals, approaches to learning, and interests based on student needs. Computers have begun to filter down into elementary schools in significant numbers in recent years. I have addressed issues and concerns that the elementary teacher may have regarding how to use the computer to the best educational advantage, and, more important, its impact on children.

Throughout the text I have presented ideas and technical details in a straightforward manner that the novice computer user will find interesting to read and easy to comprehend. Technical jargon and computerese have been kept to a minimum, although some discussions require the use of computer specific language to preserve accuracy. The glossary is provided to help the newcomer to the computer field with technical usage.

The initial chapters of this book show the reader how the computer can be used with young children, avoiding a "computer hype" style of presentation. In most cases it is a balanced presentation that reflects a middle-of-the-road approach to computers in education. The underlying philosophy of this text centers on the fact that the computer does not provide all the answers to questions we have about education, rather it is another tool to be used by teachers to enhance classroom learning.

There are also several chapters that will help both teachers and administrators evaluate the hardware and software products that are available today. Making decisions about what to purchase is not an easy one given the variety and complexity of computer products in the marketplace. The products described in these chapters are among the best that have been produced; there are others equally good that have not been described.

The chapter outlining how the computer can be used with children having special needs reflects the current state-of-the-art applications of computer technology. New materials are continuously being developed to help children with physical and psychological handicaps experience the world in new and exciting ways.

The purpose of this book is to provide present and future classroom teachers with information and ideas that will help them make well-informed decisions about how computers can be used with young children. Only by learning to use the computer in thoughtfully creative and educationally sound ways can teachers help young children maximize their learning. It is my hope this book will help make the task easier.

ACKNOWLEDGMENTS

There were many individuals, businesses, and schools that offered help and assistance in the research necessary to compile and integrate the information and ideas that have been presented. Agencies and institutions include public and private college libraries as well as personnel employed by stores selling computer hardware and software. These people and institutions are too numerous to mention.

There are some people and agencies who offered extraordinary help in allowing me to conduct the research for this book in an efficient manner and aided in the technical preparation of the manuscript. The staff of the Wheelock College library was of invaluable assistance in helping me identify source materials. Debra Sherman, a student at Wheelock College, provided significant assistance in researching articles and printing draft and manuscript copies using a computer printer.

My family was most supportive, offering encouragement and tolerating a house of papers, journal articles, and computer disks during the fifteen months I was working on this book.

I would also like to express my appreciation to the technical staff of Garland Publishing, Inc., whose efforts made this book possible. In particular, I would like to thank Marie Ellen Larcada, my editor, who answered countless questions and supervised the proofreading of the manuscript.

INTRODUCTION

Since 1980 the microcomputer industry has made home computers available to the public at prices which the average consumer can afford. Software producers have developed computer programs that have a variety of practical and educational applications. Programs are available that can help the user organize personal information ranging from keeping financial records for tax purposes to systematizing recipe files to preparing mailing lists for holidays and special occasions.

There are also programs to help your child achieve better grades at school and prepare for the SAT examinations that are given before admission to a college or university. Programs dealing with reading readiness, introduction to concepts in mathematics, and word processing are seen as vital tools by many parents and teachers.

The microcomputer and minicomputer have had a direct impact on the business community and in administrative offices in virtually all professional fields. Consumers and people in the computer industry have identified many applications, but the full impact of the computer has yet to be realized.

The children of the 1980's are growing up in this computer age. A five or six year old thinks that playing a home computer game such as those produced by Activision, Atari, Colecovision, or Intellevision is nothing mystifying. These are seen as simply another form of entertainment. Sound, motion, and color graphics are expected components of computer games. Adults are usually more impressed and in awe of these activities than are children. The days of the traditional pinball machine are gone. Now we are in the age of Mousetrap, Q-Bert, and Ms Pac Man.

These new technologies have raised serious questions for parents and teachers. We are still trying to articulate the role that the computer will play in this and in future societies, let alone the place it will have in our educational system. For the computer will have a place in elementary classrooms; the most diehard skeptics will reluctantly admit that. The question is, what will its role be?

During the past twenty-five years the computer has infiltrated its way into our everyday lives to a great extent, perhaps without our knowledge. It might be better to say that teachers and parents knew about it, but never had to directly address philosophical and educational issues related to its uses. The reason for this is quite simple. Initially computers were used only by service agencies and businesses, such as the telephone companies, banks, dating services, the Internal Revenue Service, and many automotive repair centers. It seemed that the computer did not have a direct effect on our lives, or at least we were not constantly aware of its impact. Today the situation has completely changed. Because of computer awareness and availability for people and institutions at all levels of our society, we must carefully examine this product of the technological revolution.

Today's teachers face a difficult challenge. Computers have been and will continue to be increasingly available for use in classrooms. Most teachers are not familiar with these machines and the many peripheral devices available for them. Classroom teachers are in the process of learning to use computer software, but lack the experience and expertise to evaluate a program disk in terms of its educational effectiveness and validity.

This book treats issues related to choosing a computer system and defining criteria to be used when purchasing computer software. Attention is also given to the advantages/drawbacks to learning a computer language and teaching it to children.

This book does not provide all the answers. It is my hope that this book will help teachers become more familiar with computers so that they will be able to make sound decisions on how they can be used most effectively with our children.

W.J. Burke

Computers in the
Classroom . . .
What Shall I Do?

CHAPTER ONE

HISTORY OF THE MODERN COMPUTER

Tracing the development of the computer as it
relates to education seems a simple task.
Developments that led to the evolution of the modern
electronic computer are rooted deep in history. The
fundamental question is when to begin. We can
legitimately start with the calculating device
called the abacus developed by the Chinese five or
six thousand years ago that is still used today.
Work done by Blaise Pascal during the
mid-seventeenth century that led to the development
of the first mechanical adding machine was a step
forward in the evolution of technology that led to
the formulation of the computer as we know it today.
Before the advent of electronic calculators in
the mid-1960's, mechanical calculators still used
the basic counting wheel designed by Pascal
centuries earlier. These devices played an important
role in the teaching and application of mathematics
and served many practical functions in science,
business, and industry.
In 1671 Baron Gottfried Wilhelm von Leibnitz
designed a digital machine that improved on the
mechanical calculator developed by Pascal. His
device could perform the mathematical functions of
addition, subtraction, multiplication, and division.
By the late eighteenth century the Earl of Stanhope
used the ideas of von Leibnitz to design and
construct a desk calculator. These devices laid much
of the groundwork for our modern computer, but did
not directly affect teaching and education in our
schools.
In 1790 a very significant development occurred
when Joseph Marie Jacquard used a series of punched
cards to create specific patterns in fabrics woven
on a loom. By 1820 Charles Babbage had incorporated

3

the use of punched cards into what might be called the first computer. He had developed a mechanical device powered by a steam engine that could perform calculations.

By 1890 Herman Hollerith had created the first tabulating device that was used on a large scale. His electrical machine used punched cards and was chosen to tabulate the data for the 1890 United States census. Using this tool the entire census was tabulated in one month as compared to the hand tabulated 1880 census which took seven years to complete.

These are some of the devices that played an important role in the development of the modern computer. In each case a machine was sought to perform repetitive or complex operations such as counting and sorting. It completed these tasks much more quickly and accurately than could be done by hand.

By the 1930's there were a multitude of mechanical accounting machines in use throughout the country. Technological developments continued and by 1944 Howard Aiken had developed the first automatic calculating machine called the Mark I. This calculator used electromagnetic relays and mechanical counters instead of the mechanical gears used in all earlier machines. Initially the use of electromagnetic relays posed a serious problem as a new method had to be devised to represent data. The mechanical gears currently in use could be set to represent place value positions for numbers, while electric current used in relays cannot, as it can only be set in an "on" or "off" position. This problem was resolved by the invention of machine language, a binary code reflecting the "on" or "off" conditions of electric current. Machine language provides the set of instructions by which all computers operate today.

The Mark I and Mark II computers developed by Aiken could perform about five addition operations in one second. By 1946 John W. Mauchly and Preper Eckert had invented a machine that could perform 5000 addition operations in one second. This device was called the Electronic Numerical Integrator And Computer or simply ENIAC.

The final steps leading toward the development of the modern computer were conceptualized by John von Neumann during the late 1940's. He envisioned

the computer as having three essential components.
An arithmetic logic section is needed so the machine
can perform mathematical operations. A control
component must be provided so the machine can
regulate instructions given to it in the order in
which they will be processed. The computer requires
a memory capability in order to store information,
receive input from the user, and generate output.

The first operational computer that utilized
the three computer components described by von
Neumann appeared in 1952 and was called the
Electronic Discrete Variable Automatic Computer or
EDVAC. These components are embodied in every
computer that is produced today.

Computers produced between 1946 and 1959 are
frequently called the First Generation of Computers.
The internal operations within these machines were
carried out through the use of vacuum tubes. For
example, the UNIAC computer contained more than
18,000 vacuum tubes. Input was given to these
machines by punched cards that were programmed in
symbolic machine code.

Uses of these machines in higher education was
limited to large institutions, while applications
for secondary and elementary education were
nonexistent. These computers were costly, required a
great deal of technical expertise to operate and
maintain, and, most important, applications for
school curricula had not been defined.

By 1960 the large, bulky computer had begun to
be replaced by smaller more efficient machines. This
was chiefly attributable to the invention of the
transitor which replaced many of the slower working
vacuum tubes. Computers produced between 1959 and
1964 are frequently termed Second Generation
Computers.

To communicate with these early computers one
had to provide instructions in a format which the
machine understood. These instructions defining the
way in which the computer processes information were
and still are given in what is called machine code.
Programs written in machine language require skilled
programmers familiar with technical codes that bear
little if any resemblance to spoken language. What
was needed was a more human oriented format by which
computers could be programmed, thus letting less
technically knowledgeable people program them for
scientific, industrial, and business applications.

By the early 1960's there were many computer languages in common use, many designed with specific applications in mind. For example, COBOL, meaning "Common Business Oriented Language," was designed to efficiently handle data input, analysis, and output required for business applications. FORTRAN, meaning "FORmula TRANslation," was developed in 1957 as a language to express mathematical terms. By 1960 there were about 200 computer languages that had been developed by industry, business, and universities to meet specific needs.

In 1965 the integrated circuit printed on a silicon chip became available to the computer industry. Computers having printed circuit elements were soon called Third Generation Computers. These machines were more reliable than their predecessors, operated much more quickly, were smaller in size, and were far less expensive. At this time computers were used extensively in college and universities with virtually no use apparent in secondary and elementary schools. Most educational uses centered on mathematics and applied sciences such as physics, astronomy, and engineering.

At this time several problems surfaced relating to how these large computers were being used. Work had to be submitted in batch lots in the form of stacks of punched cards. As the computer workload increased there were frequently many sets of data waiting their turn to be entered by the operator. Often users had to wait hours or days before their job was completed if there was a large backlog of work to do. This was not a cost or time efficient way to input information.

These third generation computers operated so quickly that one user could enter information while the computer was internally processing information given by an earlier user and outputting results from a third set of data entries. Computers were frequently idle waiting for user input. This problem was solved by using minicomputers as the means for data entry. These smaller, less expensive machines were electrically connected to the main computer. This concept proved to be time and cost efficient and is still used today.

Many small institutions, agencies, and businesses realized that the minicomputer offered them a realistic way to avail themselves of this new technology. Today the demand is still high for these smaller computers that can efficiently perform most operations associated with larger machines.

Colleges and universities faced a unique problem as faculty soon found that they and their students were not able to get sufficient computer time to meet their needs. The backlog of work was still too great even when using minicomputers as input devices.

Dr. John Kemeny and Dr. Thomas Kurtz, with the assistance of undergraduate students, solved this problem by developing the time-sharing system for computer use. Their system made use of typewriter-like devices for input to the main computer, as well as for output to the user. Many such devices could be connected to the computer simultaneously, thus giving computer access to many users at virtually the same time. Even though the computer can only process one set of data at a time, its speed of operation is so fast that each user has almost immediate access to the machine.

This scheme is in use today in academic settings as well as in the business and industrial community. In some cases a deckwriter, an updated version of the typewriter-like device used by Kemeny and Kurtz, is used. More commonly we find computer input substations consisting of a monitor screen and a computer keyboard connected to the main computer. These substations are not computers, but are electrically connected to the computer which may be miles away.

A second problem identified and resolved by Kemeny and Kurtz stemmed from the fact that up to this time writing programs in computer languages was very difficult and cumbersome for the beginner. Their solution to this problem was to devise a computer language that was easier to use and to learn. They called this language BASIC, meaning "Beginners All-purpose Symbolic Instruction Code."

In 1969 computer hardware manufacturers began to sell individual computer programs and not include them as part of the package purchased when one bought a computer. This led directly to the birth of the computer software industry that has experienced tremendous growth in the past sixteen years.

With the advent of BASIC and the development of a wide range of computer software programs, the scene was set for large scale use of the computer as

an educational tool in secondary and elementary
schools. Cost still presented a major stumbling
block, as both large computers and minicomputers
were still beyond the financial reach of most school
systems.

Technological developments that included more
circuitry on a single silicon chip are the first
step in the resolution of this problem. By 1972 this
technique, called Large Scale Integration or LSI,
was perfected. Computers were now manufactured that
were smaller in size but able to perform more
complex functions at a fantastic rate of speed.

In 1971 Dr. Ted Hoff developed a single chip
that could perform all the logic and arithmetic
functions associated with currently available
electronic calculators. Hoff had effectively
invented a central processing unit almost equivalent
in capability to those of the large computers used
25 years earlier. This device was named the microprocessor.

The direct impact of LSI and the microprocessor
can be seen in every facet of today's technology.
They perform the logic functions for countless
devices, such as electronic calculators, video
games, vending machines, digital watches, and sewing
machines. From our point of view the most important
use of the microprocessor was its application to the
development of the microcomputer.

Because of the impact that LSI and the microprocessor have had on the computer industry, many
historians refer to 1972 as the beginning of the
Fourth Generation of Computers. For the first time
inexpensive, efficient computers were accessible to
elementary and secondary schools on a large scale.

By 1977 there were several types of microcomputers on the market. Since that time there have
been countless microcomputer systems developed. Many
of these are single purpose machines used for
scientific, industrial, and business applications
while others are more all purpose in scope.

There has been much specialization within the
computer software industry; large companies have
educational divisions and many smaller companies
devote all of their resources toward developing and
writing educational software programs for microcomputers.

Most school systems select the microcomputer when considering bringing this relatively new technology to the classroom although minicomputers as well as mainframe computers are occasionally chosen. The reason is that microcomputers are easy to operate, relatively inexpensive to purchase, and require little maintenance. Excellent color graphics and sound are offered by most computer systems and they can be easily moved from one location to another.

For the elementary classroom the portability of the microcomputer is a prime factor, as providing machines for each classroom is often financially difficult. Classroom teachers are not required to learn a computer language like BASIC, Logo, or Pascal, instead they can use previously prepared materials and need no technical computer expertise themselves.

Secondary schools, colleges, and universities have also incorporated the microcomputer into the curriculum. Although mini- and mainframe computers are used to an appreciable extent, the microcomputer has also found its niche. This is evidenced by the number of microcomputer laboratories found in schools across the country.

Clearly, the development of the microcomputer has had a direct impact on our society as well as on our educational system. The attitude of today's children toward our computerized world is often different than that of adults. Since they have grown up with this new technology, children do not look upon the computer with awe or apprehension as do many adults. The computer has become a fixture in our educational system and is here to stay. It is up to us as educators to make the best use of this new technology.

BIBLIOGRAPHY

Berger, Melvin. COMPUTERS IN YOUR LIFE. New York: Harper and Row, 1981.

Considers use of computers in government, medicine, communication, transportation, and law enforcement, using examples of special interest to children.

Bitter, Gary G. COMPUTERS IN TODAY'S WORLD. New
York: John Wiley & Sons, 1984.

Outlines the history of the computer in a clearcut
chronological fashion.

D'Ignazio, Fred. MESSNER'S INTRODUCTION TO THE
COMPUTER. New York: Simon and Schuster, 1983.

Uses biographies to give history of the computer
and possible future applications.

Evans, Christopher. THE MAKING OF THE MICRO. New
York: Van Nostrand Reinhold, 1981.

An excellent consideration of the history of
computers. Very well illustrated with diagrams and
pictures.

Goldstine, Herman H. THE COMPUTER FROM PASCAL TO
VON NEUMANN. Princeton, N.J.: Princeton
University Press, 1972.

Offers a detailed account of the events and people
that led to the development of the modern
computer.

Hawkes, Nigel. COMPUTERS IN THE HOME. New York:
Franklin Watts Pub. Co., 1984.

Written for older children. Provides excellent
diagrams and color photographs depicting current
and possible future applications of computers.

Hopper, Grace Marie, and Steven Mandell.
UNDERSTANDING COMPUTERS. New York: West
Publishing Company, 1984.

Traces hardware developments that have given rise
to computers as we know them today.

Ledyard, Henry E., and Patrick McQuaid. FROM BAKER
STREET TO BINARY. New York: McGraw-Hill, 1983.

Treats history and concepts of computers in a
unique storybook fashion using Sherlock Holmes to
solve mysteries.

Long, Larry. INTRODUCTION TO COMPUTERS AND
    INFORMATION PROCESSING. Englewood Cliffs, N.J.:
    Prentice-Hall, 1984.

    Gives a good historical perspective on the
    development of the computer and its applications.

Randell, Brian. THE ORIGINS OF DIGITAL COMPUTERS.
    New York: Springer-Verlag, 1975.

    Offers a sound developmental perspective on
    historical foundations for today's computer
    systems.

Sanders, Donald H. COMPUTERS TODAY. New York:
    McGraw-Hill, 1983.

    Offers insight into how computer systems are
    structured and a historical perspective on how
    they were developed.

Shelly, Gary B., and Thomas J. Cashman. COMPUTER
    FUNDAMENTALS FOR AN INFORMATION AGE. Brea,
    Calif.: Anaheim Pub. Co. Inc., 1984.

    Traces the technological developments that led to
    the formulation of the computer system as we know
    it today.

Stern, Nancy. FROM ENIAC TO EDVAC. Bedford, Mass.:
    Digital Press, 1981.

    Considers technological advancements from 1946 to
    1952 that led to the First Generation of
    Computers.

CHAPTER TWO

HIGHLIGHT TOPIC
ARE COMPUTER GAMES REALLY EDUCATIONAL SOFTWARE?

Whether or not a computer activity is seen as
educational software depends on the definition of
that term. One can argue that almost any computer
activity involves learning of one type or another.
Computer games such as Q-Bert, Ms Pac Man, and all
of the adventure games involve the development of
strategies by the user. One can legitimately argue
that developing problem solving strategies is an
important aspect of any learning activity. These and
other video arcade style games also help develop
coordination skills, including fine motor control
and hand-eye coordination by the player. These too
are components of many educational activities.
    Arcade style games also involve multisensory
input as they use sound, graphics, and animation.
Memory is an important factor since one must
remember methods of solution and sequences of play
in order to improve scores. Success in computer
games requires undivided attention and concentration
by the player. Frequently the games provide a
selection of levels of difficulty from which the
user can choose. Users strive to improve on their
previous high score. These are also characterisitics
one associates with educational activities.
    There are also many computer games that provide
a game show environment for the player. Computer
programs such as Tic Tac Show, The Game Show, and
Square Pairs fit into this category. These
activities are often perceived as more
"intellectual," as they ask the user to answer
direct questions or require concentration where the
position of characters, objects, and other things
must be recalled. These games also make good use of
color graphics, sound, and animation. Software

evaluators find it easier to make decisions about the educational appropriateness of these activities more readily, as their content is more academic in scope. Evaluators must use criteria that have been clearly articulated by educators so that decisions about the appropriateness of this type of computer software is not made in a haphazard fashion. In many cases this is not being done today.

A final category of computer games includes a range of programs dealing with such activities as learning to touch-type. There are several arcade style games such as Mastertype that introduce the keyboard to the user while playing. There is also a set of "Arcademic software" available from DLM Teaching Resources that teaches subject matter from a wide range of disciplines using the arcade game format.

These programs differ from categories of software previously discussed as they have clearly defined educational goals. The player learns concrete information such as "Math Facts" while trying to achieve the highest possible game score. To score points the player must perform an educationally related activity such as responding to questions from a geography or history curriculum. These programs often provide excellent color graphics, sound, and computer animation. The games always offer immediate feedback and give the user choices among several levels of difficulty.

Teachers of young children must decide if these games can legitimately be called educational software. Many educators can justify these materials as being educational software if their subject matter is closely related to traditional academic disciplines. Whether these materials are peripherally related to education or can be seen as an integrative curriculum component is an issue that teachers must address.

Uniform methods to group these software programs have not been developed. Although there are several other ways that I could have classified the computer software, I chose my scheme because it is easy to use and provides a convenient method by which computer software can be grouped according to educational criteria.

Most computer software can be viewed as providing opportunities for one or more types of learning or skill development. A piece of computer software is educational if it has a clearly defined educational objective as an inherent part of the program goals.

Games such as Asteroids and Hard Hat Mac, although involving fine motor skill development and strategic planning, are not designed as educational activities. They are simply well-conceived and clearly presented games. Activities like these do provide learning opportunities for children, but are better used as recreational rather than educational tools.

Other computer materials that require the user to respond to questions or define patterns and sequences can frequently be identified as educational software. The content of the program itself and how it is used by the teacher is the determinant. Many of these programs let the user add words and items to lists or let the teacher create individualized lessons. The best of these programs lets the user store responses on floppy disk or cassette tape. The possibility of storing and retrieving information as well as tailoring of information to meet individual student needs is an important characteristic of good educational software.

Arcade style games that ask the user to identify objects or words or make comparisons and computations to score game points can be viewed as educational software. Although these activities do not provide a theoretical basis on which decisions can be made, they do offer an excellent format for drill and practice. Improvement in accuracy and increased speed of response are among the benefits derived from using this type of computer software in the classroom.

Software designed for educational purposes usually has extensive documentation provided. In these written materials educational objectives are discussed and guidelines are offered to assess students' progress. Frequently suggestions are made outlining how these materials can be incorporated into your curriculum.

There is no clear-cut answer to what does or does not constitute educational computer software. The final decision is yours. As with most learning materials, the determining factor should be how they are used.

HAVING A COMPUTER IN THE CLASSROOM

Elementary classroom teachers frequently experience one of two possible sets of emotional responses when the computer is first made available for classroom use. Some regard computers with enthusiasm and excitement, seeing these machines as offering another means to enhance and broaden learning by the children. Others look at these machines suspiciously, seeing them as highly technical pieces of complex equipment that will certainly be the source of frustration and anguish.

These diametrically opposed attitudes are held by many teachers who are not computer literate and have not yet learned the educational impact computers can have on children or in a very practical way how they can be best used. The computer enthusiasts will likely take it upon themselves to learn to use these machines in highly efficient and creative ways by taking courses and workshops, and spending a great deal of time in self-instruction. These individuals are relatively few in number, but clearly can create a great deal of excitement in the school.

Most teachers are very much aware of the computer explosion that has occurred in the last few years. They feel their lack of experience and expertise and hesitate to bring this new technology into the classroom until they possess a sound knowledge of how these machines can be used as well as the cognitive effects computer education will have on young children today and in their future lives.

There is a multitude of issues that must be explored and resolved before the teacher can make informed decisions on uses of computers with young children. In this section we will investigate many issues ranging from types of computer hardware and software available today to preparing the classroom for the computer. We will also note child specific factors such as the types of thinking working with the computer entails as well as cognitive issues relating to computer use by children in the classroom.

Most schools throughout the United States have found a variety of practical ways to use the computer, ranging from administrative functions to

direct classroom applications. School systems
frequently use computer database programs to
maintain attendance records, student grades,
transcript information, as well as personal student
data. Computers often aid in the development of
academic and extracurricular schedules and
administrative and academic budget projections.
School offices use computers to generate mailing
labels and word processing programs to construct a
variety of reports and letters.

Teachers also have found uses for computers,
ranging from direct classroom applications to the
many administrative and record keeping functions
they must perform. Many teachers use computer
programs to administer and keep records of students'
progress as measured by commercially available
diagnostic tests. Records of students' academic
progress, test scores, and grades are frequently
stored and updated using computer software.

Many teachers have found other practical uses
for the computer using word processing software in
personal and professional applications: ability to
write, edit, store, and print written documents such
as papers, assignment sheets, and tests. Learning a
computer language and teaching it to young children
and becoming proficient in the use of specialized
educational software is another step in the
implementation of computer literacy development.

Many teachers perceive computer software use as
a set of drill and practice and tutorial programs
for the children. These types of programs are useful
but represent a small fraction of what is available
today or likely to be on the market in the future.
There are programs that develop creative thinking
and enhance problem solving strategy development
using color graphics and sound that enthrall young
children.

There is a variety of ways through which school
systems, schools, and classrooms acquire their first
computer for educational use. The obvious method is
to buy a computer through purchase requisitions
submitted by teachers and approved by the school
administration. In other cases school systems apply
for federal or state grants for the purchase of
computer equipment or apply for grants offered
directly by the manufacturers of computer equipment.
These are usually time consuming processes that
often require months' or years' preparation and

waiting before computers are made available for classroom use. Although seemingly logical, this is usually not the way by which computers are first brought to the classroom.

Computers are often first introduced into the classroom through the efforts of teachers and parents. They frequently lend or donate a computer for classroom use. Teachers must then determine how to make the computer work in the classroom. Parent and older student volunteers may provide a temporary solution, but the issue of how to meaningfully integrate the computer into the educational curriculum still rests with the teacher.

Unfortunately, the addition of microcomputers to K-6 classrooms has not been uniform. Suburban school systems for the most part have a higher percentage of computer accessibility and use than many city and rural school systems. Affluent school districts can provide computer experiences for children while less affluent ones cannot. The amount of money available in school budgets and from community resources are among the reasons for imbalanced distribution of computer resources in school systems across the United States.

This is not a new problem in education, however it must be addressed. We must insure that all children regardless of age, gender, family economic background, race, and ethnic origin have equal opportunities to experience the impact that microcomputer technology can have on their education. There are no simple answers to providing an equitable distribution of microcomputer hardware and software to schools.

Federal, state, and local governments must play a role in helping to solve this problem. As has been true in the past, grants awarded to school systems to upgrade the classroom learning environment is a logical starting point. State budgets should be examined to insure that financial resources are being equitably distributed so that all elementary schools have equal opportunities to bring the microcomputer into the classroom.

Several microcomputer manufacturers have made computers available to school systems at significant price reductions. We must encourage industry to continue this program, and modify it to include distribution of hardware and software to

school districts lacking the financial resources to
purchase equipment. We must continue to develop ways
to insure that all children have equal access to
computer technology in our school systems. As
educators we have this responsibility.

Having gotten the computer, teachers will then
embark on a desperate search for computer software
that can be used with it. This is likely to be a
somewhat haphazard search, as most teachers at this
stage of their computer literacy development are
unaware of what is available and how it can be used.
At this time long-range plans and developmental
effects the computer may have on children are not
the issue. The teacher is and should be concerned
with what the computer can do and how it can do it.

Through conversations, reading, workshops, and
courses teachers begin to develop a sense of the
machine's potential. Computer languages start to
become a consideration for use in the classroom.
Teachers learn that a computer language such as Logo
is most frequently used in elementary schools, while
BASIC is taught in elementary, middle, and high
schools. The language Pascal is usually reserved for
the upper track divisions in high schools. The issue
of computer languages for specific age levels and
grades is not a consideration at this time. BASIC
and Logo can be effectively used at most grade
levels with the use dependent on the teacher's
knowledge of the computer language and how it can be
applied to curriculum plans and goals.

At this point teachers usually want to
communicate to others how they are using computers
in the classroom. Other teachers in the building and
teachers throughout the school system may hear and
read about what has been done. Soon visits to the
classroom and teacher directed workshops become
commonplace. Enthusiasm and formulation of concrete
objectives and positive results can be infectious,
causing computer literacy to spread.

Soon information is being distributed by a
variety of means. Perhaps the teacher will subscribe
to educational computer networks whereby a more
broad based communication about computer
applications and a sharing of resources and ideas
can be effected. Attendance at regional and national
conferences and presentations at programs become an
important issue. The next step is likely to be

contribution to computer journals and books based on the teacher's experiences using microcomputers with young children.

Clearly, all teachers who use the computer in the classroom do not experience this level of involvement nor is it necessary. Most teachers simply try to find ways to use the computer to enhance the learning of their children. The effective integration of computers into the classroom perhaps can be used as the definition of computer literacy for teachers.

Today the percentage of school systems that use computers in either an administrative or educational capacity is very high; about 15 percent of the elementary and secondary schools use computers as teaching tools, with that percentage increasing each year. The types of uses vary according to available hardware and software as well as educational intent. These programs can be generally catalogued according to three criteria regardless of the academic discipline involved.

There are uses of the computer whose primary intent is to develop concrete academic skills related to a subject area. Most of these are interactive software programs where the computer provides questions and information and the child gives responses. Examples might include identifying characters from stories and matching words to definitions. There are other programs that provide lessons in mathematics and the development of visual discrimination skills. Mathematical concepts such as numbers and mathematical operations are carried out, frequently using colorfully animated characters. The concepts of size and position are presented in many unique and creative fashions.

Generally, computer programs that address concrete academic skills involve any one of three learning components. Many of these programs ask children to make observations and in the process accumulate factual information. Others involve children in making comparisons of two or more characters or objects. Many programs help children conceptualize the classification process by grouping objects according to a set of relationships.

A relatively recent application of computer technology to the elementary classroom has been the development of computer simulation programs. The goal of these programs is to reproduce real world problems or situations for the child to analyze. The child is usually provided with information and asked to use logic and decision making skills to find a solution to the problem or situation.

There are many types of learning processes inherent in working through a computer simulation program. Data and information must be organized according to a pattern of logical sequencing developed by the child. The skill of sorting through information to ascertain what data are relevant is fostered. Children also learn to make assumptions based on logical choices while working with the program and hypothesize probable outcomes and alternatives.

The last category of programs includes activities that encourage creativity and the use of formal computer based logic. In these cases children are to some extent left on their own to pose their own questions and develop solutions. Programming languages like BASIC and Logo are used as are computer sketch pads and music keyboards. In many ways these activities represent the most sophisticated applications of the computer.

At this level of computer use children and adults can maximize their learning by applying principles they have learned to new situations. The use of activities that foster transfer knowledge is continuously being sought by teachers and is readily achieved through the use of the computer. Through the process of designing and writing computer activities children become aware of the relationship between the human thought process and its expression in written form.

In general terms the computer can be thought of as a tool through which children can be encouraged to solve their own problems. Ideas and concepts can be freely explored without inhibitions of being right or wrong. Children seldom perceive the computer as a threat, rather as a machine to ask and answer questions. The computer is infinitely patient, allowing the child to rerun the program as many times as necessary until relationships are discovered or a solution is effected. The ease with which variables can be manipulated within the structure of a computer program encourages the child to make explorations and discoveries.

One can legitimately argue that these kinds of learning make good educational sense for students in

the elementary grades, but what kinds of learning
can be anticipated when working with kindergarten or
preschool children? Whether or not these experiences
can be done using more traditional educational tools
often becomes a moot point as much of today's
software provides experiences that are unique and
are of definite cognitive benefit to the child.

Manipulative skills and the concept of
directionality are among the first areas to be
further developed through use of the computer.
Computer keys, joysticks, and paddles are used to
move objects to the left and right, up and down.
Computer programs are available that let children
design and generate intricate patterns using a
variety of colors. Other programs help develop
number and letter recognition and their
manipulations by using sets of creatively designed
objects.

The young computer user soon finds that
comparing and matching objects using a game format
and discriminating among closely related objects can
be fun and exciting. Given the appropriate computer
software, the young user can soon create and modify
shapes and solve the intricacies of moderately
complex puzzles. Explorations into the world of art
and music are distinct possibilities.

There is a multitude of educational benefits
that young children derive from working with the
microcomputer. Working in the computer environment
fosters fine motor skill development and hand-to-eye
coordination. Children can receive an infinite
amount of instruction and practice in the area of
symbolization, as this is the means through which
computers and most computer software operate.

Research has shown that the attention span of
young children working with computers is greater
than what one expects using traditional materials.
Children do not see the computer as hostile and
unfriendly, but as a patient machine that is the
source of enjoyment. Young children soon gain a
sense of independence and a feeling that they are in
control of the machine.

Studies have shown that, contrary to what one
might expect, the use of computers in groups of
young children encourages social interactions. When
working with a computer software program or writing
a program of their own, children almost immediately

begin making group decisions and developing logical
strategies. Frequently, there is no right or wrong
way to proceed with the program, as it offers
multiple options. Frustration levels are greatly
reduced because of this. The computer is another
valuable tool through which young children can
experience their world.

In most cases young children want to be
challenged and stimulated by their education. Being
taught to write programs in a computer language can
be a highly stimulating and valuable educational
experience. Of course there are several prerequisites
necessary before this can take place. The teacher
must first become conversant in the computer
language and develop an appropriate teaching
methodology for use with the children. A worthwhile
set of educational materials must be devised and the
appropriate computer resources made available.

Teachers of computer programming should be
advocates of discovery oriented learning and work
closely with students, offering advice and
encouragement as needed. There are many skills that
must be developed before programming can be
effectively taught. These skills and concepts cover
a wide range of issues. A learning unit should be
completed that deals with requisite skill acquisition
before the teaching of computer programming is
attempted.

To be able to learn computer programming
children must have a working knowledge of spatial
relationships and be able to discriminate between
left and right and up and down. They also need to
understand how integers are numerically sequenced as
well as have the ability to apply such concepts as
less than and greater than. An ability to deal with
the attributes of color, size, and shape is also
important.

Being able to recognize and use keyboard
characters is another prerequisite to programming a
computer. For many programs a fundamental knowledge
of arithmetic operations is useful. Children should
also understand differences between the notions of
"part of" and "entire." For example, letters make up
words and a programming line is part of the computer
program.

There are additional concepts that children
should learn and tasks they are able to perform that
are prerequisites to programming a computer. The

specific experiences and educational tools that are necessary directly depend on the type of computer programs that will be written and the computer language used. As in other cases the teacher must carefully plan and develop the educational curriculum to maximize learning. Given access to computers on a regular basis, children can successfully learn new concepts and ideas as well as develop a feeling of control over this machine.

Teachers must be aware when designing computer programs or using existing software that uniformly offering problems for the children to solve that provide one and only one method of solution is educationally detrimental. Children will soon learn to shape their problem solving strategies toward finding the one correct response, thus inhibiting searching for alternative responses or methods of solution. In some circumstances this type of learning may be desirable but in other instances it is clearly not the best approach.

I believe teachers should provide both types of learning experiences for young children. There is some validity in asking questions that require one specific response. Many solutions to problems legitimately demand recall or recognition memory as the principal cognitive process.

On the other hand, the teacher should provide experiences that offer more than one set response or method of solution. By doing this students learn to make generalizations and develop application skills. A combination of these two approaches represents the ideal learning environment for the young child.

The computer can easily present to the child both types of learning experiences. It is clearly up to the teacher to learn enough about how the computer and its software are designed so that the best educational plan can be developed. The computer itself is neither good nor bad; how it is used is what matters. Teachers should introduce computers to children with well-conceptualized small-scale goals in mind until they have learned more about the intricacies and applications of this new technology.

Teaching in the elementary grades presents challenges that are not as evident in junior and senior high schools. The elementary teacher must offer a broad knowledge base so that issues relating to child development, sociology, psychology, as well as content areas such as reading and mathematics can be incorporated into their teaching plans.

One can present a similar argument for the teaching of computer literacy to children in elementary schools and extend it to include computer learners of all ages. Computer literacy is a multifaceted concept that is very difficult to define. Which definition one uses depends on the particular bias of the person providing the definition. From my perspective there is no clearly defined set of tasks to master or knowledge to learn that is a requirement before one can be said to possess this mysterious entity called computer literacy.

Becoming computer literate can be compared to becoming educated. There seems to be a legitimate starting point for each, but where does your education end so that you can be described as being educated? Education is an ongoing lifelong process; there is always more to learn in terms of concepts, information, and approaches. The same argument can be applied to what constitutes a computer literate individual.

The first step in becoming computer literate entails learning how to make the computer system function. Learning to turn on the computer and how to load information onto a computer disk or cassette tape is the first step. Becoming familiar with the keys on the computer keyboard is critical. Most keys and their positions are identical to those found on a standard typewriter, but there are some special keys directly related to operations performed with the computer.

Learning to operate a variety of computer software programs is the next step toward attainment of computer literacy. One cannot run all the computer software programs available; there are too many. One should learn to run a diverse set of programs so that operating new programs does not become a monumental task. How difficult it is to master a new program frequently depends on the experience of the user.

Although there are no specific programs that must be mastered, I do believe that every computer literate person should be able to operate a word processing program. This is my personal bias. It is not reflected in every definition of computer literacy. Computer literate individuals should have a general appreciation of the history of the computer and a basic familiarity of how the computer functions. An understanding of the impact the computer has had on society in general and for teachers in particular is useful. Individuals demonstrating high order computer literacy development are able to write programs in one or more computer languages. This represents an important step, for if you can construct computer programs, you understand how to communicate with the machine and make it complete a user defined task. If you cannot perform all of these tasks and do not possess this broad based general knowledge, you can still be termed computer literate. As stated earlier computer literacy can be thought of as having developmental components with each individual at a different stage of development. How far one progresses in literacy development depends on individual and personal and professional goals. When teachers have learned to use the computer effectively, have a broad based knowledge of how it works, and understand its impact on society they will be able to pass on the idea of computer literacy to our children.

The initial experience of introducing the computer to the classroom can create many anxious moments for the teacher who is in the process of becoming computer literate. To minimize anxiety, treat the computer as you would any other new learning tool you might introduce to the children. This attitudinal perception is important; the computer is after all simply another machine. Your next step is to develop a carefully designed set of activities or lesson plans built around the computer following the same process as for any other subject matter.

Remember, you do not have to be an expert to use the computer with children in a highly effective and educationally sound manner. The computer and its software can be used in almost all subject areas in many ways with children of all ages. Your goal is to develop a program that lets the children interact with the computer and its software in educationally productive ways. Children will be more responsible for their own learning and have a greater involvement in their own learning process. Using the computer will help them learn new skills as well as develop new abilities and find new relationships to explore.

There are several concrete steps you can take to properly prepare yourself and the classroom before actually beginning to use the computer with the children. Your first step is to gain a working familiarity with the computer system that will be used. If you have a problem operating technical equipment in general, you may wish to seek out a support person to teach you the fundamentals of the machine's operation. You can carefully read the instruction manual accompanying the machine or seek help and advice from a computer store that sells your type of computer. Most computer stores are very willing to give advice and assistance. In any case, soon you will be working productively with the computer needing no outside assistance.

Learning what is currently being done using computers in elementary classrooms is your logical second step. Journals such as CLASSROOM COMPUTER LEARNING, THE COMPUTING TEACHER, and ELECTRONIC LEARNING offer countless articles on computer applications for the classroom. These journals are not technically oriented, but are written for non-experts with many articles designed for use by teachers. There are also many books available written with a focus on classroom applications. A course or workshop that is specifically designed for teachers that provides classroom applications of the computer might also be useful.

You are now ready to plan how to use the computer in the classroom. Start with a moderate set of goals rather than a grandiose program. Articulate why you have decided to use the computer to teach specific concepts rather than another means of instruction. Consider the effects computer based instruction will have on the children. You must always keep in mind that the computer is not an end in itself but just another tool that can be used to facilitate learning.

Your challenge as a teacher is to select computer activities for the children to do that will strengthen their sensory, cognitive, and social development. The programs you choose should provide multiple sets of choices for children and allow for alternative methods of solution to problems. Computer programs that require cumulative types of learning by the user are often found to be most effective. When children work with the computer, it

serves as its own reward system, therefore no
extrinsic rewards are necessary.
    Once plans have been formulated you must
consider if there are specific computer hardware and
software requirements necessary to implement your
program. There are many excellent computer hardware
and software guides available that can help you make
decisions. Conversations with personnel from a
reputable computer store about costs, service, and
performance are often productive. You should also
try to gain the support of other teachers and
administrators in your school system. Keep them
abreast of what you plan to do by sharing your plans
and goals.
    The location of the computer system in the
classroom is another important consideration. The
computer must be easily accessible to students, but
positioned so that when an individual or a small
group of students is working with the machine it
does not create a disruptive influence for the rest
of the class. This can present a dilemma as the
microcomputer should be treated as another
educational tool to enhance classroom learning, but
the equipment itself has special requirements as do
other teaching and learning aids such as slide
projectors and tape recorders.
    The choice of tables on which the equipment is
placed is important. Tables designed and sold as
computer work stations can be used, although these
specialized tables are not necessary. Any sturdy
table measuring four to five feet in length will
serve as a work station for the microcomputer. The
height of the table is an important consideration.
The table height should be the same as that for
using a typewriter, that is the child's arms should
be parallel to the floor when fingers are placed at
keyboard level.
    The table should provide free space so that
children can write, make notes, and plan work while
at the microcomputer work station. If a computer
printer is available, a larger work surface may be
needed. Ideally the table should be provided with an
electrical power strip so that all computer system
components can be plugged in without electrical
cords and cables resting haphazardly over the work
area. If electrical cords are too long, they can be
tied together. The electrical power strip can then
be plugged into a standard 110-volt outlet.

Materials such as computer disks, cassette tapes, books, and manuals should be kept near the computer work station for easy access. Standard shelving is the most efficient way to store these materials. Many software programs are provided with containers or notebooks that can be stored on standard sized bookshelves. Some materials such as student data disks or cassette tapes should be kept in containers available from computer supply stores. These boxes offer protection from accidental damage. Children should be encouraged to return computer software to its storage location after use so that computer disks and cassette tapes are not left lying about the computer environment.

Many computer software programs are provided with back-up copies. In other cases back-up copies can be purchased at greatly reduced prices. Back-up copies should never be stored in the same place as the working copy of the computer disk or cassette tape. This is to prevent damage to all copies of software in the event of hazards such as water leaks or fire. You must also provide proper security for the computer system and protect it from hazards that may cause damage to it or its software. They should not be positioned in direct sunlight or near a direct source of heat such as a radiator. Water, dirt, and excessive dust can also cause problems in the operation of the computer. Your machine should not be positioned in a distant corner, but should be placed in a safe and secure location.

You must make provisions to insure that all students have an equal opportunity to use the computer. Computer time sign-up sheets can be used and provision made for free time when any child can use the machine. You will soon develop your own style of how to answer questions posed by children and handle minor technical problems that arise from time to time. Most teachers learn to handle simple technical problems and repairs themselves, but you should get assistance in the event of a major malfunction. You may wish to purchase a service contract for your machine or rely on contracted repair services from independent vendors.

Working with children on computer based learning experiences has a very positive effect on the classroom environment. I suggest a modest start in one particular subject area. Show the children how to use the equipment, giving minimal attention to technical terminology and detail. Use interactive programs, always making sure that what is being taught is what you intend. Share your successes and failures with others. Finally, evaluate and redesign your program as needed to meet the particular needs of your students.

Many teachers question the validity of using what are frequently called educational computer games in the classroom. One cannot make a general statement about the appropriateness of educational computer games for classroom use except that they must be analyzed on a case-by-case basis, just as one would do for educational games in general.

There are several excellent educational computer games available today. They may be useful to you if they logically fit into your learning plan. Your best approach might be to preview these activities at a computer software store, or arrange for delivery of an on-approval order from a catalogue distributor. Only then can you make an informed decision about the game's educational worth.

Carefully designed educational games are well received by children, as they are both challenging and interesting. Although there should be an obvious goal, the outcome of the game itself is uncertain. In many cases the player can choose the level of difficulty for the game, resulting in user goals that become personally meaningful.

The curiosity and fantasy components of many educational games result in their being seen as particularly stimulating and exciting by children. The use of color graphics and sound add to the games' interest. In general, these games focus on a particular academic subject and superimpose a game format through which the player is attempting to attain a fantasy goal or avoid a disaster. Well-designed educational computer games may have a legitimate place in your classroom.

The colorful, animated graphics offered by many well-designed computer software programs strive to make learning interesting and fun. A computer graphic does not have to simulate an object, person, or thing from the real world to be instructional for the child. They usually provide just enough detail so their meaning is clear but not so much detail that issues become confused.

From an educational viewpoint there are several classes of computer graphics that can be part of computer software programs. Some graphics apparently serve no particular purpose and seem to have been added as an afterthought. These graphics are worse than useless as they can cause the learner to focus on extraneous and irrelevant issues. Computer programs making extensive use of extraneous graphics are to be avoided.

Some computer graphics provide a picture that directly depicts a circumstance or scene to be analyzed or interpreted. This type of graphic is frequently used in mathematics and science software and is quite effective. Many computer graphics provide a realistic portrayal of characters and situations. The majority of educationally designed adventure games use this format. Finally, some computer graphics offer a totally abstract representation of an event that has taken place. These graphics usually consist of graphs, charts, and sets of abstract symbols.

Effective computer graphics should strive to enhance and reinforce learning. Well-designed graphics can let the users know if they have made appropriate decisions; the representation for a correct response should be more stimulating than that for a wrong answer. Computer graphics provide an environment for learning that is difficult to simulate in other ways. When appropriately incorporated into a computer program they can greatly increase children's interest and make positive contributions to the learning process.

Use of microcomputers in elementary classrooms provides an opportunity for the teacher to offer unique and innovative approaches to learning. Working with the computer helps children assume a greater responsibility for their own learning by helping them become more self-reliant and independent learners.

The important issue continues to be how well the teacher can incorporate the microcomputer into the classroom learning environment. Until the teacher is able to treat the computer as other educational materials like books, paints, and music, little progress will be likely. This is the challenge.

BIBLIOGRAPHY

Alesandri, Kathryn Lutz. "A Look at Computer
   Graphics." THE COMPUTING TEACHER 12
   (February 1985): 23-24.

   Gives an analysis of the types of computer
   graphics offered on computer software and of their
   effectiveness.

Chaffin, Jerry D.; Bill Maxwell; and Barbara
   Thompson. "ARC-ED Curriculum: The Application of
   Video Game Format to Educational Software."
   EXCEPTIONAL CHILDREN 49 (1982):   173-178.

   Outlines motivational and psychological factors to
   be considered when educational software is
   developed using a game format.

Coburn, Peter.   PRACTICAL GUIDE TO COMPUTERS IN
   EDUCATION.   Reading, Mass.:   Addison-Wesley Pub.
   Co., 1982.

   Covers a wide range of topics ranging from
   philosophical issues to areas of practical
   concern.

Glenn, Allen D., and Steven J. Rakow.   "Computer
   Simulations: Effective Teaching Strategies."   THE
   COMPUTING TEACHER 12 (February 1985):   59-61.

   Outlines characteristics and strategies for using
   computer simulation software in the classroom.

Hofmeister, Alan.   "Microcomputers in Perspective."
   EXCEPTIONAL CHILDREN 49 (October 1982):   115-121.

   Considers the multitude of ways computers can be
   used in school systems.

Leron, Uri.   "Logo Today: Vision and Reality."   THE
   COMPUTING TEACHER 12 (February 1985):   26-32.

   Outlines educational factors that contribute
   toward learning when computers are used in
   elementary classrooms.

Mace, Scott. "Give the Child an Opportunity for
    Play." INFOWORLD 6 (December 1984): 52.

    Raises a series of questions that outlines factors
    related to use of computer software with children.

Malone, T.W. "What Makes Computer Games Fun." BYTE
    (December 1981): 258-277.

    Describes psychological and behavioral factors
    that contribute toward the widespread interest in
    computer game software.

Malone, Thomas W. "Guidelines for Designing
    Educational Computer Games." CHILDHOOD EDUCATION
    59 (March/April 1983): 241-247.

    Describes factors that make educational computer
    games appealing to young children.

Miller, Inabeth. "How Schools Become Computer
    Literate." POPULAR COMPUTING: GUIDE TO COMPUTERS
    IN EDUCATION (November 1984): 22-28.

    Depicts the stages of development to be followed
    for a school to become computer literate.

Moore, Omark. "Guidelines for Choosing Hardware to
    Promote Synaesthetic Learning." CHILDHOOD
    EDUCATION 59 (March/April 1983): 237-240.

    Relates child development and how children learn
    to characteristics of computer systems that are
    consistent with these goals.

Moursund, Dave. "Improve Education." CREATIVE
    COMPUTING 10 (November 1984): 180-186.

    Discusses what kind of impact computers have had
    on education and how this has affected students.

Pea, Roy D., and Midian Kurland. "On the Cognitive
    Prerequisites of Learning Computer Programming."
    New York: Report from the Bank Street College of
    Education, June 1983.

    Considers prelearning skills necessary in young
    children before they learn computer programming.

Pea, Roy D., and Midian Kurland. "On the Cognitive Prerequisites of Learning Computer Programming." New York: Report from the Bank Street College of Education, October 1983.

Provides updated and expanded information based on the June 1983 report.

Rotenberg, Leslie. "Great Adventure: How to Turn 'Just for Fun' Adventure Games into Terrific Curriculum Aids." TEACHING AND COMPUTERS 2 (May/June 1985): 20-36.

Offers many practical suggestions about how to use adventure games as curriculum aids.

Schneiderman, Ben. "When Children Learn Programming: Antecedents, Concepts and Outcomes." THE COMPUTING TEACHER 12 (February 1985): 14-17.

Describes antecedent knowledge children must have before beginning to write computer programs.

Shapiro, Leonard. "Arcades: What Are Children Learning from Videogames?" POPULAR COMPUTING 2 (February 1983): 121-124.

Discusses educational impact arcade games are having on children and how they have affected the computer software industry.

Sherman, Sallie J., and Keith A. Hall. "Preparing the Classroom for Computer-Based Education (CBE)." CHILDHOOD EDUCATION 59 (March/April 1983): 222-226.

Familiarizes the reader with practical steps to be followed to properly prepare the classroom for the computer.

Staples, Betsy. "Education or Entertainment?" CREATIVE COMPUTING 10 (April 1984): 59-63.

Presents excellent arguments justifying the educational validity of computer games.

Steffin, Sherwin A. "Fighting Against Convergent Thinking." CHILDHOOD EDUCATION 59 (March/April 1983): 255-258.

Characterizes how convergent and divergent
thinking relate to problem solving when using the
computer.

Sullivan, George. COMPUTER KIDS. New York: Dodd
Pub. Co., 1984.

Traces how eight children have learned to use the
computer in creative ways.

Vockell, Edward L., and Robert H. Rivers.
INSTRUCTIONAL COMPUTING FOR TODAY'S TEACHERS. New
York: Macmillan, 1984.

Demonstrates how computers can be used by teachers
and students.

Watson, Edward. "When Computer Literacy Becomes
Multidimensional." CHILDHOOD EDUCATION 59
(March/April 1983): 40.

Stresses integration of the computer into all
aspects of the elementary school curriculum.

Zeiser, Edward L., and Stevie Hoffman. "Computers:
Tools for Thinking." CHILDHOOD EDUCATION 59
(March/April 1983): 251-254.

Offers a system by which computer software
programs can be easily catalogued, with emphasis
on the type of learning involved.

Ziajka, Alan. "Microcomputers in Early Childhood
Education? A First Look." YOUNG CHILDREN (July
1983): 61-67.

Examines what can be done with young children
using microcomputers and the inherent educational
benefits.

CHAPTER THREE

HIGHLIGHT TOPIC
BITS AND BYTES

How the microcomputer internally processes
information such as words and numbers is often seen
by the non-technically trained user as being one of
the mysteries of modern technology. In actuality the
computer uses a very simple scheme to represent
information of all types. It is called the binary
code system.

All characters that are represented within the
machine are designated by specific patterns of zeros
and ones. As far as the computer is concerned these
representations are indicative of the "on" or "off"
condition of a particular element of electrical
circuitry. This scheme is frequently referred to as
the binary or base two notation.

We do not usually use binary notation to
represent numbers in our daily lives, as we normally
use the base 10 system for numeric representations.
In our system the first place value position to the
left of the decimal point represents 1's, the second
10's, the third 100's, the fourth 1000's, and so
forth. Thus the number 1563 can be thought of as 1
thousand, 5 hundreds, 6 tens, and 3 ones. Each
number position carries with it a specific place
value connotation.

It is important to note that the largest
numeric value at any one place value position is 9.
If a value larger than 9 occurs at a place value
position, we represent the number by moving 10 of
the elements to the next place value position.
Therefore, if we add 75 + 89 we get a result of 164,
meaning 1 group of 100, 6 groups of 10 and 4 ones.
We do not think of the result as being 15 groups of
10 and 14 ones. In mathematical terms this process
is called carrying over values to the next place
value position.

The base ten system of notation is not useful
with microcomputers as there are only two place
value representations that can be used, for
electricity can only be in an "on" or "off" condition.
The base 2 or binary system is useful as it only
uses two digits, 0 and 1. The 0 is used to represent
the off condition of an electric circuit while the 1
is used to denote the on condition. At first this
system of notation may seem a little peculiar, but
it is actually quite simple to understand.

For example, the number 15 in our base 10
system is represented as 1111 in base two binary
code. In binary the first position to the left of
the decimal point represents 1's as it does in base
10. The second position to the left of the decimal
point represents 2's, while the third 4's, the
fourth 8's and so forth. Each place value position
can only have a 0 or a 1 value represented. A
comparison of numbers and mathematical operations is
useful and is given in the table below.

BASE 10 SYSTEM   BINARY REPRESENTATION

	10'S	1'S	32'S	16'S	8'S	4'S	2'S	1'S
10	1	0			1	0	1	0
21	2	1		1	0	1	0	1
55	5	5	1	1	0	1	1	1

BASE 10 ADDITION

	10'S	1'S			10'S	1'S
10	1	0	17		1	7
+ 21	2	1	+ 35		+ 3	5
31	3	1	52		5	2

BINARY ADDITION

		16	8	4	2	1'S
1010			1	0	1	0
+ 10101	+ 1	0	1	0	1	
11111	1	1	1	1	1	

```
                        32  16  8   4   2   1'S

        10001                1   0   0   0   1
      + 100011        +  1   0   0   0   1   1
      ---------       -----------------------
        110100           1   1   0   1   0   0
```

Now that we have considered how the
microcomputer uses binary notation to represent
numbers, let us consider how this system is used by
the microcomputer microprocessor to handle
information. Each binary digit in computer jargon is
called a bit. Groups of 8 bits can be used to
represent any character and are collectively called
a byte. A byte can be conceptualized as the
fundamental unit of memory within the computer.
Some microcomputers have 16K of Random Access
Memory, while other machines may provide 64K or 128K
of RAM. One K reflects 1 Kilobyte or 1024 bytes of
workspace for the operator to use. A 64K machine
thus provides 64 X 1024 or 65536 bytes of RAM
memory. This means that up to 65536 characters can
be entered into the computer memory before it is
full. In reality less space is available as
programming instructions for software, such as word
processors and disk operating systems used with disk
drives, also use some RAM memory.
The computer language that directly represents
characters in binary is called machine code.
Computers can only process information when it is
represented in binary machine code. Computer
programs written in machine code run the fastest, as
programs written in other high level computer
languages have to be internally converted to machine
code by the computer before their instructions can
be executed.
It would seem to be logical that computer
programmers write instructions in machine code to
make most efficient use of the microcomputer. On the
other hand, learning to write programs in machine
language is a very difficult process. Characters,
words, and instructions written in machine code bear
no resemblance to numbers and words as we know them.
Early computer programmers were forced to program in
machine language, as it was the only available way
to communicate with the computer. Today few people
actually write computer programs in machine
language.

Assembly language is somewhat easier to learn
to use, but as was true for machine language, the
programmer must write programming steps in a machine
based fashion that does not closely resemble typical
English. Assembly language instructions must be
converted to machine code by the microprocessor
before instructions can be processed. Therefore, it
is a slower operating language than binary machine
code but it is still a very fast operating language.

Most computer programmers sacrifice speed of
operation for ease and clarity of writing when
giving instructions to the computer. Computer
languages such as BASIC, COBOL, Logo, and Pascal are
frequently used to give the computer instructions.
Programming steps written in all of these high level
computer languages must be first translated by the
computer into binary machine code before the
instructions can be executed. In terms of the speed
at which the computer operates, this is a slow
process, but in reality it is rather quick as it
takes but a few extra milliseconds. For most
educational applications the user will not notice
the necessary time delay for translation of
instructions into machine code.

Microcomputers use a predetermined binary code
to represent each of the characters found on the
computer keyboard. As a user you do not have to
think about what the code for a character is, for
the computer is internally programmed to translate
your typed instructions into the appropriate machine
code representation. The code for each character is
permanently programmed into the firmware found in
the ROM (Read Only Memory) chips of your
microcomputer. These instructions constitute part of
the computer's permanent memory that cannot be
altered or added to by the user.

There are several standard character sets that
can be used by a computer manufacturer when
programming the ROM memory to represent typed
characters in binary machine code. One such code is
named the American Standard Code for Information
Interchange and is usually designated as the ASCII
code. Most, though not all, microcomputers use the
ASCII code for character representation. Several
other character codes are also in common use,
including the Extended Binary Coded Decimal
Interchange Code, usually abbreviated EBCDIC. The
EBCDIC character representation is more frequently

used in Europe while the ASCII code is more prevalent in the United States. Neither character representation system is superior to the other so choice is strictly a matter of manufacturer's preference. Examples of character representations using both systems are given below.

	ASCII CODE EXAMPLES		EBCDIC CODE EXAMPLES	
	BASE 10 NOTATION	BINARY NOTATION	BASE 10 NOTATION	BINARY NOTATION
A	65	1000001	193	11000001
B	66	1000010	194	11000010
C	67	1000011	195	11000011
D	68	1000100	196	11000100
E	69	1000101	197	11000101
F	70	1000110	198	11000110
G	71	1000111	199	11000111
0	48	110000	240	11110000
1	49	110001	241	11110001
2	50	110010	242	11110010
3	51	110011	243	11110011
4	52	110100	244	11110100
5	53	110101	245	11110101
!	33	100001	90	1011010
$	36	100100	91	1011011
+	43	101011	78	1001110
a	97	1100001	129	10000001
b	98	1100010	130	10000010
c	99	1100011	131	10000011
d	100	1100100	132	10000100
e	101	1100101	133	10000101
f	102	1100110	134	10000110
g	103	1100111	135	10000111

You may wonder if there are practical applications for knowing how to use these binary representations for keyboard characters. In most cases binary codes the computer uses to represent characters are of no concern to you as the machine will automatically carry out any operation you instruct it to do. There is one notable exception. If you write a program that instructs the computer to alphabetize the words "orange, apple, watermelon, and cantaloupe, the machine will perform the task as

expected, arranging the words in alphabetical order
no matter which character set your machine is
designed to use.
    However, if your instructions were to
alphabetize the words "Florida, computer, fish, and
California," you would get an unexpected result. The
microcomputer would print words in the order
"California, Florida, computer, and fish" if your
machine used the ASCII code and "computer, fish,
California, and Florida" if it used the EBCDIC code.
    Initially this may not make sense to you unless
you carefully examine the computer binary codes for
the first letters in each word. In the ASCII system
the first letter of the word California is an upper
case C and is represented by the base 10 number 67,
similarly the upper case F in Florida is given the
base 10 number 70. Notice that the lower case letter
c in the word computer is assigned the number 99
while the f in fish is 102. The upper case letter C
comes before the upper case letter F in the
alphabet, while the lower case letters c and f
follow respectively. As far as the computer is
concerned it has alphabetized the list of words
properly.
    If your machine was programmed to use the
EBCDIC character code, the alphabetized list of
words would read "computer, fish, California, and
Florida" as the codes for c, f, C and F are 131,
134, 195 and 198 respectively. These values can be
easily read from the chart above.
    Clearly, an understanding of how characters are
structured is useful when writing sophisticated
computer programs. In the vast majority of cases
character codes need not be considered by the
programmer. In the event you need to use them, all
you need to know is the particular character set
your machine uses and the standard binary
representation for keyboard characters. Most
computer programming books provide a complete
listing of standard character codes.

                    THE MICROCOMPUTER SYSTEM

    There are many different styles of
microcomputer systems on the market today. Some
systems are self-contained so that all essential

elements are held in one housing. Other microcomputers are available as a set of components much
like those for a stereophonic tape system. Some
units are so small they can fit into an attache case
while others are much larger.
Regardless of the type of computer system you
examine, each microcomputer contains three essential
components for the system to function properly.
There must be an input device that provides a means
to communicate information to the computer itself so
that instructions can be processed. A central
processing unit is necessary to perform operations
on data that has been input, and an output device is
needed to give feedback to the user.
In principle the operation of your computer
system is simple and easy to understand, but in
reality it is very complex. To the novice the
plethora of abbreviations and use of technical
jargon make gaining a working knowledge of how the
computer system functions a seemingly impossible
task.
If one considers the apparent complexities of
the issues involved, one might ponder the validity
of including this section in a book written for a
non-technically oriented audience. The answer is
simple. Each user or potential user of a computer
system should have a fundamental grasp of how the
system functions. By having a general understanding
of the relationship among components of the computer
system and how information is internally processed,
one can make more informed decisions regarding which
computer software programs and which computer system
to buy. Many users have purchased programs that
cannot be run on their equipment or have purchased
computer systems that cannot perform the tasks that
constitute the chief reason for purchase in the
first place. This chapter addresses many of these
issues and will, I hope, help you make more informed
decisions.
The most commonly used input device used to
communicate with the computer is the keyboard. In
most cases it is housed in the same plastic case as
the computer itself, but some computer systems have
free standing keyboards. The most useful computer
keyboards are the ones whose keys have the same
position as those on a standard typewriter. A few
specialized keys are also provided to control
computer specific operations. Many computer

keyboards also provide a numeric key pad that is set
up like those found on typical electronic
calculators. The numeric key pad is particularly
useful when one is performing repeated mathematical
operations or entering large amounts of numeric
data.
       The most technologically advanced keyboards
have a built-in rollover feature so that if a second
key is depressed before the first key has been
released the second character will be entered.
Rollover capability is a useful feature, as it can
reduce input errors when one rapidly enters data or
text. Most quality keyboards have a built-in repeat
function so that if the user keeps a key depressed
that character will be repeated until the key is
released. This is a very desirable feature that is
frequently used when constructing charts, graphs,
and tables, as well as when making drawings.
       A feature that is especially useful for word
processing applications and is found in most quality
keyboards is a memory buffer. The memory buffer is a
storage location where characters can be stored
before they are transmitted to the computer. This
feature can radically reduce errors in data entry
when keys are pressed in rapid succession. Most good
keyboards also have a built-in debouncing routine.
This means varying pressures can be applied to keys
without causing input errors. A memory buffer and
debouncing routine are very desirable keyboard
features to have to insure easy and accurate data
entry.
       Computer keyboards are available in many sizes
and offer a variety of key styles and
configurations. Your best choice is a keyboard
having keys of the same size, quality, and shape as
those found on a good typewriter. Very small
keyboards are very difficult to use as are those
having a peculiar key configuration.
       There are many touch sensitive keyboards on the
market today. These keyboards lack mechanical keys
as the keyboard characters are imprinted on the
surface of a plastic sheet. These keyboards are very
inexpensive but have the distinct characteristic of
being easily prone to user errors. If you
accidentally touch or rest your fingers on the
keyboard you will be making erroneous data entries.
Your fingers must be kept above the keyboard at all
times.

As you can see the keyboard is a vital part of
your computer system. Before purchasing a computer
examine its keyboard carefully to determine if it
has the features you consider important. Most
keyboards are directly connected to the computer as
they are housed in the same plastic case. Some free
standing keyboards communicate with the computer
with no wire or cable connections required. Other
free standing keyboards are connected to the
computer by means of a cable.

There are two types of cables used to connect
free standing keyboards to computers. There are
round cables that resemble plastic coated wires and
ribbon type cables. Ribbon type cables are generally
found to be superior. The connecting points between
cable and keyboard as well as between cable and
computer should be secure, preferably having a
locking mechanism.

There are two means by which computer programs
and data values are frequently input into the
computer. A cassette recorder can be used as an
input device to pass programs stored on cassette
tapes to the computer or a disk drive can be used to
transmit information stored on computer disks. Both
of these methods are in common use today. There are
advantages and drawbacks to each system. Which
system you choose is directly dependent on your
particular needs as well as your budget.

Of the two methods for data input, the cassette
recorder system is by far the less expensive. A
cassette recorder that produces high quality
stereophonic sound is not necessary. Any good
quality cassette recorder is fine. The recorder can
be purchased separately from your computer as long
as an interface cable is available so that it can be
connected to the computer. Use 15- or 30-minute
tapes that are moderately priced. The reason for not
using 60- or 90-minute tapes will soon become
apparent.

Cassette storage is a sequential method of data
storage that records information as a series of
tones representing computer characters. Each
computer file is linearly stored on the cassette
tape. You must use the counter on the cassette
recorder to locate the exact position of the
computer program or file you wish to use. Failure to
do this will cause the computer to improperly read
the file from the tape, resulting in a program that

will not function or operate properly. The program
itself, stored on the cassette tape, is not lost or
damaged and can be reread from the tape into the
computer.
    Cassette recorders can read computer programs
from tapes and pass the instructions to the computer
at the rate of 10 to 1000 characters per second,
depending on the type of information to be read and
the cassette recorder used. This may seem fast to
you, but in terms of the speed at which a computer
operates this is exceedingly slow. As cassette tape
data storage is linearly sequential, if the program
you wish to access is near the end of the tape you
may have to wait five minutes to reach the program
you wish to use.
    Cassette recorders work well as a means to
input data into the computer. I do find them to be
frustrating because of the time necessary to find
and enter programs. However, extreme care must be
taken to locate the exact position on the tape where
programs are located or a great deal of frustration
can result. In spite of this, cassette tape storage
does represent an efficient and economical way to
store computer programs and input data into the
computer.
    A disk drive unit offers another method by
which stored computer programs can be input into the
computer. Some computer systems provide one or two
disk drives that are built into a housing containing
the keyboard, computer, and the computer monitor
screen. Many machines offer disk drives as an add-on
peripheral device, one that can be connected to the
computer by cable connections. Many users utilize
two, three, or four disk drives with their computer
system. In general one disk drive is sufficient,
although in some cases two disk drives are required
for the operation of more sophisticated computer
programs. Additional disk drive units can be easily
added to your computer system as the need arises.
    Use of a disk drive requires the inclusion of a
disk drive interface printed circuit card that
allows information to pass between the computer and
the disk drive. Disk drives can be purchased as part
of the computer system from the manufacturer or
distributer or they can be purchased as separate
items from an independent vendor. The source of your
disk drive is immaterial provided the cable
connection and interface card are compatible with

your machine. Frequently, disk drive units purchased
as individual items are less expensive than those
provided by the manufacturer of your computer.
Most microcomputer disk drive units are
designed to accommodate 5 1/4-inch floppy disks
although some machines use 3-inch mini floppy disks.
In both cases these soft plastic disks are covered
with a stiff cardboard envelope to give them
rigidity. The larger minicomputers often use an 8-
inch hard disk in conjunction with a 5 1/4-inch
floppy disk. (Still larger hard disks are frequently
used with mainframe machines, but these computers
are not generally found in common use in elementary
classrooms so we don't have to be concerned with
them.)
Floppy disks seem to have many characteristics
of typical phongraph records, but they actually
function in an entirely different way. Phonograph
records are provided with a set of spiraling grooves
on which music is recorded. To listen to a
particular song on the record, you must first listen
to all the songs recorded on the grooves preceding
the song you wish to hear. In other words phonograph
records behave like cassette tapes, as they provide
sequential information storage capabilities. Floppy
disks as used with the computer store information in
a completely different fashion.
Floppy disks are not provided with a set of
spiraling grooves, rather they more closely resemble
a smooth, blank surfaced record. Before information
can be stored on a floppy disk the disk must be
prepared to hold that information. The process of
of disk preparation to store computer programs
is called initializing or formatting the disk. Each
brand of computer has its own technical procedure
for preparing a disk to store information. Although
a floppy disk can be used with any computer disk
drive unit, once it is initialized it becomes
machine specific and can only be used with similar
machines made by the same manufacturer. There are
exceptions, but this is the general rule. Similarly,
when purchasing computer software one must use
programs that are designed for use with your brand
of computer as they have been prepared with
instructions for use with that particular disk
operating system.
Many computer software programs offer a built-
in routine that will automatically initialize a

48 MICROCOMPUTERS

blank disk so that it can store information. You can also format a disk by following the set of simple instructions given in your computer manual. A word of caution. Only initialize a computer disk once, as reinitializing the disk erases all information stored on it. No technical expertise is needed to initialize a disk. When a disk is initialized it is electro-magnetically divided into a series of tracts that can be thought of as a series of concentric circles. Each tract is subdivided into smaller units called sectors, and each sector is further divided into still smaller units called bytes. A byte represents the memory location of a character as you type it on the keyboard. Each byte has a memory location called an address associated with it so that it can be readily and accurately accessed by the computer.

Information is stored and recalled on disk in a random access fashion rather than in a linear sequence as found with cassette tapes. This means that information stored on disk is found by looking for that particular information without having to read in a linear sequence all the data previously saved. This is called random access memory and is much faster than cassette tape storage. Simply stated, the disk drive head can read information contained on any part of the disk at any time.

Disk heads are able to read between 1000 and 10000 characters per second, depending on the computer system you use. This is 10 to 100 times faster than the read capabilities using a cassette recorder system. Hard disk drive systems operate at a still faster rate, being able to read one million or more characters per second. Clearly the disk drive system offers tremendous speed advantages over cassette tape storage. In most cases the floppy disk system is preferable for use in elementary and secondary school applications.

There are many types and brands of 5 1/4-inch floppy disks on the market today. I suggest using a moderately priced disk for classroom applications. Floppy disks can be purchased singly, in two and ten packs, or in bulk lots of 50, 100, or more. If your need warrants it, the best buy may be to purchase disks in bulk.

Which type of disk to purchase can also be a confusing issue. Single and double sided disks are available and are termed single, double, and quadruple density. They are also available having hard or soft sectors. Check your computer to determine which type of disk your machine is designed to accommodate. The disk density reflects how tightly information can be packed on them. A double density disk can hold more information than a single density one. I find that single sided soft sector double density disks are the most convenient to use.

There are many other peripheral devices to give input to the computer. In many cases acoustical modem units are used that allow you to interface your computer using a telephone with another distant computer also provided with an acoustical modem. This technique allows you to access computer bulletin boards which serve the function of newspapers and information exchanges. The acoustical modem also allows you to send information directly to another computer. One important point to note is that communication from computer to computer via telephone lines constitutes a telephone call and your telephone company will bill you accordingly. Many computer bulletin boards are free while other services provided by modems must be purchased.

Music synthesizers can also be interfaced with your computer system, giving you the capability to program your computer to play music. Music scores can be written, saved, edited, and played back at a later time. Quality music synthesizers are relatively easy to use if you have a working knowledge of the techniques and procedures followed when writing music. The quality of sound generated by these devices varies according to the sophistication of the individual music synthesizer and its speaker system.

Several types of graphics tablets are currently available that easily allow you to create drawings and designs with no prior knowledge of computer language. Your drawings are literally drawn on the graphics tablet and the results appear on the monitor screen. A wide selection of colors is offered by most graphics tablets provided you have a color monitor. Drawings can be saved on disk or tape, edited, and retrieved at a later time. Some graphics tablets allow you to make composite drawings from those you have saved.

Some computers and computer software programs offer a touch sensitive monitor screen whereby instructions can be given and choices made using the monitor screen as an input device. In many cases computer input can be directed through the use of joysticks, paddles, or a computer mouse. The most advanced large-scale computers are frequently provided with optical readers which use light as a means to evaluate user input values. For many years punched cards were the primary means of data input to large computer systems, but today they are becoming increasingly difficult to find. The industry is beginning to develop voice activated computer input devices for microcomputers. These devices will likely come into prominence in the future as our technology advances to meet growing needs.

The microcomputer has within it a central processing unit, usually abbreviated CPU, that contains a control unit, an arithmetic logic component, and primary computer memory. These elements are contained on a single microprocessor chip and can be thought of as the computer itself. A similar microprocessor chip is built nowadays into calculators and other devices. In essence the microprocessor acts as the brain of the computer as it contains integrated circuits that allow the CPU to carry out all of its functions.

The control unit called the compiler performs a multitude of important functions necessary for the computer to operate properly. It regulates computer operations, reads programming instructions, and tells other components of the computer system what to do and how to do it. The compiler also keeps a record of which parts of the computer program instructions have been completed as well as those parts that have not yet been executed. It also collects output and sends it to the appropriate output device. When a computer program is run, the compiler translates into machine language program instructions given in a high level computer language like BASIC that are stored in the main memory of the computer. Machine language is the coded set of instructions by which the computer actually operates.

The arithmetic logic section of the microprocessor chip executes all mathematical and logic operations as required within the computer

program. Mathematical operations such as addition,
subtraction, multiplication, and division are
regulated by this component. It makes logical
comparisons and evaluations such as the evaluation
of relationships using concepts like greater than,
less than, and equal to. Program comparisons and
evaluations made from programming statements such as
FOR ... NEXT, REPEAT ... UNTIL, WHILE ... DO, and IF
... THEN are carried out within the arithmetic logic
unit so the program can be directed to proper
programming loops.

The primary computer memory within the
microprocessor consists of silicon chips on which
information can be stored. These chips constitute
what is commonly called RAM or random access memory.
It is a non-permanent type of memory that can be
read or written by the user. In many cases the user
can add more RAM chips to the central processing
unit.

RAM provides the compiler with a place for
temporary storage of computer program instructions
and data. It has no moving parts and its speed of
information transfer approximates the speed of
light. When a program is entered into the computer,
the compiler sends it to primary computer memory.
The control unit then retrieves the program one line
at a time as it is needed from the primary core
memory. When the computer is turned off all
information contained in RAM memory is lost.

Microcomputers vary radically in the amount of
RAM memory they have available. Available memory is
determined by the number of bytes present, where one
byte represents a single character or letter. As the
number of bytes present in computer memory is large,
a shorthand notation for the number of available
bytes of memory available is often used. The term
kilobyte is used to represent 1024 bytes of memory
and is usually abbreviated as 1K of memory.

The smallest computers on the market today
offer 4K or 4096 bytes of random access memory.
Machines providing 16K, 32K, 64K, 128K, 256K, and
512K are very common. Given the applications and
programs computers carry out today, a computer with
fewer than 16K RAM memory is practically useless.
Most educational computer programs require a minimum
of 32K and many need 64K to be able to be run. I do
not recommend the purchase of a computer for
educational purposes having fewer than 64K of RAM
memory.

The central processing unit also contains a set of chips that constitute the read only memory or ROM unit. These chips contain complex functions that are built into the computer by the manufacturer. These functions are permanently wired into this memory and cannot be altered or added .to by the user. These instructions are not lost when the computer is turned on or off.

As you can see, the central processing unit of the computer is a complex and integrated entity. We have not explored all of its components nor have we identified precisely how it works. For our purposes it can be thought of as the receiver of a program written by you in a computer language such as BASIC. It can also work with previously written and stored programs or purchased programs such as the word processing program WordStar. The CPU is the part of the computer system that carries out instructions, interprets and evaluates results, and directs the computer output.

There are several means by which the user can receive output from the computer. The most common output device used with microcomputer systems is the computer video monitor called the CRT (for cathode ray tube). The monitor is connected to the computer using a plastic coated wire cable. If your computer system is a self-contained single piece unit, the connection between the computer and the monitor will not be apparent.

Many component computer systems offer the choice of purchasing a video monitor or using your standard television set. If you plan to use your television set as a video display unit, the television is connected to the computer using a RF modulator. The RF modulator is connected from the computer video outlet to the antennae leads of the television set in the same manner in which home video games are connnected.

Computer video monitors provide better picture and character resolution than television sets using RF modulators. The graphics and characters viewed on monitor screens are much crisper. Both black and white and color monitors are available. If you are purchasing a single computer system I would recommend one providing a color monitor. Color monitor systems are significantly more costly, but the additional expense is worthwhile as many educational computer programs offer excellent color

graphics. However, if you are going to have several
computer systems, you might have some with black and
white monitors. When you use word processing
programs a color monitor is not necessary.
Cassette tapes and computer disks are often
used as recipients of computer output. The ability
to save information is an important aspect of the
computer system. These electromagnetic media storage
systems are almost always used for long-term storage
programs, data, and text files. The procedure to
follow for storing data is given in your computer
manual. Files can be erased from disk or tape so
it can be used repeatedly. One difference between
this type of storage and RAM memory is that you do
not lose the contents of the tape or disk you have
saved when the computer is turned off.
Frequently you will want a paper copy of work
done at the computer. We call this "hard" copy in
contrast to the "soft" copy of the electronic images
generated on the monitor screen. To get a hard copy
of your computer results you need a printer, a cable
that connects the printer to the computer, and the
proper printer interface circuit board.
Some electric typewriters can be interfaced
with a microcomputer system. This seems to be a cost
efficient decision as the typewriter could serve two
purposes, but in general there are more drawbacks
than advantages in using a typewriter rather than a
standard computer printer. The cost of an electric
typewriter that can be used with a computer is
greater than that for a printer. Typewriters print
characters at the rate of about 15 characters per
second, while typical printers generate between 25
and 100 characters per second. This is particularly
important if you are printing a long document.
The dot matrix printer is most commonly used in
homes, schools, and offices. It generates characters
by printing patterns of closely spaced dots. The
quality of output is not as good as an electric
typewriter, but it prints characters quickly at the
rate of 70 to 100 characters per second. More
sophisticated dot matrix printers print characters
at a much faster rate. There are many dot matrix
printers available for about $200 list price.
Letter quality printers do what their name
implies. They print characters that are
indistinguishable from those formed by a good
electric typewriter. These devices use a daisy wheel

character element containing 96 characters. The
wheel rotates each time a character is to be
printed. They operate much more slowly than dot
matrix printers and generate characters at the rate
of 25 to 50 characters per second. There are more sophisticated printers
available, such as the laser printer, but they are
not generally used in the classroom settings because
of their cost and the fact that they are not
necessary. If your facility has a computer, it is
necessary for you to have a printer. Your first
printer choice should be a dot matrix printer. Each
computer station does not require a printer, but if
a second printer were being considered I would
choose a letter quality printer.

There are several other output devices that are
used for special purposes with microcomputer
systems. Speech synthesizers can be used with some
computer software programs and are necessary when
working with vision impaired students. As mentioned
earlier, acoustical modems, music synthesizers, and
graphic tablets are used to meet special needs. In
general computer monitors, printers, and
electromagnetic storage media are the types of
computer output that you are likely to use.

BIBLIOGRAPHY

Cline, Ben E.   MICRO-PROGRAMMING: CONCEPTS AND
   TECHNIQUES. New York: Petrocelli Books, 1981.

   Offers a well-written discussion about computer
   architecture with emphasis on how circuit
   elements function.

Gear, C. William.   COMPUTER ORGANIZATION AND
   PROGRAMMING. New York: McGraw-Hill, 1980.

   Provides an excellent treatment of how a
   computer system functions, including input,
   output, and data storage.

Gorsline, G.W.   COMPUTER ORGANIZATION
   HARDWARE/SOFTWARE. Englewood Cliffs, N.J.:
   Prentice-Hall, 1980.

   A technically oriented treatment of computer
   components. Not for the novice.

Greenfield, S.E. THE ARCHITECTURE OF MICRO-
COMPUTERS. Cambridge, Mass.: Winthrop, 1980.

Gives a technical treatment of the structure and
design of computer systems with good
applications.

Khambata, Adi J. MICROPROCESSORS/MICROCOMPUTERS:
ARCHITECTURE, SOFTWARE AND SYSTEMS. New York:
John Wiley and Sons, 1982.

Provides an in-depth treatment of the design,
structure, and components of the microcomputer
system.

Osborn, Adam, and David Bunnell. AN INTRODUCTION TO
MICROCOMPUTERS. VOL 0, THE BEGINNERS BOOK.
Berkeley, Calif.: Osborn/McGraw-Hill, 1982.

Presents a very well written discourse on
components of a microcomputer system that is
geared toward the novice.

Richard, Ian. COMPUTERS. New York: Watts Pub.
Co., 1983.

A well-written volume for young people describing
computer functions and operations.

Schneiderman, Ben. SOFTWARE PSYCHOLOGY: HUMAN
FACTORS IN COMPUTER AND INFORMATION SYSTEMS.
Boston: Little, Brown, 1980.

Treats psychological factors that must be
considered when designing computer information
systems.

Shelly, Gary B., and Thomas Cashman. COMPUTER
FUNDAMENTALS FOR AN INFORMATION AGE. Brea,
Calif.: Anaheim Pub. Co., 1984.

Gives an excellent treatment of the component
functions of computer systems and how they are
integrated.

Sturvidge, Helena. MICROCOMPUTERS. New York:
Watts Pub. Co., 1984.

Outlines the hardware and software components of
the microcomputer system.

Tatchell, Judy, and Bill Bennett. THE BEGINNERS'
COMPUTER HANDBOOK. Burlington, Ontario, Canada:
Hayes Publishing Co., 1983.

Good for use with older children. Provides
introduction to the microcomputer and its
components and gives an introduction to computer
programming.

CHAPTER FOUR

HIGHLIGHT TOPIC
PURCHASING A COMPUTER SYSTEM

Before deciding whether or not to purchase a
computer system there are several child related
issues that must be considered. This obvious step is
frequently overlooked when one is examining the
computer systems, peripheral devices, and software
programs that are available for them. We must keep
child related issues clearly in mind, as the effect
computers can have on the education of young
children is our primary concern.
    Children are excited and enthusiastic when
working with electronic media in the home or
classroom setting. What we can easily forget is that
it is not necessarily the computer hardware that
generates interest in children. What the computer
can do and the software that can be run on it are
the key issues. As educators we can use this
emotional response to our advantage by creating
legitimate learning experiences for children using
currently available computer technology as it has
been applied to hardware and software development.
    The high level of positive emotional response
to the computer can often help the child learn
educational material more quickly. Children feel
challenged but not threatened when working with a
computer. The machine provides immediate feedback,
letting the child know if the answer is correct or
incorrect. There is a sense of privacy evident when
one works with a machine that demonstrates emotional
neutrality.
    If the teacher carefully plans computer based
activities, they can be used to complement other
academic work being done in the classroom. In this
case computer programs are used to supplement,
broaden, or provide a different approach to the

57

teaching of conceptualizations or factual material.
The computer can also be used to introduce
principles and ideas that will be further developed
using more traditional approaches. The computer
system can further be used to provide supplemental
information or offer extensions of principles that
have been previously introduced. The uses and
applications of the computer to the classroom seem
endless. Your goal should be to provide a computer
system that children can easily use and for which
there is appropriate software available to meet your
academic needs.

The computer provides tremendous variety and
versatility in the way that information and ideas
can be presented to children. The concepts that are
presented are frequently not unique and are usually
treated using other materials. The style of
presentation is what makes computer based
instruction different. It is very difficult to
emulate by other means the color graphics, motion,
sound, and variety of shapes that are used in
computer software programs. These secondary features
are what have direct appeal to children and
stimulate them to remain actively involved in the
learning experience.

The active participation in their own learning
and the sense of control over the machine they
develop are very positive impacts that using
computers can have on children. Working with
well-designed computer activities can help children
develop a positive self-image and enhance their
personal esteem. This is what we are always striving
to achieve as we teach our classes.

The type of computer and the kinds of software
chosen also have educational implications for the
types of learning that will take place in the
classroom. A computer system is an expensive piece
of equipment so you must try to insure that your
choice of machine clearly suits your intended
purposes. The machine should be easy for a child to
operate when using software or writing programs in a
computer language. Instructions should be stated on
the monitor screen in an easy-to-understand fashion
and not require complex responses by the user.
Statements to the user should be positive and
reinforcing rather than being abrupt and
intimidating. Programs and computer systems that
have these attributes are said to be user friendly.

You should also decide if the computer system being considered will meet your future needs. This can be difficult for the beginning user to do as you are likely to be concerned with today's applications and how to operate the computer system. There are a few precautions you can take to try to insure that the system will address current and future needs.

The computer system should be expandable so that it can grow to meet new tasks you require it to perform. For example, a machine having a relatively small amount of internal user accessible memory should allow for the easy addition of more memory units. In technical terms this means that a machine providing 16K RAM memory can be easily expanded to incorporate 48K or 64K RAM memory. This is very important as many software programs such as word processors require this level of computer memory in order to function.

The computer should also provide external jacks and/or internal electrical slots to allow for the simple incorporation of peripheral devices into the computer system. As an example, although telecommunications from computer to computer may not be a current concern, it may be an important issue in the future. Your system should allow for the addition of other accessories, such as printers, joysticks, game paddles, speech synthesizers, and graphics tablets. If these types of devices are not compatible with the computer system or are simply not available, this computer system cannot grow to meet your future needs. My advice is to look for another type of computer.

If your school is considering the purchase of several computers to perform similar functions, it is often wise to purchase identical machines rather than computers from different manufacturers. Although there are distinct advantages to letting children work with different machines as each machine has unique characteristics and software programs to use, at the outset it makes more sense to have a collection of similar computers.

By your choosing several similar machines the computer store or manufacturer may frequently allow a price discount. Furthermore, your software will be compatible so that computer programs can be shared and used on all of the equipment. In general, software produced for one type of computer cannot be run on other machines. Training is much easier if

one type of machine is used. Finally, in the event
of a malfunction it is more convenient to get repair
services if you are working with one type of
computer system.
    State-of-the-art computers have a wide variety
of computer software programs available for use with
them. The availability of appropriate software to
meet your educational goals should be the underlying
issue that determines which computer system is to be
purchased. Once more the novice is at a disadvantage
as much confusion can arise when one looks through
software catalogues because of the number of
available programs covering a wide range of subject
areas.
    This problem can be resolved if we examine ways
to cluster computer software into logical groupings.
The most versatile computer systems have software
available that has been produced to meet curriculum
and administrative needs. Identification of useful
computer software is usually most efficiently done
by reviewing computer software directories or
catalogues published by computer software
manufacturers or vendors.
    Tutorial programs are very useful as they
provide ways for children to review material
presented in class or introduce a new approach in
terms of presenting ideas and concepts. Similarly,
drill and practice software can be effectively used
to help children develop and master many important
skills.
    Microcomputers should have software available
for using different computer languages. Computers
usually have the language BASIC built into the
system, but software should also be available so
languages like Logo can be used. Using computer
languages helps develop logical and systematic
thinking skills and can help the cognitive
developmental process in young children. There
should also be ample software produced so one can
use many of the utility programs discussed in
Chapter Seven. These include word processing
programs as well as programs that help teachers
carry out administrative functions of the classroom.
    Simulation software are useful as they present
children with real or hypothetical circumstances and
ask them to make decisions that lead to solutions.
These programs typically provide multiple sets of
options and ask children to make choices. Computer

games at times can be used as educational software.
These activities help develop hand-to-eye
coordination and can often present educational
material in interesting and creative ways.
There are also computer programs presenting
arts software that let children explore drawing,
painting, and music in diverse and creative ways. If
the computer system you purchase has these types of
software available for use, it is very likely that
your system will meet today's academic needs as well
as those in the future.
There are several advantages to having the
computer as part of the educational classroom
environment. As we have seen, the computer can
provide an innovative way to introduce principles
and ideas on a wide range of subjects. The immediate
feedback this tool provides for children as well as
the non-threatening atmosphere it creates are
important considerations.
The computer can let the teacher assess students'
progress and test their understanding of lessons
that have been taught. By using existing software
programs or writing tailor-made ones, the teacher
can provide learning experiences for children that
address individual needs.
I hope this brief outline of issues relating to
uses of a computer system in the classroom will help
provide information that will allow you to choose
the best computer system to meet your needs. There
are a multitude of factors to consider, but if
approached systematically you can better make
appropriate decisions. Being well informed and
willing to ask questions are key factors that will
help you make the most appropriate decisions.

CHOOSING YOUR COMPUTER SYSTEM

Deciding which computer system to purchase can
result in an agonizing decision making process as
there are so many systems from which to choose. To
further compound the problem, each manufacturer's
system will likely offer one or more unique features
that are desirable. Of course, no one computer
system incorporates all the characteristics that

have been described to you by salespeople or you
have read about in literature. There must be a more
rational approach to purchasing a computer system
than going from store to store or catalogue to
catalogue.
There are a few steps to follow and tasks to
perform that will make your computer purchase
satisfying instead of being a fear ladened
experience. This is especially true for the
non-technically oriented person. The key step is to
be prepared, knowing what you are looking for and
why you want it. Once you have identified your
particular needs, you will know what questions to
ask, thus making the task much simplier.
Your first task is to clearly articulate what
you want the computer to perform today, and try to
predict future uses and applications of the computer
system. If you need the computer system to do word
processing, database management, and spread sheet
analysis the machine must have at least 48K of RAM
memory (random access memory). The reason for this
is simple. When many software programs are loaded
into the computer, they take up significant amounts
of memory themselves before you begin to enter your
data. These programs frequently use up to 30K of
memory, so you need extra memory to store
information within the computer before saving it on
cassette tape, cartridge, or floppy disk. Many
sophisticated programs require 64K of memory. Having
enough user available memory is an important issue
to consider when making a computer purchase.
The next step involves a small amount of
research. You should investigate the quality and
quantity of computer software available for each
system being considered for purchase. Computer
software directories and literature available from
software vendors and the computer manufacturer
should be adequate sources of information. Since
your goal is to use the computer system for
educational computing, there must be sufficient
software available at the time of your purchase.
Only the best computer systems are supported by a
wide variety of quality software that takes
advantage of state-of-the-art computer graphics and
sound capabilities available today.
If you plan to use or teach a programming
language, be sure that the computer system is able
to use that language. Learning to use a computer

language may not be your immediate goal, but most
users ultimately find uses for computer programming
when working with young children.
     Computers can utilize many useful accessories
that are called peripheral devices. These devices
are connected to the computer using external jacks
or by inserting printed circuit cards into accessory
slots within the computer. Adding peripheral devices
to the computer should not require special technical
knowledge and should be easy for the novice to use.
The computer should permit the addition of several
accessories to the computer environment. Be sure
that peripherals such as printers, disk drives,
modems, graphics tablets, and speech synthesizers
can be used with the computer system.
     Having a well-designed computer keyboard is
another feature of the best computer systems. The
best computer keyboards provide keys designed much
like those found on quality electric typewriters.
Some computer keyboards have keys similar to those
found on electric calculators or use a pressure
sensitive membrane onto which the keys are printed.
The typewriter-like keys are far superior to other
types as they are more convenient to use. Many
computer keyboards offer numeric keypads like those
used with calculators as well as special function
keys. These are luxuries that can make your work
easier.
     Your computer should be able to produce both
upper and lower case letters and provide a screen
display of at least 40 columns and 24 rows of type.
The computer should also contain a good quality
audio speaker system able to produce multiple
octaves. These characteristics are useful when
running a great many computer software programs.
     The computer should also provide an external
means for storing programs and information. Cassette
tapes, cartridges, and floppy disks are all
frequently used. A computer disk system is far
superior to cassette tape or cartridge storage. Data
stored on disk can be retrieved in seconds while
other means of data storage can take several minutes
to access. There are also many more educational
computer programs available on floppy disk than on
cassette tape or cartridge.
     The computer disk holds more information than
other means of data storage and is easier and more
convenient to use. When using a disk drive system

the user can easily receive a catalogue of disk contents making it very easy to search for a particular file. This is not the case when using other data storage systems. Disk drive systems are, however, much more expensive than cassette or cartridge storage since they cost six to eight times as much. I believe the extra cost represents a worthwhile investment.

Prices quoted for a computer can be deceiving as you will also need to purchase peripheral devices for the computer system to function. You will need an external memory device such as a disk drive or cassette recorder. A video display unit like a computer monitor or a television set is a necessity. A computer printer is another requirement although it is not necessary when running the system. The printer will be used to generate hard copies of your work. You will also need software to use with the computer system as well as miscellaneous items such as computer paper and cassette tapes or floppy disks. Frequently the total cost for these peripheral devices is more than two or three times the price of the computer itself.

The computers described in this section are representative of microcomputers used in schools and homes. Minicomputers and mainframe systems are not included because they are not in common use due to their high cost. These data are not intended to provide complete profiles of the machines, but to give general characteristics and unique features. Photographs of selected computers and computer systems are also included.

Acorn Computer

        Provides excellent graphics and offers 32K of RAM memory expandable to 256K. It can display up to 16 colors giving a screen format having 25 lines and 20, 40, or 80 columns. It can generate 3 voices, 4-channel music, and has a speech synthesizer. Compatible peripherals such as light pens, musical keyboards, modems, and graphic tablets are available. It has a moderately good selection of educational software available and can use several computer languages, including BASIC, FORTRAN, Logo, Pascal, Pilot, and Forth. The retail price of

the computer is $995.00, with a complete
computer system including computer, monitor,
and disk drive selling for $1790.00. Offers an
excellent networking system at a moderate cost.

Adam Computer

Offers very good graphics using 16 colors
and 3 voices. Has 80K RAM memory that is
expandable up to 144K. Provides a 24-line text
screen with 36 or 80 columns. Keyboard has a
numeric key pad. Can use BASIC and Logo as well
as many peripheral devices such as modems.
Limited educational software available for this
system. At a price of $700.00 the system
includes the computer, tape storage, monitor,
and letter quality printer.

Apple IIe

Provides very good graphics with a 24-line
text screen and 40 or 80 columns. Offers 16
colors in low resolution graphics and 8 colors
in high resolution graphics and a small audio
speaker. Has 64K RAM expandable to 128K.
Accessories including speech synthesizers,
printers, and graphics tablets are available.
Can use many computer languages with the
system, including BASIC, Logo, Pascal, Cobol,
Assembly language, Pilot, and FORTRAN. Has the
most extensive educational software library
available. The most commonly used computer in
school systems across the country at a price of
$895.00

Atari 600XL Computer

Has exceptional color graphics, offering 16
colors and 256 hues. Provides 4 voices over a
3 1/2-octave range and can use all commonly
available peripherals including disk drives and
musical keyboards. This machine has 16K RAM
memory expandable to 64K. It can use BASIC,
Logo, Pascal, and Pilot and offers a 24-line

Apple IIe Computer System
Photograph supplies courtesy
of Apple Computer, Inc.

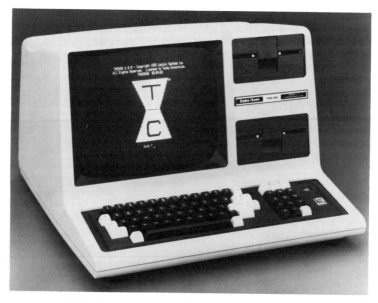

TRS-80 Model 4 Microcomputer
Photograph supplied courtesy
of Radio Shack,
A Division of Tandy Corporation

text screen with 40 columns. The unit retails
for $249.00, with a good selection of
educational software available.

Atari 800XL Computer

A more powerful machine than the Atari
600XL. It has a 64K RAM memory expandable to
128K. Offers the same features as the 600XL,
but is much more versatile and quicker to
operate. Cost of the Atari 800XL is $329.00
and it too offers a good selection of
educational software.

Atari 1200XL Computer

A versatile computer, having 64K RAM memory
expandable to 128K. Offers 256 color options
and has a built-in 4-voice system. Provides
both help and computer function keys. Has
excellent color and graphics. Can add
peripheral devices. Priced at $229.00, with
good educational software available.

Commodore-64 Computer

A very popular machine with home users.
Provides 64K of RAM memory and a 40-character
width screen having 25 lines of text. Very good
graphics and offers 16 colors and 3 voices over
9 octaves. Can use the computer languages
BASIC, Logo, and Pilot with this machine as
well as most accessories, including joysticks,
printers, modems, and light pens. Priced at
$225.00, with a moderately good selection of
educational software available.

Commodore-128 Computer

A new model having 128K RAM memory and
providing a 40- or 80-column screen display.
Has a good keyboard, including a numeric keypad
and several dedicated keys to perform special
functions. Offers very good color and graphics

capabilities. Can run all Commodore-64 software. An excellent computer sold at a retail price of $300.

Epson HX-20 Notebook Computer

Uses a microcassette tape storage system and has a built-in word processor. Has typewriter style keys as well as several programmable function keys. Provides 16K RAM memory expandable to 64K. Includes accessible jacks for peripherals, including telecommunication equipment and printers. This is a portable computer that can fit into a briefcase and costs $795.00.

Epson QX-10 Computer

A very easy-to-use computer having a typewriter-like keyboard with print, help, and store keys for user convenience. Offers built-in software, including word processing, database management, and spread sheet. A fast operating system providing a very good visual display. System includes a computer, monitor, and disk drive. Priced at $2995.00, it is an excellent machine for non-technically oriented users.

Franklin Ace 1000 Computer

Has a typewriter-like keyboard including a numeric keypad. Offers 64K RAM memory expandable to 512K and a 40-, 70-, or 80-column screen having 24 text lines. Provides good graphics and includes a small audio speaker. Offers 16 colors in low resolution graphics and 8 in high resolution graphics. Handles most peripherals such as musical keyboards, game paddles, and voice synthesizers as well as the computer languages BASIC, Logo, FORTRAN, Pascal, Pilot, and C-BASIC. Priced at $700.00, with an excellent collection of educational software available.

Acorn Computer
Photograph supplied courtesy
of Acorn Computer Corporation

Apple IIe Computer
Photograph supplied courtesy
of Apple Computer, Inc.

Franklin Ace 1200 Computer

A 64K RAM memory machine expandable to
512K, offering 40, 70 or 80 characters per line
and a 24-line text screen. A faster machine
than the Franklin Ace 1000 it provides the same
color and graphics capabilities. Priced at
$1495.00, with same peripheral possible
interface as the Franklin Ace 1000, as well as
computer languages and software.

Franklin AcePro Plus Computer

Includes an Ace 1000 computer, monochrome
monitor, disk drive, and 80-column text card.
Software provided includes a word processor,
database management, and spread sheet program.
Has a clear quality video display and at a
price of $1495.00 is an excellent value.

IBM PC Computer

Provides 256K RAM memory expandable to
640K and an 80-column screen having 25 lines of
text display. Has fair graphics using 16 text
colors and 8 graphics colors. Provided with a
single voice speaker with an 8-octave range.
The IBM PC can utilize all typical peripherals
and use several computer languages including
BASIC, Fortran, Pascal, and Logo. Retail cost
is $1265.00, with a fair collection of
educational software available.

IBM PCjr Computer

IBM has discontinued the manufacture of
this machine but there are many available. It
has an 80-column screen with 25 text lines.
Graphics are fair, using 16 text colors and 8
colors for graphics. Has a sound generator with
3 voices over a range of 7 to 8 octaves. A 128K
RAM memory is provided and the machine can run
most IBM PC software that includes a fair
collection of educational software. Price is
listed at $999.00.

Macintosh Computer

A computer providing 128K RAM memory and
having 80-character columns per line, with the
number of text lines dependent on the character
size. Does not provide color, but has good
graphics and a sound generator. Peripherals
such as modems and printers can be used with
this machine as well as computer languages like
C, Forth, and Pascal. The computer is priced at
$2495.00 and has a limited collection of
educational software available for it.

Sanyo SN550 Computer

Has 128K RAM memory expandable to 256K. A
fast operating computer providing good graphics
resolution. Has 8-color capability and provides
jacks for accessories. Priced at $699.00,
including word processing and spread sheet
programs. Includes one disk drive using single
sided disks.

Sanyo SN5502 Computer

A fast operating machine with jacks for
peripherals. Provides very good text resolution
and offers 8 colors. Has 128K RAM memory
expandable to 256K. Priced at $749.00, with one
disk drive using 2-sided disks. Has good
graphics.

Sinclair QL Computer

Includes built-in software, including word
processing, spread sheet, and database
management, as well as a graphics routine. Has
jacks available for accessories such as
monitors, printers, and television sets. Has
128K RAM expandable memory and is provided with
a typewriter-style keyboard. Retail cost is
$499.00; offers good screen instructions for
computer operations.

Texas Instruments Professional Computer
Photograph supplied courtesy of
Texas Instruments, Inc.

Texas Instruments
Portable Professional Computer
Photograph supplied courtesy
of Texas Instruments, Inc.

TRS-80 Color Computer II

Provides 16K RAM memory expandable to 64K
and offers a 32-column screen with 16 text
lines. Has good graphics using 8 colors and
capable of generating 255 different sound
tones. Can interface with modems, graphics
tablets, printers, and other peripherals and
use computer languages such as Assembly
language, BASIC, Logo, and Pilot. Priced at
$120.00, with a fair collection of educational
software available.

TRS-80 Model 4 Personal Computer

Is a completely self-contained single unit
computer system. Provides a 12-inch diagonal
screen giving green characters on a black
background with very good uniformity of
characters. Has a typewriter-style keyboard
including a numeric keypad. Provides 64K RAM
memory expandable to 128K. Can interface with
most peripherals. A moderately good educational
software collection is available.

A video display unit is a necessity when using
a microcomputer system. One can use a computer
monitor or a television set to view images on the
screen. I firmly believe that in terms of quality of
screen display, the computer monitor is far superior
to a television set. Most television sets only
provide for a 40-column width character display,
although in some cases there are attachments
available that let you achieve 80 characters per
screen line of text. Television sets are not able to
clearly display defined sets of closely spaced
characters and graphics, as their picture tube
resolution is not adequate to perform this task.
Many computer programs such as word processors and
spread sheet software are easier to use with an
80-column text screen. For these reasons I prefer
the computer monitor to the television set for a
computer video display unit.
There are several important features and
characteristics to consider before purchasing a
monitor for your computer system. The first step is

Epson Computer System
Photograph supplied courtesy
of Epson America

Epson Notebook Computer
Photograph supplied courtesy
of Epson America

to view the images formed on the monitor screen
while the monitor is connected to the computer you
are examining. Fill the screen with characters to
check for uniform character clarity and to see if
some characters are cut off at the edges of the
screen. Overscanning is the term used to describe
the cutting off of computer characters at the edges
of the screen.

Similarly, there should not be large areas of
unused space along the borders of the screen. This
is called underscanning. Quality computer monitors
can be adjusted to compensate for over- or
underscanning. There should also be a good contrast
between the characters on the monitor screen and the
background color. Most monochrome monitors provide
white or green characters against a black
background. Some color monitors give the user
choices among several background colors.

In any case the best monitors allow you to
adjust for brightness, contrast, and color as on a
television set. Many monitors also have vertical and
horizontal hold adjustments and are provided with an
antiglare screen. Adjustment control panels are most
convenient when they are positioned at the front or
side of the monitor rather than at the back.

Clarity of images and contrast between
characters and background color are among the most
important features to consider when purchasing a
monitor. How the picture aesthetically appeals to
you is the important issue. The monitors described
in this section all provide good quality pictures
and are in common use today. Although they are
significantly more expensive, you should consider
purchasing a color monitor to take full advantage of
the advanced color graphics available in educational
software. If, however, your primary application is
word processing, choose a monochrome monitor.

Amdek Color 300 Monitor

       A color monitor having a 12-inch diagonal
picture. Has excellent uniformity of characters
and a good control panel. Has a built-in
speaker and audio amplifier for sound
production and a headphone jack for individual
use. A tilt/swivel stand base is available.
Cost is $350.00.

Amdek Color 600 Monitor

Provides excellent text and graphics resolution. User can change from white to green characters for text with a switch on the front of the monitor. Has very good character quality and includes a speaker, audio amplifier, and headphone jack. An excellent monitor priced at $650.00.

Amdek Video 300 Monitor

Provides a black-and-white picture on a 12-inch diagonally measured antiglare screen. Has good brightness and excellent contrast. Does not give horizontal overscanning and features excellent uniformity of characters at all screen positions. Provides green characters on a black background for text. Priced at $179.00.

Apple Color Monitor

Offers a crisp picture with good character resolution. No over- or underscanning when used with an Apple computer. Provided with a 12-inch diagonal picture with no character distortion. Very good uniformity of characters. Retail price listed at $375.00.

Apple III Monitor

A monochrome monitor priced at $249.00 providing a 12-inch diagonal screen. Has green characters against a black background. Has an antiglare screen with very good brightness and contrast. Very good uniformity of characters and no over- or underscanning when used with Apple computers. Some adjustments can be made if used with other machines.

BMC Composite Monitor

This color monitor has a 13-inch diagonal screen. Has good text resolution and a clear

crisp picture. Priced at $239.00. No character
distortion. Overscanning and underscanning not
a problem.

Commodore 1702 Color Monitor

Has very good picture resolution and offers
good colors. Provides a 14-inch screen and has
good image clarity. Designed for use with
Commodore computers. Does not show over- or
underscanning problems. List price is $255.00.

Comrex 5600 Monitor

A monochrome monitor priced at $179.00
providing a 12-inch diagonal screen. Has good
brightness and excellent contrast. Significant
horizontal overscan is possible but it can be
adjusted. Offers green characters on a black
background showing excellent uniformity of
characters. Includes a video jack.

Hitachi MM1270P Monitor

A monochrome monitor producing green
characters against a black background. Has a
12-inch screen showing good character
resolution and uniformity of characters. Does
not show overscanning or underscanning. Priced
at $185.00.

NEC 1201 Monitor

A monochrome monitor providing a green
background and a 12-inch screen. Has good
character resolution. Gives 80 columns of text
per line and 25 lines of text on the screen.
Priced at $139.00; jacks provided at the back
of the machine.

NEC 1216 Color Monitor

Has good colors and clear character
resolution. Allows for 80 characters across the

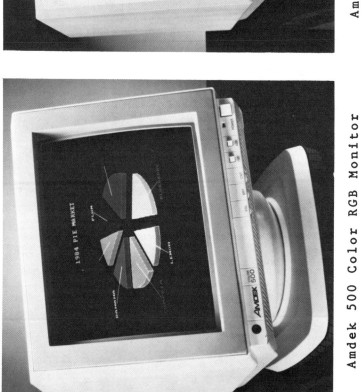

Amdek 700 Color RGB Monitor
Photograph supplied courtesy
of Amdek Corporation

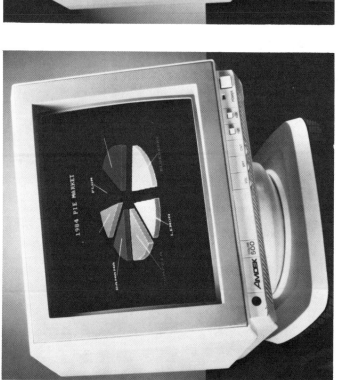

Amdek 500 Color RGB Monitor
Photograph supplied courtesy
of Amdek Corporation

screen and 25 lines of text on the 12-inch
screen. Offers a clear crisp picture with no
overscanning or underscaning at a price of
$429.00.

Panasonic D1300 RGB Color Monitor

Has excellent color and graphics, with
good adjustment capabilities for picture. Very
good uniformity of characters and can adjust
internally to compensate for over- or
underscaning. Priced at $359.00 and provided
with a 12-inch picture.

Panasonic D1300D Monitor

Has a 13-inch diagonal screen and provides
both front and rear panels for many picture
adjustments. Has very good brightness and
contrast and shows very good character
resolution. Priced at $380.00.

Panasonic S101 Monitor

An inexpensive color monitor priced at
$250.00 that lets the user switch from color to
black and white. Provided with a 10-inch screen
and a built-in speaker and amplifier. Gives a
clear picture and sharply defined characters.
Includes front and rear control panels. User
can internally adjust for over- and
underscanning.

Princeton HX-12 Monitor

A color monitor having excellent text
resolution. Has a 12-inch screen offering 80
columns per line. Priced at $489.00; very good
colors and picture quality; overscanning and
underscanning not a problem.

Quadchrom Color Monitor

A color monitor showing excellent
character resolution on a 12-inch screen.
Provides 80 characters per line of text and 24
lines per screen. Has good colors and does not
show overscanning or underscanning. Priced at
$499.00.

Sakata SC100 Monitor

A composite color monitor providing a
13-inch screen. Has good colors and clear
images. Priced at $249.00, with audio speakers
and earphone jack included. Gives 80 columns of
text per line.

Sakata SC200 Monitor

A color monitor offering superior color
graphics. Has very good screen resolution and
provides very good brightness and contrast.
Priced at $499.00 and offers 80 columns of text
per line.

Sanyo CRT70 Monitor

Has a 12-inch screen offering 80
characters per line and 25 lines viewable at
one time. Has excellent color and good text
resolution. Priced at $589.00; shows uniform
image clarity on all parts of the screen.

Sanyo DM5109CX Monitor

Offers very good brightness and excellent
contrast on a 9-inch diagonal screen. Has
excellent uniformity of characters but may have
some non-adjustable horizontal overscanning.
Priced at $175.00; provides green characters on
a black background.

Sanyo DM8012CX Monitor

Has a 12-inch diagonal screen offering
black characters on a white background.
Antiglare screen gives very good brightness and
contrast. Some horizontal overscanning is
possible but it is internally adjustable.
Excellent uniformity of characters; cost is
$240.00.

Sanyo DM8112CX Monitor

A monochrome monitor providing a 12-inch
diagonal antiglare screen with very good
brightness and contrast. Offers green
characters on a black background with some
horizontal overscanning possible. Priced at
$250.00; shows very good uniformity of
characters.

Sony CPD120 Monitor

A monochrome monitor offering excellent
contrast and brightness on a 12-inch diagonal
screen. Has good clarity of characters and
picture resolution. Does not demonstrate
overscanning or underscanning. Priced at
$375.00.

Tandy CM-2 Color Monitor

Provides excellent graphics and character
resolution. Offers a front control panel for
picture adjustments. Has a 12-inch diagonal
screen with clear crisp colors. Does not
demonstrate overscanning or underscanning. List
price is $549.95.

Tandy VM-3 Monochrome Monitor

Provides a 12-inch diagonal screen with a
front control panel for picture adjustments.
Gives white characters on a black background

Amdek Color Monitor
Photograph supplied courtesy
of Amdek Corporation

and provides good picture resolution. Has good
graphics capabilities and does not show over-
or underscanning. List price is $219.00.

Taxan 400 Monitor

A color monitor having very good colors
and good screen resolution. The 12-inch screen
gives good uniformity of characters with no
distortions. Priced at $269.00.

Taxan RG Bvis III Monitor

A color monitor providing a 12-inch
screen. User can choose among four screen
background colors. Has good colors for graphics
and a front control panel for color adjustment.
Has good brightness and picture resolution.
Priced at $630.00.

USI 1400 Monitor

A color monitor providing a built-in
speaker and giving 16 screen colors. Has good
picture resolution with no distortions. Priced
at $279.00; overscanning and underscanning not
a problem.

USI 900G Monitor

A monochrome monitor having a 9-inch
screen. The green screen provides a clear
picture. Offers 80 characters per line of text
and 24 lines of text on the screen at one time.
Priced at $99.99.

Zenith M123 Monitor

A monochrome monitor providing a 12-inch
diagonal screen and green characters against a
black background. Has good character resolution
and picture clarity for graphics. Priced at
$169.00 and offers good brightness and
contrast.

Zenith M135 Monitor

        A color monitor offering a 13-inch screen
and having good graphics and color. Allows for
80 columns of text and 25 lines per screen. Has
16 colors with very good resolution and uniform
image clarity across the screen. Priced at
$269.00.

        Choosing a printer to use with your computer
system can be an exasperating process as there are
so many types of printers available that have a wide
range of options. As was true for other components
of the computer system, you must first identify your
specific needs to address current tasks and make
predictions for future requirements. Although a
printer is not necessary for the functioning of the
computer system, it is highly unlikely that a user
can efficiently use a computer system without a
printer being available.
        Printers are used to perform a variety of
computer related tasks. They are used to obtain
paper copies of reports, letters, and material that
have been written using a word processor. When
writing programs in a computer language like BASIC
users typically use a printer to get a copy of
programming instructions as well as sample program
runs. The hard copy a printer provides makes editing
documents and debugging computer programs a much
simpler task. Similarly, data and results from
statistical analyses, computations from spread sheet
software, and sorts generated from database
management programs are obtained using a computer
printer. Many printers are also able to print graphs
and charts in both black and white and color. These
applications and the fact that the printer can
produce typed documents at a much greater speed than
even a good typist make it an invaluable tool.
        Computer printers most frequently used for
home, business, and educational applications are
generally called impact printers. These machines
produce characters by having a print element strike
an inked ribbon forming characters on paper in the
same manner as an electric typewriter. There are
other types of printers including laser jet printers
that generate characters at a tremendous rate of

speed. These devices are very expensive and are not
generally used in educational settings. They are not
considered in this discussion.

There are two types of impact printers in
common use. Dot matrix printers produce characters
by moving a distinct set of pins or wires against an
inked ribbon that touches the computer paper. The
print element moves back and forth across the page
printing material at a fast rate. Printed letters
are formed by a unique set of closely spaced dots
which are detectable by the naked eye.

The majority of dot matrix printers offers a
variety of character forms. Frequently the user can
choose between pica and elite typeface and can use
bold type, enlarged and reduced character modes.
Features such as the ability to underline text and
use superscripts and subscripts are available with
these machines. Instructions for using these
features are provided in printer manuals and often
as routines within computer software programs.

A second class of impact printers are called
letter quality printers. These machines print
characters much slower than dot matrix printers but
the characters are indistinguishable from those
formed by a quality electric typewriter. Most of
these printers are called daisywheel printers as
print characters are mounted on a central hub like
spokes on a wheel. As characters are typed the
daisywheel rotates to accommodate the new character
position on the wheel. Generally, letter quality
printers are more expensive than dot matrix printers
but produce superior looking documents.

The best printers are able to print letters
with descenders, that is, characters like the
letters "j" and "p" where part of the letters extend
below the line of type. This gives the type an
appearance much like that seen in a book or magazine
and is easy to read. Quality printers are also able
to proportionally space letters. This means that a
letter like "i" takes up less space than a "w"
making for much easier reading.

All computer printers generate characters at a
faster rate than most typists. Better printers can
do this in part because they print characters
bidirectionally, that is, from left to right and
right to left across the printed page. This reduces
the time necessary to print a document. The most
sophisticated printers move the print head to the

exact location on the line where characters are to
be printed. In general dot matrix printers generate
characters at a rate three to four times faster than
letter quality printers.

There are three types of paper that printers
can use. Some printers use continuous roll paper,
others single sheets, and still others continuous
form tractor fed paper. Tractor fed paper has
perforated edges which are easily torn off after the
document is printed. The most convenient printers to
use are those that permit the user to print single
sheets and can also use tractor fed paper. Some
letter quality printers require the addition of a
tractor feed unit before tractor fed paper can be
used.

The best printers provide a switch that lets
you go from one type of paper to another. These
printers allow you to use a variety of paper types
and widths, ranging from 5-inch note paper to
mailing labels to standard 8 1/2-inch width
stationery. Versatility is an important issue to
consider before purchasing your computer printer.

Computer printers that provide a control panel
for line and paper feed functions are the easiest to
use. The printers described here are relatively
inexpensive and can perform a wide range of
functions. Before purchasing the printer be sure
that it is compatible with your computer. You can
read the specification literature for this
information or you can simply ask your computer
dealer.

Amdek 5025 Printer

          A very quiet running letter quality
printer priced at $899.00. It offers friction
paper feed for single sheets of paper but a
tractor feed attachment is available. Print
rate is good, offering bidirectional printing.
Has a control panel and generates good quality
print.

Apple Imagewriter Printer

          A fast operating dot matrix printer
offering a variety of type styles and character

widths. Provides good graphics and has
descenders and proportional spacing. Price is
$695.00; has a 15-inch carriage and a front
control panel.

Atari 1025 Printer

A dot matrix printer offering both single
sheet and tractor fed paper. Prints 80
characters per line at a moderate speed. Has a
price of $189.00 and provides multiple
character sizes.

Axion 700 Color Printer

A dot matrix printer that can print up to
four colors. Operates at a moderate print speed
and can print up to 20 graphics symbols. Can
make 3 carbon copies at a time. List price of
$483.00.

Daisywriter 2000 Printer

A letter quality printer with excellent
type quality. Operates at an average speed and
has descenders and proportional spacing. Both
tractor feed and sheet feed attachments
available. List price is $949.00.

Datasouth Personal Printer I

A dot matrix printer priced at $695.00,
offering very good print quality approaching
that of a letter quality printer. Has both
friction and pin feed capabilities. Has
descenders, can print various sized characters
using multiple character sets. Can print
graphics and is provided with a control panel.

Diablo 620 Printer

A letter quality printer having excellent
print quality, priced at $1050.00. Provides

friction feed for single sheets of paper but a
tractor feed attachment is available. A fast
operating machine providing descenders and
proportional spacing. Can print graphics and is
provided with a good control panel.

Epson FX-80 Printer

A dot matrix printer providing good
quality print, priced at $699.00. Can use
single and continuous form paper. Can print
graphics as well as varying sizes and
darknesses for characters. Has good print speed
with descenders and proportional spacing. Has
an excellent control panel.

Epson JX-80 Printer

A fast operating dot matrix printer that
can print up to seven colors, priced at
$800.00. Offers 128 type styles, including
elite and pica, with enlarging and underlining
features for them. Has full descenders and
proportional spacing. An excellent machine that
produces accurate graphics and can use both
tractor fed and friction fed paper.

Epson MX-80 Printer

A good quality dot matrix printer having
good speed, able to print graphics. Can use
tractor fed or single sheet paper. Has multiple
print features including: large and small
character sizes, extra dark print, special
characters, subscripts, and superscripts. A
very versatile machine having a good control
panel.

Epson RX-80 Printer

A dot matrix printer able to print
graphics characters, priced at $299.00.
Provided with tractor feed which can be removed

for friction feed. Can print multiple character
sizes, types, and darknesses. Has very good
print quality and good print speed.

Gemini 10X Printer

A dot matrix printer providing good
quality print and showing very good
versatility. Can use single sheet, roll, or
tractor fed paper. List priced at $399.00. Has
good print speed and gives 80 characters of
text per line.

Juki 6300 Printer

A letter quality printer priced at $995.00
that has average print speed. It can print
multiple sized characters with proportional
spacing. Variety of type forms, including
superscript and subscript, boldface and
underlining. A good quality printer offering
bidirectional typing.

Mannesmann Tally Printer

A dot matrix printer priced at $259.00
that operates at a good type speed. Can use
both single sheet and tractor fed paper. A
quiet running machine, printing in multiple
character modes and offering good graphics.

Microline 80 Printer

A dot matrix printer having good quality
type, priced at $499.00. Has good typing speed
and can handle standard sheet paper or
continuous form paper. Can print graphics and
offers both large and small sized characters.
Provided with a control panel.

Microline 82A Printer

A dot matrix printer providing very good
quality print, priced at $549.00. Has slow type

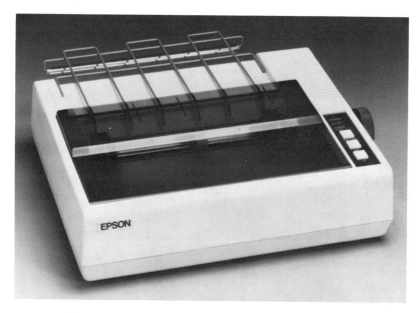

Epson RX-80 Dot Matrix Printer
Photograph supplied courtesy
of Epson America

Epson FX-80 Dot Matrix Printer
Photograph supplied courtesy
of Epson America

speed but provides descenders and an excellent
control panel. Has both small and large
character print modes and can print graphics
and special characters. Can use both single
sheet and tractor fed paper.

Microline 92 Printer

A daisywheel printer offering very good
quality print, priced at $699.00. Has average
speed and can use single sheet and tractor fed
paper. Can print graphics as well as various
sizes and darknesses for characters. Provides
proportional spacing and can combine print
modes. Has an excellent control panel.

Olympia Electronic Compact RO Printer

A versatile and inexpensive letter quality
printer priced at $550.00. Has fair print speed
with proportional spacing and full descenders.
Offers both tractor and friction paper feed.
Can use 2 1/4 to 15-inch wide paper and
provides bidirectional printing. Has an
easy-to-use control panel.

Olympia Needle Point Printer

A dot matrix printer priced at $329.00
that can use both single sheet and tractor fed
paper. A fast operating printer that prints
bidirectionally. Provides descenders and
proportional spacing and gives good type
quality.

Panasonic P1090 Printer

A dot matrix printer providing for
multiple paper widths, priced at $395.00. Can
print graphics characters having very good
print quality. Prints characters of varying
sizes and darknesses. Prints bidirectionally
and can underline and print special characters.
Has a control panel.

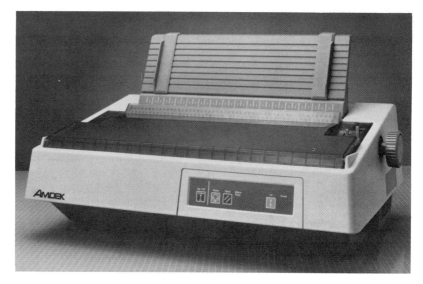

Amdek 5040 Letter Quality Printer
Photograph supplied courtesy
of Amdek Corporation

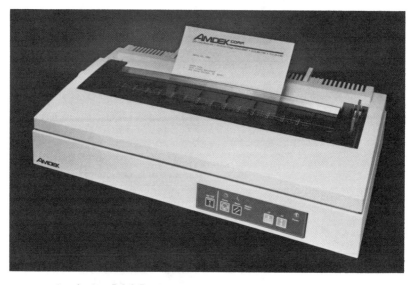

Amdek 5025 Letter Quality Printer
Photograph supplied courtesy
of Amdek Corporation

Radio Shack DMP-100 Printer

A dot matrix printer providing fair
quality type at a price of $399.00. Has
moderate type speed and can use multiple sized
tractor fed paper. Can print graphics and extra
large character sizes.

Radio Shack DMP-120 Printer

A dot matrix printer that can print
graphics characters. Is a fast printer
generating good quality characters. Can print
bidirectionally and will underline and give
variable sized characters, including elongated
and condensed forms.

Radio Shack DWP-210 Printer

A letter quality printer offering fair
print speed and providing very good quality
type, priced at $599.00. Has proportional
spacing and prints bidirectionally. Can print
up to 115 characters per line and has a control
panel with excellent features. Provided with
single page paper feed but a tractor feed
attachment is available.

Microcomputer Networks

Another consideration to address when you are
using several computers in one classroom or have
several microcomputers scattered in classrooms
throughout your building is whether or not your
computers should be networked. A microcomputer
network consists of several computers that are
connected to one master control computer. The
control computer contains all of the software used
by individual microcomputer stations.
Each machine still functions as a typical
microcomputer allowing you to word process
information, write computer programs, create music,
or perform any other computer assigned task. The
principal difference between a networked system and
free standing computers is that all software used by
networked machines are loaded from the master

computer. Similarly, data to be stored are loaded into the master computer. Computer printers are frequently connected to the control computer.

The individual computers communicate with the master computer on a time sharing basis. This means that if five users wish to access information stored in the master computer, the master computer processes the requests on a first-come first-serve basis. Microcomputers process information so quickly that in most cases users hardly realize that they do not have immediate access to the control computer. Some microcomputer network systems let the operator prioratize computers that are part of the network system. For example, if computer #3 were given first priority, a user operating this machine will get immediate access to the master control computer even though other users had asked for access first.

The key to understanding how a microcomputer network functions is to realize that the only time you must communicate with the control computer is when you wish to access programs or store data values. At all other times your computer station functions as any other microcomputer. You might then ask why one might wish to establish a microcomputer network.

The primary reason for using a network is the cost savings that can result. Your system software needs can be greatly reduced as you will not require multiple copies of programs for use with computers in different classrooms. You will simply need a single networked version of the program that can be down loaded to any computer that is part of the network. Individual student or classroom disks for information storage are not needed as this function is also carried out by the master control computer. A school or classroom having several networked computers can function nicely with one printer connected to the control computer.

Networked computer software has the advantage of letting teachers in different classrooms use the same software program simultaneously. The storage capability of the master computer is usually much greater than that for individual microcomputers. Recent trends indicate that networked microcomputer systems are beginning to use hard disks as the primary means of data storage. Hard disks can store tremendous amounts of information and access these data at fantastic rates of speed.

Almost any number of microcomputers can be networked, ranging from three or four to 100 or 200, depending on the type of networking system you are using. Schools in Great Britain have been using the Acorn computer network system with great success for the last three years. In general, microcomputer network systems have not been used to an appreciable extent in United States elementary schools. These systems have been more common in secondary education and in college and university settings.

If there are advantages to the microcomputer network system there must also be drawbacks. One principal disadvantage relates directly to technical breakdown of equipment. If a technical problem arises with the master computer, the entire network cannot function. Another disadvantage is that there is not a diverse collection of educational software available for microcomputer network systems.

To build a computer network some specialized equipment is needed. Each network requires a network control unit as well as cables and a disk drive unit for the master computer. Two disk drives usually are included that can read double sided disks, or a hard disk system is used. One must also purchase standard software for the network system.

These items can represent a considerable capital outlay for a school, depending on how many computers are being networked. However, cost analyses for networking computer systems indicate that in the long run networking is cost effective. Several types of microcomputers can be networked, including Acorn computers, Apple computers, and TSR-80 Radio Shack computers. For detailed information about the purchase and installation of specific microcomputer networks contact your computer dealer.

Additional Computer Peripherals

There is also a collection of computer peripherals that can greatly increase the number of ways in which your computer system can be used. Some of these accessories help protect equipment or let you store disks and cassette tapes in a more organized and safe fashion. In many cases these items reflect the hidden costs of owning a microcomputer system, but they are worth the financial investment as they increase the quality of work that can be done. Technical specifications and sources of these products can be readily obtained from computer and office supply dealers, as well as from catalogues. You will find many practical applications for these materials as you explore new ways and techniques for using your microcomputer system.

Cassette tape and floppy disk storage devices become important as increased numbers of computer software programs are purchased and the number of data and programming disks grows. There is a wide variety of plastic containers designed for storing magnetic materials available at computer stores, office supply dealers, as well as from department stores and from catalogue sales. They are an inexpensive way to protect your programs and a convenient way to organize them. Back-up copies of computer software should be stored in these containers and kept at a distant location.

There are several cursor control devices that can be used with some computer software such as for games and creating music programs. Devices like game paddles, joysticks, and the mouse greatly simplify instructions the user gives to the computer. Some software requires the use of a cursor control device. This equipment is relatively inexpensive and can be particularly useful when working with children with physical disabilities.

Data storage devices are a must for your computer system. They are usually included as part of the package when you purchase a complete computer system, but if you buy individual components they frequently are not. A cassette tape recorder is the least expensive way to store computer programs on cassette tape. You must also provide the appropriate interface cable to connect the recorder to the computer. A disk drive unit serves the same function but is much more costly; however, it is a much more efficient and easy means of data storage. Many computers require the addition of an interface card when the disk drive is connected to the computer. Many users find that having two disk drives connected to the computer is useful when running some computer software programs. The addition of a second disk drive does not require the purchase of an additional disk controller card. Disk controller cards are not generally included in the price of the disk drive as they are machine specific.

In many cases users wish to add additional circuitry to their computer system. Some systems allow the easy plug-in addition of RAM memory cards that increase the internal user accessible memory within the computer. In other cases memory chips can be added. This new circuitry frequently allows you to run more sophisticated programs or lets you use existing software more efficiently.

The 80-column text card is among the most frequently used pieces of circuitry that is added to the computer. Many machines do not allow for 80 columns of text to be seen on the screen at one time. This can be very inconvenient when using some word processing programs since the typical stationery and computer paper allows for eighty columns of text to be printed. If needed these devices can usually be plugged into internal jacks provided in the computer.

Most computers allow for the inclusion of graphics tablets as peripheral devices. These tools permit the user to draw and paint computer pictures without using computer type commands. Instead the user is provided with a stylus or a light pen which is used in conjuction with the graphics tablet itself. Creations made with graphics tablets can be saved on cassette tape or floppy disk and later edited or combined with other creations. This equipment is relatively expensive, typically priced between $100 and $300. Graphics tablets have been used very successfully when working with disabled children.

Modems have become increasingly popular as a telecommunication device for use with microcomputers. A modem is simply a mechanical device that lets the user connect the computer to a telephone line in order to communicate with other machines that are provided with this device. They provide a convenient means for information exchange as programs and data can be passed from one machine to another very quickly. You can easily communicate with a machine located hundreds of miles away, but you will be billed by the telephone company as if you had made a typical telephone call, so this can be expensive. Computer user groups, bulletin board services, and educational databases frequently use modems as the means for communication.

Quality musical keyboards can be valuable educational tools when connected to the microcomputer. Using these piano-like keyboard one can write music and store it on cassette tape or floppy disk. The composition can be retrieved and edited at a later time. If a graphics printer is used the musical score can be printed as sheet music. These expensive instruments provide very good quality sound, much better than that offered by computers using audio speaker systems.

A numeric keypad like that found on calculators can be very useful if you are dealing extensively with numerical data. Some machines, including Franklin computers, IBM PC computers, and TRS-80 Radio Shack computers include a numeric keypad as part of the computer keyboard but most machines do not. Some computer manufacturers offer a numeric keypad as an accessory device.

A power strip is an inexpensive and very practical device to use with a computer system. A power strip is a set of, usually, six electrical receptacles mounted in a rectangular box. It is provided with a single switch that turns on all of the receptacles at one time. All electrical components of your computer system can be plugged into the power strip. This lets the user turn the system on or off by pressing a single switch. The better power strips are also provided with a light that indicates when the strip has been turned on. This can prevent computer equipment from being accidentally left on for long periods of time. The best power strips are also provided with line filters that can protect the equipment against minor electrical power fluctuations. The purchase of a power strip is a worthwhile investment.

There are several items that are used to provide security and protection for the computer system. Many microcomputers have specially designed locking systems available by which your computer and many of its components can be attached to a table or bench. This prevents accidental moving of the equipment and to some degree computer theft. Other devices are available that help protect the computer system from environmental hazards. Electrically grounded antistatic mats are often used if there is excessive static electricity in the room. If your city or town is subject to radical power fluctuations, relatively sophisticated line filters

may be needed. Last, dust covers can be purchased
for individual components of the computer system.
Many users find one or more of these devices to be
practical additions to the computer environment.
     A quality speech synthesizer is an expensive
piece of computer hardware that has been found to be
extremely useful when visually impaired people use
the microcomputer system. Inexpensive speech
synthesizers produce peculiar speech patterns with
inflections that take significant amounts of time
for the user to learn to understand. The best speech
synthesizers produce much more human-like sounds.
     There are many computer supplies that are
necessary additions. You will need a collection of
cassette or floppy disks to store and save
information. Computer printer ribbons and computer
paper have to be replaced periodically. If you are
using a letter quality printer a collection of
daisywheels offering a selection of type faces may
be desirable. Each of these items is available from
most computer supply dealers or from stores selling
office equipment. The best advice is to check prices
in several stores and catalogue sales vendors, as
prices fluctuate radically. If you use large
quantities of materials you may find that buying
these materials in bulk is the most economical
solution.

HARDWARE DIRECTORY

Acorn Computer Company
     400 Unicorn Park Drive
     Woburn, MA 01801

Amdek Corporation
     2201 Lively Blvd.
     Elk Grove Village, IL 60007

Apple Computer, Inc.
     20525 Mariani Ave.
     Cupertino, CA 95014

Atari, Inc.
     1312 Crossman Ave.
     Sunnyvale, CA 94086

Axion, Inc.
    1287 Lawrence Station Rd.
    Sunnyvale, CA 94089

Coleco Industries
    999 Quaker Lane South
    West Hartford, CT 06110

Commodore Business Machines
    1200 Wilson Drive
    West Chester, PA 19380

Comrex International, Inc.
    3701 Skypark Dr. #120
    Torrance, CA 90505

Daisywriter
    3540 Wilshire Blvd.
    Los Angeles, CA 90010

Datasouth Computer
    4216 Stuart Andrew Blvd.
    Charlotte, NC 28210

Diablo Systems, Inc.
    901 Page Ave.
    Fremont, CA 95438

Epson America, Inc.
    3415 Kashiwa St.
    Torrance, CA 90505

Franklin Computer Company
    1070 Busch Memorial Highway
    Pennsauken, NJ 08110

Hitachi America
    401 West Artesia Blvd.
    Compton, CA 90220

International Business Machines, Inc.
    P.O. Box 1328
    Boca Raton, FL 33432

Juki Industries
    299 Market St.
    Saddle Brook, NJ 07662

Micro Peripherals, Inc.
    4426 S. Century Dr.
    Salt Lake City, UT 84123

NEC Home Electronics
    1401 Ester St.
    Elk Grove, IL 60007

Olympia International
    P.O. Box 22, Route 22
    Sommerville, NJ 08876

Panasonic Industrial Company
    One Panasonic Way
    Secaucus, NJ 07094

Princeton Graphics Systems
    1101-I State Rd.
    Princeton, NJ 08540

Quadram Corp.
    4357 Park Dr.
    Norcross, GA 30093

Sakata U.S.A. Corp.
    651 Bonnie Ln.
    Elk Grove Village, IL 60007

Sanyo Business Systems Corp.
    51 Joseph St.
    Moonachie, NJ 07074

Sinclair Research Limited
    50 Staniford St.
    Boston, MA 02114

Sony Video Communications
    Sony Drive
    Park Ridge, NJ 07656

Tandy Corp./Radio Shack
    1400 One Tandy Center
    Fort Worth, TX 76102

TSK Electronics
    18005 Cortney St.
    City of Industry, CA 91748

USI Computer Products Div.
150 N. Hill Dr.
Brisbane, CA 94005

Zenith Data Systems Corp.
1000 Milwaukee Ave.
Glenview, IL 60025

BIBLIOGRAPHY

Anderson, John J. "Commodore." CREATIVE COMPUTING
10 (March 1984): 56, 60.

Gives a history of the development and
philosophy of the Commodore computer
corporation.

Arrants, Stephen. "Apple Computer." CREATIVE
COMPUTING 10 (March 1984): 42-46.

Provides a general discussion about the Apple
computer company's products.

Bird, Pristin, et al. "Tracking Down the Right
Computer." ELECTRONIC LEARNING 3 (January
1984): 39-45.

Provides very useful information about
characteristics and operating features of
computer systems.

Blair, Majorie, and Sharon Lobello. "People Sharing
Educational Computing." ELECTRONIC EDUCATION 3
(May/June 1984): 14-16, 26-27.

Considers the positive effects the computer can
have on education, in terms of individual
students' needs.

Burke, Robert L. "Selecting Microcomputers for
Schools." ELECTRONIC EDUCATION 3 (April 1984):
18, 23.

Considers educational, public relations, and
morale implications of purchasing a computer
system for schools.

Byers, T.J. "Micro to Micro Communications."
    POPULAR COMPUTING 3 (February 1984): 113-119.

    A non-technical article describing the
    structure and operation of microcomputer
    network systems.

Coburn, Peter, et al. PRACTICAL GUIDE TO COMPUTERS
    IN EDUCATION. Reading, Mass.: Addison-Wesley,
    1982.

    Introductory guide to choosing hardware and
    software and how to incorporate them into the
    curriculum.

Countermine, Terry, and Mary Lang. "Assessing the
    Hidden Costs of a Personal Computer."
    CHILDHOOD EDUCATION 59 (March/April 1983):
    248-250.

    Stresses types of preparation and planning that
    should be done before purchasing a computer
    system.

Daughenbaugh, Richard L. "The Acorn: BBC'S
    Educational Microcomputer." THE COMPUTING
    TEACHER 12 (December/January 1984-1985):
    66-67.

    A well-written article describing features and
    networking capabilities for this computer.

Dyrli, Avard Egil. "Choosing Your Educational
    Computer System." POPULAR COMPUTING (October
    1984): 131-136.

    Describes important features to look for when
    choosing a computer system for educational
    purposes. Includes 14 specific examples.

Hoffmann, Thomas V. "IBM PCjr." CREATIVE COMPUTING
    10 (March 1984): 74-94.

    Gives rigorous treatment of the design,
    structure, and applications of this machine.

"How to Choose a Monitor." CONSUMER REPORTS 48
    (October 1983): 537-539.

Outlines qualities inherent in good monitors
and what image characteristics to look for.

"How to Choose a Printer." CONSUMER REPORTS 48
(October 1983): 531-536.

Outlines characteristics of quality printers
designed for non-technical uses.

McMillan, Tom. "Best Buys in Computers." POPULAR
COMPUTING 2 (February 1985): 70-75.

Considers features of four computers than can
be used in educational setting, costing less
than $700.00.

McMurrar, Pamela, and Loretta W. Hoover. "The
Educational Use of Computers: Hardware,
Software and Strategies." JOURNAL OF NUTRITION
EDUCATION 16 (Spring 1984): 39-43.

Traces developments, trends, and strategies of
computers used in education. Also considers
hardware and software selection and uses.

Sloan, M. INTRODUCTION TO MINICOMPUTERS AND
MICROCOMPUTERS. Reading, Mass.:
Addison-Wesley, 1980.

A good introductory text geared toward problem
solving applications using mini- and
microcomputers.

Spencer, Mima, and Linda Baskin. "Computers in the
Classroom." CHILDHOOD EDUCATION 59 (March
1983): 293-294.

Discusses advantages of having computers in the
classroom and outlines categories of software.

"The Bits and Pieces of a Computer System."
CONSUMER REPORTS (September 1983): 462-473.

Outlines characteristics to look for when
purchasing a computer system, with technical
information presented in a very readable way.

Titus, R. "Local School Support for Micros is Alive and Growing." INFOWORLD 4 (November 1982): 36.

Shows how the use of microcomputers has begun to grow in school systems.

Watt, Dan. "Selling Micros to Schools." POPULAR COMPUTING 4 (February 1983): 48-54.

Compares hardware and software products with special emphasis on educational computing.

Ziajka, Alan. "Microcomputers in Early Childhood Education? A First Look." YOUNG CHILDREN (July 1983): 61-67.

Describes characteristics to be considered before purchasing a computer system.

CHAPTER FIVE

MAINTENANCE FOR YOUR COMPUTER SYSTEM

After purchasing a computer system, finding a suitable location for it, and learning to use it, the user seldom considers the importance and necessity of cleaning, maintaining, and protecting this valuable equipment. Generally speaking, today's computers are durable and not susceptible to frequent malfunctions due to environmental factors such as heat and cold, but care must be taken to insure the longevity of the equipment as well as the software you use. In most cases common sense prevails if one follows the maintenance and safety precautions outlined in the manual provided with the machine.

Since the 1960's many large mainframe computers have been housed in protected and controlled environments. Specially designed rooms have been built for them where factors like humidity, temperature, and air purity can be carefully regulated. With the advent of minicomputers and microcomputers in homes, schools, and offices, many of these precautions to protect equipment are no longer feasible. We must find ways to handle problems resulting from dirt and contamination in the typical living and working environments.

Possible detrimental effects of high and low temperature and humidity are among the first concerns expressed by most computer users. In general, micro- and minicomputer systems will function properly over normal ranges of temperature from 50-80 degrees farenheit (10-26.6 degrees celcius). If operating temperatures are too low, mechanical problems can result, as disk drives and printers may behave sluggishly. Overheating can also cause the system to operate improperly, resulting in computer errors and, in the extreme, a total

shutdown of the computer system. Exceedingly high
humidity can result in similar problems.

A typical thermostatically controlled heating
system is sufficient to regulate the temperature.
High humidity ordinarily does not pose a problem,
but if one does encounter difficulties a portable
dehumidifier offers the best solution. A more costly
solution entails use of a dehumidifier that is
connected to the heating system itself.

The most common heat related problems are
associated with the computer system itself. The
monitor and computer generate significant amounts of
heat. Because of this the placement of your computer
system is important. It should not be positioned
against a wall or in any non-ventilated area.
Instead place it so that air can freely circulate
around and behind it. Many computers have built-in
fans to prevent excess heat build-up. Most machines
are provided with sets of vent holes to allow for
the free circulation of air. These vents should be
kept clean and free of clutter.

Peripheral devices such as printers, electronic
keyboards, and speech synthesizers further
contribute to the problem of localized heat
build-up. In many cases several computer systems are
housed in the same room, further contributing to the
problem. Other electrical elements such as electric
lighting and radios also add to the heat build-up.
Direct sunlight is one of the greatest sources of
heat, and the computer system should never be
positioned directly in its path.

The best method you can use to prevent heat
damage is to spread out the components of your
computer system as much as possible rather than
stacking them vertically in a closed cabinet. Allow
for good air movement by providing free space around
your equipment. If problems still develop install a
fan or a portable air conditioner to remove excess
heat.

Dirt and related contaminants are among the
worst offenders to cause havoc with the operation
of your computer system. As microcomputers are not
kept in isolated and protected quarters, they are
exposed to a wide range of contaminants, such as
dirt, dust, small pieces of food, smoke, and
airborne household and office chemicals. The problem
can be more serious than simply having dirty

equipment, as dirt build-up can result in declining performance or computer failure. As you might suspect contaminant build-up occurs slowly and may not be noticed until a problem arises.

Dirt on the outer surfaces of your computer equipment doesn't usually pose a serious problem. However, a dirty monitor screen makes characters difficult to read, while dirty keys and surfaces are unsightly. Dirt and dust that block cooling vents can be more serious, as this can lead to unwanted heat build-up. Fireplaces, wood stoves, and hot air furnace ducts are primary sources of dust contamination. Computer systems should be placed as far as possible from these offenders and filters for hot air furnaces should be replaced at regular intervals. Commercially available dust covers can be used to prevent dust and dirt accumulation on printers, monitors, and computers.

A periodic cleaning of the area surrounding your computer system is important. Rugs should be vacuumed, drapes and windows washed, baseboards and woodwork cleaned, as you would any other area of your school, home, or office. Do not apply regular cleaning solutions or materials to the surfaces of your computer system, as they may cause damage.

There are many computer component cleaning solutions commercially available from stores selling computer accessories or from catalogues. Cleaning solutions are available in bottled containers, pump sprays, and in aerosol cans. Treated lint-free paper cloths are excellent for cleaning monitor screens. Cleaning pads and cotton tipped applicators are a must for cleaning the edges of the keyboard keys and the air vents of your machine. Avoid using chemical solvents like degreasers and detergents, as they may damage your equipment. Be sure your computer system is unplugged when cleaning components.

If the chassis of your computer can be opened, you should periodically open it and inspect for dirt and contamination. Be sure that the computer system is unplugged when doing this. A pair of tweezers and an aerosol can of pressurized air are the best tools to use when removing debris and cleaning the inside of your computer. Check to see if the integrated circuit elements are properly seated and the cables are firmly connected. Remove any foreign objects like scraps of paper and paper clips that always seem to find their way into computers and printers. Your computer manual provides additional information

about how to carry out a more complete maintenance
check. If you feel unable to do this, take your
machine to a technician at a computer store for a
complete check-up about once a year.
Magnetic and electromagnetic fields as well as
static electricity can adversely affect the
operation of your computer since they can disrupt
the internal operations of the machine. At times
they can alter data values currently being processed
and erase data stored on floppy disks or cassette
tapes.
Every electronic device generates an
electromagnetic field that can present a problem to
the proper operation of your computer. In general
electrical devices that contain motors and
transformers are most likely to cause problems.
Telephones, stereo speakers, and video terminals are
among the devices that should be kept as far from
your computer as possible. Problems resulting from
magnetic and electromagnetic fields are easily
rectified by simply removing the particular item
from the computer environment and the computer's
stored data on disk or cassette tape.
Problems resulting from static electricity are
frequently among the most difficult to identify and
resolve. Up to 2500 volts of charge can be
transferred when one walks across a rug in stocking
feet, touches a metal object, and feels a spark
jump. Static charge can affect the internal
operations of the computer, cause alterations in
data values being internally processed, and damage
magnetic media being stored on disk or cassette
tape. In extreme cases electrostatic charge can burn
out elements on printed circuit boards and
physically damage computer disks and tapes.
Unfortunately static electricity cannot be
entirely eliminated, but its effects can be
minimized so that it will not impact on your
computer system. It is best to use protective
measures against possible damage resulting from the
transfer of electrostatic charge.
Most computer elements are provided with a
three-pronged grounded outlet. Using this grounded
plug in a grounded electrical receptacle reduces
many problems related to static electricity
build-up. Be sure that all components of your

computer system that are provided with grounded
cables are in fact grounded and not left unattached.
Cables should be positioned so that they do not rub
other elements and cannot be stepped on. Use of
commercially available antistatic sprays on areas
around your computer system may be helpful. These
sprays should never be used directly on the computer
or its peripherals. Finally, good quality grounded
antistatic mats can be used on floor or table areas
around the computer and a humidifier provided if the
air typically has a very low moisture content.

Variations in the amount of electrical power
being provided to you by your electrical utility
company can cause damage to or problems with your
computer system. Micro- and minicomputers are
designed to operate at the standard 115-volt energy
level, with a slight variation being acceptable.
Power companies usually provide electrical power
with some range so in most instances no problems
result.

Sometimes electrical power is momentarily shut
off, as seen when your radios, televisions, and
lights go off for a second or two. For household
appliances this does not present a problem, but for
an operating computer this is a much more serious
issue. A momentary loss of electrical power
typically causes the computer to erase what is
stored in its internal RAM memory, allow meaningless
data values to be stored, or give faulty
transmission of data values. This means that
whatever you are currently working on is rendered
useless.

This does not mean that your computer or the
computer software you were using has been damaged in
any way, rather that whatever is stored in the
internal memory of the computer is now inaccurate.
Materials on computer disk or cassette tape will not
be affected, nor will information you have stored on
them. A similar effect is observed when you receive
low voltage power from the utility company providing
your electricity. This is the case when your
lighting dims and is called a brownout.

An increase in voltage beyond the 130-volt
level can cause similar problems. These short-term
moderate increases are commonly called spikes. A
radical increase in electrical power being supplied
to your machine can cause physical and circuitry
damage to your computer as well as damage to your
computer disks and tapes. Fortunately this problem
is exceedingly rare.

In general any abnormalities in the quality and quantity of electrical power being supplied to your computer system can cause problems. It should be noted that it is your responsibility and not that of the computer distributor or manufacturer to protect the computer system against such occurrences.

Fortunately protection against most variations in electrical power is readily available and inexpensive. To protect your work against possible minor power fluctuations simply develop the habit of periodically saving your work, rather than completing the task and then saving the results. For example, if you are word processing a report, save what you have done after every hour of computer time. If a minor electrical disturbance occurs you have lost a relatively small amount of information.

Protection against slight as well as major fluctuations in electrical power also involves the purchase of equipment. Surge protectors and line filters are available at most computer stores and computer supply outlets. Inexpensive but adequate line filters can be purchased for between $40 and $80 and offer protection against minor electrical surges. Sophisticated line filters and surge protectors offer greater protection but typically cost between $100 and $3000. These are not generally used with individual computer stations because of cost considerations. The installation of an inexpensive line filter is simple, as it resembles an electrical power strip. The computer and its peripherals are plugged into the receptacles of the line filter and the line filter is plugged into your electrical outlet.

One aspect of computer system maintenance that is frequently ignored is the proper cleaning of the heads for disk drive units and cassette recorders. Disk head cleaning kits and cassette recorder cleaning solutions are available from stores selling computers and computer supplies as well as through catalogue sales.

Removing dirt, oil, grease, and other contaminants from cassette recorder heads is a relatively simple operation that can be done using dust-free cloths, cotton tipped applicators, and a proper cleaning solution. The proper technique is outlined in the user manual accompanying the cassette recorder. Cleaning disk drive heads

presents a different challenge, as they are not
readily accessible and are susceptible to damage by
poking and prodding with foreign objects.
The computer industry has solved this problem
by developing head cleaning kits that can be easily
used by the non-expert. Cleaning is accomplished by
placing the cleaning disk in the disk drive and
running the disk drive for about 30 seconds. During
this time dirt, grease, and other contaminants are
removed from the heads of the disk drive. The
recommended frequency of cleaning varies according
to the type of product used and the extent of
computer usage and that can be after between 8 and
40 hours of use. If cleaning is not periodically
done read and write errors can result when the
computer is saving or loading a computer program. If
extensive deposits build up on disk heads the disk
may be damaged. Disk head cleaning kits are most
effective when contaminant build-up is light to
moderate.

There are three types of disk head cleaners in
common use today. Wet-dry cleaners use a disk in a
cardboard jacket that has a cut-out window to which
2 ml of cleaning solution are added. In general 1/3
of the disk is wetted while 2/3 remains dry.
Cleaning is accomplished when the disk rotates over
wet and dry areas. Most of these cleaners are run
for 30 seconds while the disk drive is rotated.

Dry cleaners use a standard floppy disk to
which a piece of cleaning material has been
attached. As the disk is rotated for typically 60
seconds, the disk heads are cleaned by a rubbing
action at the position of the cut-out window.

Wet cleaners use disposable cleaning disks
which are placed in a cardboard disk jacket. The
entire cleaning disk is wetted with 2-3 ml of
cleaning solvent and the disk is rotated for 30-60
seconds. Each of these cleaning procedures provides
a safe, reliable method of disk head cleaning that
should be periodically done.

Cleaning solutions can be purchased in bottles
where the user measures the quantities of solvent
for each application, or in premeasured dosage
packets. My preference is for premeasured solvents
with a wet cleaner disk head cleaning system. This
system causes less disk head abrasion and is easy
for the new computer user to handle.

Use common sense when it comes to the care and storage of computer cassette tapes and floppy disks. Each cassette tape and disk should be labeled and stored in a container; these are available in computer supply stores as well from catalogues. These materials should be stored in an area not exposed to direct sunlight, electromagnetic fields, or heat. Many programs you may purchase come with a back-up copy. This back-up copy, as well as back-up copies of text and data files you make, should be stored in a location far from your primary storage, preferably in another room or building. This is important. In the event of fire or some other tragedy you won't lose all of your computer programs and stored materials.

Cassette tapes are very well protected by the plastic cases in which they are enclosed. The exposed portion of tape from which information is read and to which information is written should not be handled in any way. Scratches, smudges, and the like can destroy the information stored on that section of tape, rendering it useless.

Most disk drives used with microcomputers use single sided 5 1/4-inch floppy disks. The side on which information is stored is the side opposite to that on which you will find the disk label. This feature has led to many cases of damaged disks, as users typically remove the disk from the disk drive and place it label side up on a table surface. The disk is then subject to damage from scratching, dirt, and any other materials on the table surface. The best policy when you have finished using a disk is to place it in its protective disk sleeve and put it back into its storage container.

Disks can be damaged in other ways. Bending and pressing disks against surfaces are the greatest offenders. Disks can be erased by being placed near magnetic fields such as those produced by permanent magnets, stereo speakers, or bulk erasers used in libraries. Sensors used in building entrances for security purposes and metal detectors at airports do not affect computer disks. If you are shipping disks by mail, package them between two stiff sheets of cardboard or use commercially available computer disk mailers. Computer disks should not be cleaned with any solvent as this may result in disk damage.

In general computer disks and cassette tapes are very rugged and durable when handled properly.

Their shelf life is estimated to be 20-30 years
although no one is certain precisely how long they
will last. Cassette tapes should be periodically
rewound if stored for long periods of time while
disks require no maintenance. Both methods are
effective to store computer information for long
periods of time.
General maintenance of your computer system is
not time consuming and it is easy to do. Your
computer manual provides information regarding
proper lubrication of moving mechanical parts. It is
important to follow these instructions, as damage to
components of your computer system might result. If
this happens your computer must be serviced by a
technician, often resulting in expensive repairs and,
more important, temporary loss of your computer
system. Prevention and regular care will minimize
problems and let the machine carry out tasks you
assign in a quick, accurate, and efficient manner.

BIBLIOGRAPHY

Ahl, David H. "Floppy Disk Handling and Storage."
     CREATIVE COMPUTING 9 (December 1983): 205-206.

     Provides useful, practical information on the
     care, handling, and storage of floppy disks.

L'Hote, John D. "Glitchproof." AMERICAN SCHOOL AND
     UNIVERSITY (June 1983): 20-24.

     Outlines adverse effects electrical and
     environmental factors can have on computer
     system.

Man, Ernest E. "Taking Care of Your Computer."
     CREATIVE COMPUTING 9 (December 1983): 184-202.

     Makes excellent suggestions for general care
     and maintenance of computer systems by
     non-professionals.

Weinberg, Sandy. "Antistatic Tactics." AMERICAN
     SCHOOL AND UNIVERSITY 57 (February 1985): 69.

     Gives suggestions on how to prevent
     electrostatic build-up around the computer
     environment.

Whitaker, Lew. "Keep It Clean." CREATIVE COMPUTING
    9 (December 1983): 211-215.

    Offers sound suggestions and cleaning
    techniques for the computer and the computer
    environment.

Zaks, Rodnay. DON'T (OR HOW TO CARE FOR YOUR
    COMPUTER). Berkeley: Sybex, 1981.

    Provides practical suggestions for the care and
    maintenance of the computer system and the
    computer environment.

CHAPTER SIX

HIGHLIGHT TOPIC
CHOOSING YOUR EDUCATIONAL SOFTWARE

Whether or not you are an experienced computer user, purchasing quality educational software is at best difficult. A logical starting point is to review descriptions of programs given in catalogues and sourcebooks. There is information that should be included with each program to make your task easier. Each program description should include: 1) program name, 2) producer/distributor, 3) cost, 4) availability by type of computer, 5) ages for which the program is intended, 6) type of computer graphics used, 7) whether or not sound is used, 8) if adaptive hardware such as joysticks are required, 9) a statement of program goals, 10) a description of how the program functions, 11) the academic discipline for which the program is intended. If the catalogue you are using does not provide these data, try another one. There are many good catalogues available.

A good second step is to try to learn more about how the program actually functions. Descriptions can be deceiving as the program may do what is stated, but how it functions may not be acceptable. Asking a colleague who has the program to run the program with you is a logical step. This is particularly useful if you can observe the program being tried by young children.

It is frequently difficult to identify someone who has previously purchased the computer program in which you are interested. Call your local software store to see if it is available. Most computer stores will let you spend considerable time reviewing a program, often providing assistance and advice. Some software manufacturers, although their numbers are few, have a preview policy that you can

take advantage of. This is the ideal situation.
If, after purchasing a software program, trying it
with children, and finding that it does not meet
your needs, you may be allowed by many computer
stores to return the program. Ask dealers about
their return policy before purchasing computer
software.

One problem that confronts the buyer of
computer software is learning to identify the
characteristics and attributes that will maximize
the likelihood that the programs will meet your
needs. Many teachers have developed software
evaluation forms that are used when reviewing
software for purchase. For the beginner it is more
useful to have a set of questions and issues to
consider. After working with computer software, you
will be able to identify the characteristics and use
of computer programs that are most important to you.

The evaluation criteria discussed here include
a wide range of topics and issues. It is highly
unlikely that any computer program will meet all of
these criteria. This does not mean that the program
is somehow deficient, rather that these criteria are
all encompassing. They can be applied to computer
programs designed for use in any academic
discipline. For a particular subject area, it is not
necessary or particularly desirable for all criteria
to be met.

The first criterion concerns program validity.
A good piece of computer software has its
educational goals stated in the written
documentation provided with the program. These goals
should be implemented in the program. Examine the
program carefully to check that it addresses the age
group for which it is intended. After trying the
program, you should be able to identify whether or
not the stated program goals were met. From an
educational viewpoint the topics should be well
chosen and the information provided technically
accurate.

The program should have a focus directed toward
problem solving. Note whether using a computer is
the best way to teach the concepts and information
that are presented. The computer program should
provide encouraging comments to the child for both
correct and incorrect responses. Finally, the topics
should be presented in a creative and innovative
fashion.

Ease of use is another criterion to be
considered when previewing educational software.

Instructions for running the program and directions given in the program should be clearly stated and easy to follow. If you type in an inappropriate data entry, a number when a word is needed, for example, the program should handle this mistake and let you reenter the correct information. Ideally the program's instructions should be presented in an interactive mode and include a tutorial section so that the user can practice following them. Good software lacks flaws and mistakes commonly called "bugs." The best software lets the user return to the main program menu at any time during its execution. If the instructions for operating the program are unusually complex, a "text window" should be provided on the monitor screen. The text window tells the user how to get additional instructions and/or how to enter desired responses.

The third evaluation criterion is to insure that the program itself is non-discriminatory. When appropriate, computer software should allow for the use of adaptive hardware such as joysticks, game paddles, enlarged screen character mode, and speech synthesizers so that the program can be used by disabled individuals. Non-discriminatory software portrays graphics characters of all ages. There should be equal representation of people from all races and individuals of both sexes should be depicted with equal frequency.

The fourth criterion is whether or not the software program fully utilizes the capabilities of the computer. For example, does the program make use of state-of-the-art color graphics, sound, and animation? The best software offers editing features that let users change responses to questions posed in the program. Frequently users are given a second chance to respond to a question. The most advanced programs let teachers modify and create lessons as well as enter in a simple fashion their own data lists. The best software also provides ways to store data and results so that they can be retrieved and used at a later time.

The last criterion concerns issues related to user involvement with the computer program. The user should be able to choose the rate at which the program instructions are executed, meaning how quickly activities and examples are presented. All quality computer software provides an interactive format so the users are not simply watching, rather they are actively involved with the program.

Ideally, the program should let the user choose from a selection of levels of difficulty when executing it. Good programs are challenging and able to hold your interest and attention. When applying evaluation criteria to educational software, many teachers find it useful to list criteria for each category in vertical rows. Number scales such as 1 ... 5 can be used to indicate how well each criterion is met. This process eliminates some of the guesswork when deciding what constitutes worthwhile computer software. Regardless of the method of evaluation chosen, the decision rests with you. Knowing what to look for in computer software will make your decision making process easier and more reliable. A sample software evaluation form is given below.

SOFTWARE EVALUATION FORM

Product name
Producer
Availability by type of computer system
Hardware requirements
    a. disk, cassette, or cartridge
    b. RAM memory needed
    c. peripheral devices necessary (printer,
       joysticks, light pen, etc.)
Cost
Back-up/Preview/Replacement policy
Recommended age level
Academic discipline
Type of program (drill and practice, simulation,
       tutorial, writing etc.)

Are instruction manual and documentation provided?
Warranty and guarantee information provided?
Does manual suggest computer and non-computer based
    activities?
Are educational objectives stated in the
    documentation?

Is the program easy to load?
Is the program easy to use?
Does software effectively handle user input errors?
Does the program maintain user interest?
Are visual instructions clearly presented?

Can user control rate at which information is
     presented?
Can child "escape" from the program at any time?
Are text windows giving specific instructions
     provided throughout the program?
Are help menus available in the program?
Are multiple levels of difficulty offered?
Are there no errors in the program?

Is information presented accurately?
Is program developmentally designed?
Is difficulty level appropriate for specified ages?
Is quality of graphics good?
Can child's program input be stored?
Can software be modified by the teacher?
Is a summary of the child's performance provided?
Do screen images portray multi-cultural and
     multi-racial people?
Do screen images portray people of all ages and both
     sexes?
Are program content and pedogogical applications
     sound?
Can concepts presented be taught better in other
     ways?
Do the educational advantages warrant the spending
     of funds?

EDUCATIONAL SOFTWARE

     Computer software can be good or bad, but given
a good computer program, whether or not you perceive
it as being educationally effective frequently
depends on how you use it. The software included in
this section is valuable as educational tools.
Without doubt, there are additional programs
available that are equally effective. I have not
included computer games for entertainment's sake,
but rather programs that provide a positive learning
environment for the child.
     The more you learn about how a computer program
functions and the range of options it offers, the
better this tool can be incorporated into your
learning plan. In order to make best use of
educational software it is necessary to test it out

before using it in the classroom. As with any
materials, the better the teacher understands them
the more effective they will be when used with
students. Each program included here provides
instruction manuals and/or teacher's guides that
make the learning process easier for you.

Precisely how, when, and where to incorporate
the computer into day-to-day lesson plans frequently
is a problem for the classroom teacher. Computers
are relatively new educational tools that do not
have a history of classroom use. Similarly, quality
computer software using state-of-the-art technology
is new to the consumer market. Probably the most
important factor is that elementary teachers are
just beginning to learn to use these machines
themselves. Microcomputer use in pre-school through
upper elementary grades may pose more questions than
provide answers.

One can find evidence for this by examining
educational computing journals that illustrate how
microcomputers can be used in elementary grade
settings. Articles show clever and innovative ways
that microcomputers and their software can be used
for specific applications. These reports are usually
written by computer enthusiasts who have spent
considerable time learning how to operate the
microcomputer system and use its software. Generally
what is lacking is a long-term set of teaching
strategies indicating how to incorporate learning
with the microcomputer into a curriculum unit.

The central issue for teachers is often whether
to use microcomputer software to introduce a
curriculum unit so that the microcomputer is central
to the teaching strategy, or use it as a tool to
provide supplemental information and review concepts
that have been taught. Teachers who are just
beginning to learn to use microcomputer technology
should take the latter approach. There are no simple
answers to how this can be most effectively done, as
this will depend on the curriculum unit being
presented, the quality of available software, and
the state of computer literacy development the
teacher has attained.

For example, if a mathematics unit dealing with
set relations and the concept of attributes and
values is being presented, use of the software
program Gertrude's Secrets would be appropriate.
This program can be used as a tutorial for children

experiencing difficulty mastering concepts dealing
with characteristics and relationships, or serve as
a review for children having completed the unit.

Fifth or sixth grade children who have just
completed a unit on geography of the United States,
would find the simulation program Geography Search
stimulating. In this activity children learn to use
what they have learned, applying this knowledge to
many situations where they must make choices and
decisions.

It is easy to say that children can use a piece
of software as part of a curriculum unit, but this
assumes that each child can operate the
microcomputer system. This will not be true until
each child receives instruction. Furthermore, will
these computer activities be done with the entire
class as a group, or will they be done in small
groups? I believe that teachers should start by
introducing the computer to the class as a whole.
Several opportunities should be provided for
students to observe how the computer is used while
they suggest values for data entries. Perhaps
letting a child enter data suggested by classmates
would be a good starting point. Children can then be
taught by example how to care for and use the
microcomputer and its software. Many teachers
construct cards for the children that show how to
start up and use the microcomputer.

The next step is to let small groups of
children use the microcomputer for an activity. This
should be done under close teacher supervision.
There are always children who try to monopolize the
equipment because of enthusiasm, interest, and
ability. The teacher must insure that all children
have equal opportunities to use these materials.
When first introducing the microcomputer system to
small groups of children, teachers find that it is
practical to enlist the help of other teachers,
teacher's aides, or classroom volunteers.

The age of the children is another factor to
consider when using the microcomputer in the
classroom. One can expect an 11- or 12-year-old
fifth or sixth grade child to display a much greater
independence and proficiency of use than a 5- or 6-
year-old kindergarten or first grade child. Computer
operating instructions as well as computer software
instructions will have to be demonstrated much more
frequently for younger children. Choosing software
that is age-appropriate is the foremost
consideration.

Given the many problems that can and will arise, use of microcomputer software in elementary classrooms may seem an insurmountable task. Once the teacher becomes familiar with the equipment and computer software programs, it is not. The computer will soon become just another learning and teaching tool. The quality of computer software designed for classroom use has shown a significant improvement in the past two or three years. I believe that this is directly attributable to teachers and educators being involved with the conceptual design and writing of computer software programs. Curriculum units having sound pedogogical foundations have just begun to be available for classroom use.

Other types of computer software such as teacher utility programs, word processing systems, and software for use with special needs children are included elsewhere in the text. Some of these programs have direct applicability for use with children, while others can make your work as a teacher easier.

For ease of use, the educational software included here has been grouped into categories including: General Purpose Software, Language Arts, Mathematics, Science, and the Arts. Each software selection includes the name of the program, producer, availability by type of computer, cost, and ages for which the program is intended. A short description of program content and goals is also included with each program description.

General Purpose Software

Computer software included in this section does not relate directly to a particular academic discipline. Many of them deal with readiness skills while others offer an excellent way to introduce the computer to the young child in a non-threatening, educational way. Other programs offer a puzzle/game format where students develop logical problem solving strategies. Some programs allow the teacher to change items so that particular needs can be addressed.

The color, sound, graphics, and animation provided by these programs are exceptional. They hold the interest of the user and provide positive

and frequently dramatic reinforcement for correct
responses. These programs are among the best
currently available and are worthy of consideration
as additions to your software collection.

Better View A Zoo
        Producer: Sunburst Communications
        Availability: TRS-80 Color Computer
        Cost: $55.00
        Ages: 5-8

        Designed for beginning readers. Uses
animated graphics, sound, and music built into
six theme activities. Offers practice in
identifying numbers, letters, and directions
such as up and down. Provides practice in
reading simple stories. Contains back-up disk
and teacher's guide.

Body Awareness
        Producer: Learning Well
        Availability: Apple 48K
        Cost: $49.95
        Ages: 5-7

        Gives practice in identifying and locating
parts of the body as well as seasons of the
year and clothing worn. Uses color, sound, and
graphics. Game options can be set by the
teacher. Uses one key for input. Provides
teacher's guide with suggested activities.

Code Quest: Strategies in Problem Solving
        Producer: Sunburst Communications
        Availability: Apple 48K, Atari 48K, TRS-80
                      Color Computer
        Cost: $55.00
        Ages: 9-13

        User breaks a series of codes that allow
identity of mystery objects. Allows teacher to
enter codes and clues from any subject area.
Develops discrimination, pattern
identification, and classification skills.
Offers practice in solving problems of varying
complexity. Contains back-up disk and teacher's
guide.

Facemaker
    Producer: Spinnaker Software Corporation
    Availability: Apple IIe, Atari cartridge,
                  Commodore-64 cartridge and disk,
                  IBM PC, IBM PCjr
    Cost: $34.95
    Ages: 5-8

        Allows children to create faces from a
    prepared selection of features. Children can
    add animation and play a game by repeating a
    series of movements generated by the computer.
    Includes color graphics, sound, and instruction
    manual.

Fun House Maze: Strategies in Problem Solving
    Producer: Sunburst Communications
    Availability: Apple 48K
    Cost: $55.00
    Ages: 9-adult

        Provides practice in pattern recognition
    and develops skills in building problem solving
    strategies. Format is a journey through a
    three-dimensional maze. Offers color graphics.
    Includes a back-up disk and instruction manual.

Juggles Rainbow
    Producer: The Learning Company
    Availability: Apple IIe, Commodore-64
    Cost: $29.95
    Ages: 5-7

        Lets children use a computer before they
    can read. Offers color graphics. Provides math
    and reading readiness skills. Includes an
    instruction manual.

Moptown Hotel
    Producer: The Learning Company
    Availability: Apple IIe, Atari, IBM PC,
                  IBM PCjr
    Cost: $39.95
    Ages: 8-12

        Lets children test hypotheses, use
    analogies, and develop strategic thinking
    skills. Offers a game format using colorful
    characters. Includes an instruction manual.

Moptown Parade
      Producer: The Learning Company
      Availability: Apple IIe, Atari, IBM PC,
                    IBM PCjr
      Cost: $39.95
      Ages: 6-11

      Offers seven games having colorful
characters. Emphasis on logic, game strategy
development, and pattern recognition. Includes
an instruction manual.

Odd One Out
      Producer: Sunburst Communications
      Availability: Apple 48K
      Cost: $55.00
      Ages: 5-12

      Offers five programs to develop
classification skills: Pictures, Words,
Letters, Numbers, and Word Problems. Has
varying levels of difficulty with color
graphics, animation, and sound. Teacher can
modify items. Lets children find order and
relationships by looking for a pattern.
Includes back-up disk and teacher's guide.

Square Pairs
      Producer: Scarborough Systems
      Availability: Apple IIe, Atari disk and tape,
                    Commodore-64 disk and tape
      Cost: $39.95
      Ages: 7-13

      Based on the game concentration where
players look for matches or things that go
together. Four sample games are provided.
Teachers can create their own games. Includes a
teacher's guide.

Stickybear Opposites
      Producer: Xerox Corporation
      Availability: Apple IIe
      Cost: $39.95
      Ages: 5-8

      Considers opposites such as: full/empty,
up/down, and in front of/behind. Offers color
graphics and sound. Includes a "Look Book,"
poster, and stickers.

Stickybear Shapes
      Producer: Xerox Corporation
      Availability: Apple IIe
      Cost: $39.95
      Ages: 5-8

      Offers three games: Name a Shape, Pick a
Shape, and Find a Shape. Provides color
graphics, sound, and animation. Includes a
"Look Book," poster, and stickers.

Language Arts Software

      There are a great many programs available that
teach and offer drill and practice in isolated
skills areas such as the proper handling of nouns,
verbs, and punctuation. A genuine challenge is to
find computer programs that encourage the child to
think creatively about language and its application
to diverse situations. Programs included in this
section meet these educational criteria.
      The software described below covers a wide
range of topics and includes a range of levels of
difficulty. Programs range from letter recognition
and alphabetization to word and part of speech
recognition. There are also programs that let the
user write simple sentences and stories. Many of
these programs easily permit the teacher to add
customized word lists and modify lessons.
      A few of the programs provide a game format,
but most just build sound and color graphics into
the learning environment. Since children frequently
perceive computer programs simply as fun, they
command their attention and interest. This makes
language arts software a valuable teaching tool for
use in the classroom.

Academic Skill Builders in Language Arts
      Producer: DLM Teaching Resources
      Availability: Apple IIe
      Cost: $44.00 per program
      Ages: 6-10

      Is a series of six separate disk programs
including: Spelling Wiz, Verb Viper, Word
Invasion, Word Man, Word Master, and Word
Radar. Drill and practice programs using

keyboard or game paddles. Offers sound effects
and speed and time variability. Includes an
instruction manual.

Alphabetizing
    Producer: Learning Well
    Availability: Apple IIe, Atari disk
    Cost: $49.95
    Ages: Red version 8-10, Blue version 9-12

        Students place words in alphabetical
order. Offers four levels of difficulty for
each version. Includes instruction manual.

Alphabet Beasts and Company
    Producer: Readers Digest Services, Inc.
    Availability: Commodore-64 disk
    Cost: $34.95
    Ages: 5-8

        An unusual alphabet program. Uses animal
characters and graphics, poems, and sounds.
Builds alphabet and number skills, manual
dexterity, and hand/eye coordination.
Instruction manual included.

Early Games: Matchmaker Reading Readiness Games
    Producer: Counterpoint Software
    Availability: Apple IIe, Atari disk,
                  Commodore-64 disk, IBM PC,
                  IBM PCjr
    Cost: $29.95
    Ages: 5-7

        Teaches colors, direction, shape, and size
discrimination. Offers musical sounds and
color graphics. Instruction manual included.

Extra Extra
    Producer: Milton Bradley
    Availability: Apple IIe
    Cost: $39.95
    Ages: 7-12

        Uses clues to track down facts such as:
who, what, why, where, when, and how to write a
story. Instruction manual included.

Getting Ready to Read and Add
    Producer: Sunburst Communications
    Availability: Apple IIe, Atari 16K,
                 Commodore-64
    Cost: $55.00
    Ages: 5-7

        Offers color graphics, animation, and
    sound. User identifies and matches shapes,
    upper/lower case letters and numbers. Teacher
    can control selection of objects. Teaches shape
    discrimination and letter and number
    recognition. Uses game paddles or joysticks.
    Includes back-up disk and teacher's guide.

Letter Recognition and Alpabetization
    Producer: Milliken Publishing Company
    Availability: Apple 48K
    Cost: $75.00
    Ages: 5-14

        Offers upper and lower case letter
    discrimination and alphabetization. Several
    programs have animated graphics. Can
    individualize assignments and mastery levels.
    Includes two disks, teacher's manual, and
    binder.

Magic Spells
    Producer: The Learning Company
    Availability: Apple IIe
    Cost: $34.95
    Ages: 6-12

        Offers an adventure game format with
    castles, demons, and wizards. User spells and
    unscrambles words from 14 word lists to unlock
    treasure chests. Can create your own word
    lists. Teacher's guide included.

Rapid Reader
    Producer: Silicon Valley Systems, Inc.
    Availability: Apple IIe, Atari disk
    Cost: $39.95
    Ages: 8-adult

        Provides five reading options: words, word
    pairs, phrases, short sentences, and long

sentences. Five word banks provided in English
and Spanish. Three word banks are modifiable.
Includes teacher's manual.

Rhymes and Riddles
    Producer: Spinnaker Software Corporation
    Availability: Apple IIe, Atari disk,
                  Commodore-64, IBM PC, IBM PCjr
    Cost: $29.95
    Ages: 5-10

        Contains three letter guessing games as
    well as jokes and riddles, nursery rhymes, and
    famous sayings. Includes color graphics and
    sound. Instruction manual provided.

Space Waste Race
    Producer: Sunburst Communications
    Availability: Apple 48K, Atari disk, TRS-80
                  cassette, disk, and network
    Cost: $55.00 Apple, $49.00 TRS-80 cassette,
          $165.00 network
    Ages: 5-8

        Designed for beginning readers. Program
    includes: music and animation, counting, number
    and letter order, and directionality. Includes
    a back-up disk and teacher's guide.

Spelling Bee and Reading Primer
    Producer: Edu-ware
    Availability: Apple IIe
    Cost: $39.95
    Ages: 5-6

        Contains two programs dealing with: double
    vowels, consonants, simple two- and
    three-letter words, four-letter one-syllable
    words, simple and difficult multisyllable
    words, and more. Instruction manual included.

Stickybear ABC
    Producer: Xerox Corporation
    Availability: Apple IIe
    Cost: $39.95
    Ages: 5-6

Is an alphabet program offering color graphics, sound, and computer animation. Includes a "Look Book," poster, and stickers.

Story Machine
    Producer: Spinnaker Software Corporation
    Availability: Apple IIe, Atari cartridge and
                  disk, Commodore-64 cartridge,
                  IBM PC, IBM PCjr
    Cost: $34.95 for Apple, Atari, and IBM; $39.95
          for Commodore-64 cartridge
    Ages: 5-9

    Contains a forty-word dictionary with parts of speech. User writes sentences, paragraphs, and simple stories. Has full color graphics and sound. Instruction manual included.

Story Maker
    Producer: Bolt, Beranek and Newman
    Availability: Apple 48K
    Cost: $30.00
    Ages: 8-13

    Lets user compose original stories, change stories, or attain a program defined goal. Provides good practice in making inferences and decisions. Back-up disk and instruction manual included.

The Puzzler
    Producer: Spinnaker Software Corporation
    Availability: Apple IIe, Atari cartridge and
                  disk, Commodore-64 cartridge,
                  IBM PC, IBM PCjr
    Cost: $34.95 for Apple and IBM; $39.95 for
          Atari and Commodore-64 cartridge.

    Offers five stories where children use skills of prediction, confirmation, and integration to solve mysteries. Focuses on comprehension and expression of ideas. Includes back-up disk and teacher's manual.

Wizard of Words
    Producer: Advanced Ideas
    Availability: Apple IIe, Commodore-64, IBM PC,
                  IBM PCjr

Cost: $39.95
Ages: 8-13

Contains five word games using over 20,000
words keyed to age levels. Teacher can
customize games and add words and lessons.
Teacher's manual included.

Word Detective
    Producer: Sunburst Communications
    Availability: Atari 48K
    Cost: $55.00
    Ages: 8-adult

Computer provides a collection of letters
and user forms as many words as possible. Any
words missed are listed. Teacher can provide
letter selection. Designed to enhance spelling
and stimulate interest in new words. Includes
back-up disk and teacher's manual.

Word-Pak
    Producer: Sandpiper Software
    Availability: TRS-80 16K Computer
    Cost: $23.50
    Ages: 8 to adult

A vocabulary program using a game format
to identify words. Includes three games.
Teacher can enter words and phrases, save,
edit, and print materials.

Mathematics Software

Mathematics software was among the first of the
academic disciplines to which computer technolgy was
applied. Because of this, there is an abundance of
software in the field. Initially math programs were
written to solve computational types of problems, as
these are relatively easy to develop and make good
use of the immediate reinforcement capabilities of
interactive computer programs.
    Due to the recent advancements in computer
technology leading to color graphics, sound, and
animation, more interesting and creative programs in
mathematics have become available. There are many

drill and practice and tutorial programs on the
market today. These are often presented in
interesting ways that are difficult to duplicate
using traditional math materials. There are also
many simulation programs that let the student try
multiple solutions to problems and situations.
Abundant software has been written that help
teachers diagnose conceptual problems a student has
with mathematics and keep a record of the student's
progress.

There has been a marked improvement in the
quality of math software available in the past few
years. As in most fields, there are many excellent
programs available, as well as many that are of a
much lesser quality. The software listed here
includes the best available in terms of cost, age
applicability, and educational appropriateness.

It is not that traditional materials such as
paper and pencil, Attribute Blocks, and Deans Blocks
are being supplanted by the computer. Rather, the
computer can be used as another tool to present
mathematical concepts and to let students further
develop skills they have learned. In many cases the
computer lets the teacher do things that are
otherwise difficult or not practical to simulate.

Basic Number Facts
    Producer: Control Data Publications-Plato
    Availability: Apple IIe, Atari disk
    Cost: $60.00
    Ages: 6-13

        Offers practice in addition, subtraction,
    multiplication, and division with single digit
    numbers. Has increasing levels of difficulty.
    Statistical results from each practice session
    are given. Instruction manual included.

Bumble Games
    Producer: The Learning Company
    Availability: Apple IIe, Atari disk,
                  Commodore-64 disk
    Cost: $39.95
    Ages: 5-12

        Deals with positive numbers and number
    pairs. Numbers are plotted on a number line or
    on map and grid locations. Instruction manual
    included.

Bumble Plot
  Producer: The Learning Company
  Availability: Apple IIe
  Cost: $39.95
  Ages: 8-13

       Builds on skills developed in Bumble
  Games. Uses positive and negative numbers
  plotted as number pairs on grids. Instruction
  manual included.

Challenge Math
  Producer: Sunburst Communications
  Availability: Apple 48K, Commodore-64
  Cost: $55.00
  Ages: 7-13

       Provides practice in estimating whole
  numbers and decimals. Three game formats are
  included: Alien Intruder, Digitosaurus, and
  Math Mansion. Sound and color graphics are
  offered. Includes back-up disk and teacher's
  manual.

Counters: An Interactive Approach to Counting and
          Arithmetic
  Producer: Sunburst Communications
  Availability: Apple 48K
  Cost: $55.00
  Ages: 5-7

       Considers counting, addition, and
  subtraction, using colorful animated objects.
  Includes a back-up disk and teacher's manual.

Decimals
  Producer: Control Data Publications-Plato
  Availability: Apple IIe, Atari disk
  Cost: $60.00
  Ages: 6-13

       Uses a dart game format to show decimal
  intervals on a number line. Darts are thrown to
  burst balloons. Offers increasing levels of
  difficulty. Back-up disk, worksheets, blackline
  masters, and teacher's guide included.

Early Games for Young Children: Nine Learning Games
    Producer: Counterpoint Software
    Availability: Apple IIe, Atari disk,
                Commodore-64, IBM PC, IBM PCjr
    Cost: $29.95
    Ages: 5-7

        A menu driven program that includes nine
    learning games. Games include: counting,
    addition and subtraction of blocks, letters,
    and alphabet, comparisons of shapes, and
    creating pictures. Offers sound, animation, and
    color graphics. Instruction manual included.

Early Games for Young Children: Fraction Factory
    Producer: Counterpoint Software
    Availability: Apple IIe, Atari disk,
                Commodore-64, IBM PC, IBM PCjr
    Cost: $29.95
    Ages: 7-13

        Considers fraction concepts such as: see
    and describe, finding equal values with
    different denominators, and multiplication,
    addition, and subtraction of fractions. Sound,
    animation, and color graphics provided.
    Includes instruction manual.

Exploring Metros: A Metric Adventure
    Producer: Sunburst Communications
    Availability: Apple IIe
    Cost: $55.00
    Ages: 9-adult

        Explores a colorful planet where students
    learn estimation skills. Concepts of mass,
    length, temperature, and capacity are treated.
    Back-up disk and teacher's manual included.

Exploring Tables and Graphs
    Producer: Xerox Corporation
    Availability: Apple IIe
    Cost: $34.95
    Ages: 8-10; 11-13

        Programs for two age groups sold
    separately. Has many applications for subject
    areas. Uses tables, bar graphs, pictures and

area graphs. Includes blackline masters and
teacher's guide.

Flip Flop
    Producer: Milliken Publishing Company
    Availability: Apple 48K, Atari 16 & 32K
    Cost: $39.95
    Ages: 7-12

        Shows two pictures on the screen. Children
    learn concepts of transformational geometry by
    comparing figures on the screen. Documentation
    provided.

Fractions
    Producer: Control Data Publications-Plato
    Availability: Apple IIe, Atari disk
    Cost: $60.00
    Ages: 6-13

        Uses a dart game format to show fractions
    on a number line. Has over 50 levels of
    difficulty. User throws darts to burst
    balloons. Back-up disk, worksheets, blackline
    masters, and teacher's guide included.

Gertrude's Puzzles
    Producer: The Learning Company
    Availability: Apple IIe
    Cost: $44.95
    Ages: 6-13

        Expands concepts from Gertrude's Secrets.
    Puzzles are more complex and develop high level
    reasoning skills. Offers color, sound, and
    animated graphics. Instruction manual included.

Gertrude's Secrets
    Producer: The Learning Company
    Availability: Apple IIe
    Cost: $44.95
    Ages: 5-10

        Develops planning and logical thinking
    skills by having children guess rules to solve
    puzzles. User can create puzzle pieces. Has
    color graphics, sound, and animation.
    Instruction manual included.

Math Blaster
> Producer: Davidson and Associates
> Availability: Apple IIe, Commodore-64, IBM PC,
> IBM PCjr
> Cost: $49.95
> Ages: 6-13
>
> Has 25 data files that can generate
> problems in addition, subtraction,
> multiplication, and division for whole numbers,
> decimals, and fractions. User can add original
> problems. Instruction manual included.

Memory Math
> Producer: Hartley Courseware
> Availability: Apple 48K, IBM PC, IBM PCjr
> Cost: $39.95
> Ages: 6-10
>
> Has 25 lessons using concentration game
> format with three levels of difficulty for
> each. Teachers can modify existing lessons or
> create their own. Good graphics. Keeps student
> records.

Money! Money!
> Producer: Hartley Courseware
> Availability: Apple 48K, IBM PC, IBM PCjr
> Cost: $39.95
> Ages: 6-11
>
> Provides experiences with counting money,
> making change, and dealing with money based
> word problems. Has multiple sets of lessons and
> teachers can modify existing ones or create
> their own. A very flexible program.

Place Value--Ones, Tens, Hundreds
> Producer: Educational Materials and Equipment
> Company
> Availability: Apple 48K
> Cost: $43.00
> Ages: 8-13
>
> Helps children develop place-value
> concepts. Uses groups of blocks to show
> place-value notation. Provides a place-value
> game. Has good graphics. Documentation
> provided.

Stickybear Numbers
    Producer: Xerox Corporation
    Availability: Apple IIe
    Cost: $39.95
    Ages: 5-7

        Emphasizes number recognition and counting
    skills. Offers color, sound, and animated
    graphics. Includes a "Look Book," poster, and
    stickers.

Teasers by Tobbs
    Producer: Sunburst Communications
    Availability: Apple 48K, Atari disk,
                  Commodore-64, TRS-80 Computer
                  cassette
    Cost: $55.00 disk, $49.00 cassette, $165.00
          network
    Ages: 9-adult

        Offers two programs with six levels of
    difficulty. Reinforces mental arithmetic skills
    and constructs math relationships between
    operations. Contains back-up disk and teacher's
    manual.

The Right Turn: Strategies in Problem Solving
    Producer: Sunburst Commuications
    Availability: Commodore-64
    Cost: $55.00
    Ages: 9-adult

        User creates patterns and does spatial
    transformations on them. Emphasizes prediction
    and experimentation while teaching concepts of
    rotation and transformation. Uses color
    graphics and includes back-up disk and
    teacher's guide.

                    Science Software

        The computer programs included in this section
    emphasize student skills of making predictions and
    developing logical strategies for problem solving.
    There are several programs that offer laboratory
    simulations where children can learn more about the
    world of science when real life experimentation is
    difficult.

These software programs offer good animation
and color graphics. For effective use, the programs
should be incorporated into a curricular unit after
the basics of the topic have been discussed with
students.
There are many additional programs available
that offer review of specific content information
using a drill and practice format. In general the
programs listed here are developmental and thought
provoking in nature. They force the user to apply
the information and ideas learned in new situations.
They represent the best of what is currently
available. In any case, science is best learned by
doing. These programs offer lessons that are usually
difficult to undertake through a hands-on experience
and are therefore valuable learning tools.

Basic Facts Package
    Producer: Milliken Publishing Company
    Availability: Apple 48K, Atari 40K
    Cost: $150.00
    Ages: 5-14

        Provides drill and practice activities
    using many different problem formats. Offers
    individualized assignments and mastery levels.
    Contains four disks, teacher's manual, and
    binder.

Classification
    Producer: Educational Materials and Equipment
             Company
    Availability: Apple 48K
    Cost: $33.00
    Ages: 8-12

        Provides practice in classification, using
    three attributes: shape, number of sides, and
    number of dots shown. Uses colored, animated
    graphics. Includes teacher's guide and
    worksheets.

Electric Circuits
    Producer: Educational Materials and Equipment
             Company
    Availability: Apple 48K
    Cost: $33.00
    Ages: 10-13

Shows children how simple circuits are constructed using batteries, bulbs, and switches. Considers such concepts as: insulation, conduction, open and closed circuits. Has good graphics and provides teacher's guides and worksheets.

Gears: Strategies in Problem Solving
    Producer: Sunburst Communications
    Availability: Apple 48K
    Cost: $55.00
    Ages: 9-adult

To learn problem solving skills of prediction and analysis by experimenting with gears. One chooses number of gears and number of teeth for each and builds models to predict rotation of gears and number of turns made. Offers animated color graphics, back-up disk, and teacher's manual.

Physical or Chemical?
    Producer: Educational Materials and Equipment
             Company
    Availability: Apple 48K
    Cost: $33.00
    Ages: 9-12

Helps children learn differences between chemical and physical properties of matter. User develops rules to determine which type of change occurs. Has good graphics and includes teacher's manual and worksheets.

Rocky's Boots
    Producer: The Learning Company
    Availability: Apple IIe
    Cost: $49.95
    Ages: 7-13

Develops logical thinking skills by providing elements to build working machines. Game points are scored based on the efficiency of the machines formed. One learns about principles of computer logic circuits. Includes instruction manual.

Science Middle School Volume 3
    Producer: Minnesota Educational Computer
        Consortium
    Availability: Apple 48K
    Cost: $49.00
    Ages: 11-14

        Contains a five-part biology/physical
    science program. Topics include: fish,
    minerals, Odell Lake, and Quakes Ursa.
    Instruction manual and back-up disk included.

Shadows and Light
    Producer: Educational Materials and Equipment
        Company
    Availability: Apple 48K
    Cost: $33.00
    Ages: 8-12

        Provides light ray diagrams to show how
    objects reflect light and how shadows of
    multi-shaped blocks are formed. Has very good
    graphics and includes teacher's guide and
    worksheets.

Sound
    Producer: Educational Materials and Equipment
        Company
    Availability: Apple 48K
    Cost: $33.00
    Ages: 10-13

        Considers cause and nature of sound.
    Illustrates how sound travels through solids,
    liquids, and gases. Has clearly depicted
    graphics and provides teacher's guide and
    worksheets.

The Digestive System
    Producer: MRRA
    Availability: Apple 48K
    Cost: $39.95
    Ages: 7-13

        Uses animation and colorful drawings to
    show anatomy of the digestive system. Includes
    text material and a dictionary of terms.
    Instruction guide included.

The Ear
        Producer: MRRA
        Availability: Apple IIe
        Cost: $24.95
        Ages: 9-15

                Considers anatomy and physiology of the
        ear. Has color graphics and a tutorial. Test
        questions and instruction manual included.

The Factory: Strategies in Problem Solving
        Producer: Sunburst Communications
        Availability: Acorn 32K, Apple 48K,
                        Commodore-64, IBM PC, IBM PCjr,
                        TRS-80 Color Computer
        Cost: $55.00
        Ages: 9-adult

                A three-level program using color graphics
        and animation to let students create products
        on a simulated machine assembly line. Levels
        include: test a machine, build a factory, and
        make a product. Instruction manual included.

The Human Body--An Overview
        Producer: Brain Bank
        Availability: Apple IIe
        Cost: $90.00
        Ages: 9-15

                Learn body systems, their parts, and how
        they work together. Eight lessons provided on
        two disks. Includes a tutorial, test questions
        in text, and instruction manual.

The Incredible Laboratory: Strategies in Problem
Solving
        Producer: Sunburst Communications
        Availability: Apple 48K, Atari 48K,
                        Commodore-64
        Cost: $55.00
        Ages: 8-adult

                See cause/effect relations of mixing
        chemicals. Encourages trial and error learning.
        Offers varying levels of difficulty, color
        graphics, and animation. Back-up disk and
        teacher's manual provided.

The Pond: Strategies in Problem Solving
    Producer: Sunburst Communications
    Availability: Apple 48K, Atari 32K,
                  Commodore-64, IBM PC, IBM PCjr,
                  TRS-80 Color Computer
    Cost: $55.00
    Ages: 7-adult

        Students learn to recognize patterns from
observed data. Uses game format to get a frog
across a pond of lily pads. Varying levels of
difficulty. Game points awarded on efficiency
of pattern. Back-up disk and teacher's manual
included.

The Respiratory System: A Puff of Air
    Producer: MRRA
    Availability: Apple 48K
    Cost: $39.95
    Ages: 7-13

        Uses animation and colorful drawings to
show anatomy of the respiratory system. Shows
relationship between respiration and
circulation. Asks questions, includes a quiz
and dictionary of terms. Instruction manual
provided.

Water in the Air
    Producer: Educational Materials and Equipment
             Company
    Availability: Apple 48K
    Cost: $37.00
    Ages: 11-14

        Considers evaporation and condensation of
water, and how frost is formed. Has excellent
animated graphics illustrating behavior of
water vapor in the air. Includes teacher's
guide and worksheets.

Social Studies Software

        Compared to the other academic disciplines,
there is relatively little available for social
studies. In general, social studies programs tend to
deal with individual concepts but do not fit into

any particular curriculum context. Many of the drill and practice programs are clever and well designed, but in terms of content do not significantly differ from what is done through traditional means.
On the other hand, there are some excellent computer programs available. There are many well-constructed simulation programs that let the student try many possible solutions to a problem. These activities are very difficult and time consuming to replicate in other ways. Other programs deal with geography, history, the calendar, and map reading. Many of these programs are innovative and serve as excellent review, drill, and practice materials.
Social studies software makes use of the advanced color, sound, and animation capabilities of the microcomputer. Many of these computer programs hold the interest of children while they learn new information, develop strategies for problem solving, and review factual information.

Elementary Volume #3
        Producer: Minnesota Educational Computer
                Consortium
        Availability: Apple 48K
        Cost: $39.95
        Ages: 7-13

        Contains seven simulation programs including: Civil War, States, States 2, and four programs that simulate running a business, including Lemonade Stand. Well-designed programs, some having color, sound, and graphics. Instruction manual included.

Elementary Volume #6
        Producer: Minnesota Educational Computer
                Consortium
        Availability: Apple 48K
        Cost: $40.00
        Ages: 8-14

        Contains five simulation programs: Furs, Nomad, Oregon, Summer, and Voyager. Topics include: trading, map reading, conservation, and economics. Includes lesson plans, learning objectives, and worksheets.

Energy Search
    Producer: McGraw-Hill Book Company
    Availability: Apple 48K
    Cost: $180.00
    Ages: 11-adult

        Students manage a simulated energy factory
    and try to develop new energy sources.
    Excellent as a class activity. Has good
    graphics and includes teacher's guide, student
    worksheets, and a data disk.

Game of the States
    Producer: Milton Bradley
    Availability: Apple IIe
    Cost: $39.95
    Ages: 7-adult

        Contains five games: recognizing states
    from maps, learning state capitals, learning
    abbreviations for states, and learning major
    cities. Has realistic graphics. Instruction
    manual included.

Geography Search
    Producer: McGraw-Hill Book Company
    Availability: Apple 48K, TRS-80 Computer
    Cost: $180.00
    Ages: 10-adult

        Students search for the New World on
    sailing ships. Navigation is done using stars,
    sun, weather, and more. An involved but
    educationally valuable program. Includes
    student workbook and teacher's manual.

Geology Search
    Producer: McGraw-Hill Book Company
    Availability: Apple 48K
    Cost: $180.00
    Ages: 11-adult

        A simulation program in which the user
    searches for oil by performing geology tests.
    Decisions on drilling for oil are made on what
    has been learned about rocks, fossils, and
    underground structures. Each student in the
    class can be assigned a part of the project to

do. Includes teacher's guide, student
worksheets, and data disk.

Introduction to Geography
Producer: Orange Cherry Media
Availability: Apple 48K
Cost: $55.00
Ages: 9-adult

A two-part program that uses color
graphics to teach information about the 50
states, and develops global map reading skills.
Provides tests to help the teacher assess
student progress. Documentation provided.

Map Maker
Producer: D.C. Heath and Company
Availability: Apple 48K
Cost: $59.00
Ages: 10-adult

Lets users create and explore their own
maps. Provides maps for cities, states, and
and countries. User is asked to locate and
identify features. Uses good graphics and
includes teacher's guide illustrating how to
incorporate this program into the curriculum.

Regions of the United States
Producer: Evanstron Educators, Inc.
Availability: Apple 48K, Commodore-64
Cost: $39.95
Ages: 10-adult

A geography program treating states as
parts of regions. Considers climate, cultural
factors, and terrain. Provides three games and
facts on each region. Information is
educationally significant. Documentation
included.

The Oregon Trail
Producer: Intellectual Software
Availability: Apple 48K
Cost: $19.95
Ages: 11-13

Offers a simulated wagon trip to Oregon
set in the 1800's. User encounters many

obstacles and must use conservation measures.
Instruction manual included.

The Railroad Works
    Producer: CBS Software
    Availability: Apple 48K, Commodore-64 disk
    Cost: $49.95
    Ages: 10-adult

        Students plan and implement the
    development of a railroad system. Children plan
    track layouts and develop production schedules
    for use of the railroad by businesses. A clever
    program that offers good graphics with
    instruction manual provided.

Tic Tac Show
    Producer: Advanced Ideas
    Availability: Apple IIe, Commodore-64, IBM PC,
                  IBM PCjr
    Cost: $39.95, $19.95 for each additional
          subject disk
    Ages: 7-adult

        Provides an animated game show format for
    one or two players. Has color graphics and
    sound and offers 14 subject areas. Teachers can
    write their own lessons. Additional subject
    disks include: Fun With Facts I, Fun With Facts
    II, Foreign Language, History, Sports Facts,
    and Young Explorer. Instruction manual
    included.

World Atlas Action
    Producer: Developmental Learning Materials
    Availability: Apple 48K
    Cost: $44.00
    Ages: 9-adult

        Users are given 13 maps of regions of the
    world. They are asked to identify salient
    geographic features and important information
    about a country or geographic region. Includes
    blackline masters and teacher's guide.

                        The Arts Software

        As with many other academic disciplines,
    children learn music, painting, drawing, and other

art forms best by doing rather than enacting a
simulation. There are several excellent software
programs included in this section that let the user
do things that are otherwise difficult to emulate.
     These music and drawing programs let the
children create, save their work, then modify, and
add to it at a later time. This allows for
creativity and experimentation. These programs
frequently encourage children to work together, with
each member of the group contributing ideas. This
facet makes the programs valuable teaching tools.
     Many programs include special adaptive hardware
which is literally plugged into the computer. No
computer or technical knowledge is necessary to do
this. There are additional, more costly, and
comprehensive products available today. Most
computer stores can provide information on them.

Delta Drawing
        Producer: Broderbund Software
        Availability: Apple 48K, Atari cartridge,
                      Commodore-64 cartridge, IBM PC,
                      IBM PCjr
        Cost: $49.95
        Ages: 5-13

        User creates colorful drawings on monitor
screen using single key commands. Can integrate
up to five pictures into a complex drawing.
Drawings can be saved and printed using a
graphics printer. Includes lesson cards and a
teacher's manual.

Koala Pad
        Producer: Koala Technologies Corporation
        Availability: Apple IIe, Atari, Commodore-64,
                      IBM PC, IBM PCjr
        Cost: $125.00 Apple, $110.00 Atari, $110.00
              Commodore-64, $149.95 IBM PC and
              IBM PCjr
        Ages: 5-adult

        A video sketch pad that is connected to
the computer. Commands are given on sketch pad,
not on computer keyboard. Teaches drawing and
logical thinking. Knowledge of a computer
language not required. Includes an extensive
instruction manual.

Micro Maestro
    Producer: Chalkboard, Inc.
    Availability: Atari cartridge, Commodore-64
                 cartridge
    Cost: $24.95
    Ages: 5-adult

        Converts Power Pad by Chalkboard, Inc., to
    piano keyboard. Covers two octaves. Lets user
    hear what is played and see notes on monitor
    screen. Includes instruction manual.

Painter Power
    Producer: Microlab Learning Center
    Availability: Apple 48K
    Cost: $39.95
    Ages: 10-adult

        Can create designs. Using keyboard,
    joysticks, or game paddles can cause motion or
    changes in shapes. Two levels of difficulty,
    multiple speed settings, and ability to save
    designs on disk. Documentation provided.

Picturewriter
    Producer: Scarborough Systems
    Availability: Apple IIe, Atari disk, IBM PC,
                 IBM PCjr
    Cost: $39.95
    Ages: 8-adult

        Requires joysticks to draw lines, shapes,
    and pictures. Can fill areas of pictures with
    colors. Pictures can be saved on disk and
    edited. Shapes and pictures can be set to
    music. Includes instruction manual.

Power Pad
    Producer: Chalkboard, Inc.
    Availability: Apple IIe, Atari cartridge,
                 Commodore-64 cartridge, IBM PC,
                 IBM PCjr
    Cost: $99.95
    Ages: 5-adult

        A touch sensitive pad that is connected
    to the computer. Serves as a drawing pad,
    painting canvas using colors, and a piano

keyboard. Knowledge of a computer language not necessary. Includes an extensive instruction manual. See Starter Kit.

Songwriter
    Producer: Scarborough Systems
    Availability: Apple IIe, Atari,
                  Commodore-64, IBM PC, IBM PCjr
    Cost: $39.95
    Ages: 8-adult

        Offers a player piano-like graphics mode to illustrate music and music theory. Deals with both simple and complex music. Songs and ideas can be stored on disk and later edited and synthesized. Has a library of more than eight songs. Includes an instruction manual.

Starter Kit
    Producer: Chalkboard, Inc.
    Availability: Apple IIe, IBM PC, IBM PCjr
    Cost: $49.94 Apple, $79.95 IBM PC, IBM PCjr
    Ages: 5-adult

        Required to connect Power Pad by Chalkboard, Inc., to Apple and IBM computers.

Computer Software Producers

Advanced Ideas
2550 Ninth Street, Suite 104
Berkeley, CA 94710

Apple Computer, Inc.
10260 Bandley Drive
Cupertino, CA 95014

Atari, Inc.--Computer Division
60 E. Plumeria Drive
San Jose, CA 95150

Automated Simulations, Inc.
1043 Kiel Center
Sunnyvale, CA 94089

Beagle Brothers
4315 Sierra Vista
San Diego, CA 92103

Bell & Howell
7100 McCormick Street
Chicago, IL 60645

Bolt, Berman and Newman
10 Moulton Street
Cambridge, MA 02238

Brainbank, Inc.
220 Fifth Avenue
New York, NY 10001

Broderbund Software
17 Paul drive
San Rafael, CA 94903-2103

Commodore International
1200 Wilson Drive
West Chester, PA 19380

COMPress
P.O. Box 102
Wentworth, NH 03282

Computer Headware
P.O. Box 14694
San Francisco, CA 94114

Control Data Publications--Plato
8100 34th Avenue
South Minneapolis, MN 55440

Cybertronics International, Inc.
999 Mount Kremble Avenue
Morristown, NJ 07960

Data Command
329 E. Court Street
Kankakee, IL 60901

Davidson and Associates
6069 Groredac Place #2
Rancho Palas Verdes, CA 90274

Designware, Inc.
185 Berry Street
San Francisco, CA 94701

Developmental Learning Materials
One DLM Park
Allen, TX 75002

Earthware Computer Services
P.O. Box 30039
Eugene, OR 94703

Educational Activities, Inc.
1937 Grand Avenue
Baldwin, NY 11510

Educational Materials and Equipment Company
P.O. Box 17
Pelham, NY 10803

Eduware Services, Inc.
28035 Dorothy Drive
Agoura, CA 91301

Ginn and Company
191 Spring Street
Lexington, MA 02173

High Technologies Software Products, Inc.
1611 N.W. 23rd Street
P.O. Box 60406
Oklahoma City, OK 73146

Insoft
10175 Barbur Boulevard
Suite 202B
Portland, OR 97219

Intellectual Software
798 North Avenue
Bridgeport, CT 06606

Krell Software Corporation
1320 Stony Brook Road
Stony Brook, NY 11790

L&S Computerware
1589 Fraser Drive
Sunnyvale, CA 94087

Learningways, Inc.
98 Raymond Street
Cambridge, MA 02140

Learning Well
200 S. Service Road
Roslyn Heights, NY 11577

McGraw-Hill Book Company
1221 Avenue of the Americas
New York, NY 10020

Merian Scientific
247 Armstrong Avenue
Georgetown, Ontario
Canada L7G 4x6

Microcomputer Workshops
225 Westchester Avenue
Port Chester, NY 10573

Milliken Publishing Company
1100 Research Boulevard
P.O. Box 21579
St. Louis, MO 63132-0579

Milton Bradley Educational Division
443 Shaker Road
East Longmeadow, MA 01028

Minnesota Educational Computing Consortium
2520 Broadway Drive
Saint Paul, MN 55113

On-Line Systems
36575 Mudge Ranch Road
Coarsegold, CA 93614

Penguin Software
830 4th Avenue
Geneva, IL 60134

Random House School Division
400 Hahn Road
Westminster, MD 21157

Scarborough Systems
25 N. Broadway
Tarrytown, NY 10591

Scholastic, Inc.
901 Sylvan Avenue
Englewood Cliffs, NJ 07632

Silicon Valley Systems, Inc.
1625 El Camino Real #4
Belmont, CA 94002

Sirius Software
1537 Howe Avenue #106
Sacramento, CA 93614

Software Masters
3330 Hillcroft
Houston, TX 77057

Software Publishing Corporation
1901 Landings Drive
Mountain View, CA 94043

Spinnaker Software Corporation
215 First Street
Cambridge, MA 02142

Sunburst Communications
Washington Avenue
Pleasantville, NY 10570

SVE/Society for Visual Education, Inc.
1345 Diversey Parkway
Chicago, IL 60614

Synergistic Software
5221 120th Avenue S.E.
Bellevue, WA 98006

Tandy Corporation/Radio Shack
1400 One Tandy Center
Fort Worth, TX 76102

Telephone Software Connection
P.O. Box 654B
Torrance, CA 90504

Terrapin, Inc.
380 Green Street
Cambridge, MA 02139

The Learning Company
4370 Alpine Road
Portola Valley, CA 94025

Visicorp
1330 Bordeau Drive
Sunnyvale, CA 94086

Window, Inc.
460 Pleasant Street
Cambridge, MA 02172

Xerox Educational Publications
Computer Software Division
245 Long Hill Road
Middletown, CT 06457

BIBLIOGRAPHY

Ahl, David. "Software for Learning Mathematics."
CREATIVE COMPUTING 10 (October 1984):   76-91.

   Provides analysis and detailed descriptions of
   25 software programs for mathematics.

Anderson, John J. "Drawing Conclusions." CREATIVE
COMPUTING 9 (December 1983).

   Reviews characteristics and attributes of several
   programs for turning the computer into a sketch
   pad.

Balajthy, Ernest. "Computer Simulations and
Reading." THE READING TEACHER 37 (March 1984):
590-593.

   Describes how software written for academic
   disciplines is useful for teaching reading. Gives
   examples of specific programs.

Brown, Peter D. "English and the Computer."
ENGLISH QUARTERLY 16 (Winter 1984):   55-62.

   Compares computer learning to language learning.
   Makes effective analogies and developmental
   comparisons.

Chomsky, Carol. "Finding the Best Language Arts
  Software." CLASSROOM COMPUTER LEARNING 4 (January
  1984): 58-63.

  Gives criteria for evaluating software, what to
  look for in software, and sample programs that are
  analyzed.

Cohen, Mollie L. "Educational Software: A Taste of
  What's Available for Social Studies." THE
  COMPUTING TEACHER 10 (December 1982): 11-15.

  Gives descriptions of types of software available,
  by category, including sample programs.

Dewey, Patrick R. "Searching for Software."
  POPULAR COMPUTING 3 (Mid-October 1984): 137-141.

  Outlines how to use computer software directories
  for software searches. Gives a good listing of
  software directories.

Fraser, Sherry. "The Learning Software Awards."
  CLASSROOM COMPUTER LEARNING 4 (January 1984):
  52-59.

  Examines several computer programs and considers
  criteria that can be applied when evaluating them.

Jarchow, Elaine McNally. "Teaching Literature with
  the Help of Microcomputers." THE COMPUTING
  TEACHER 11 (November 1983): 35-45.

  Describes software program author developed for
  use as a tool to review and discuss literary
  works.

Kayser, Roger, and George King. "7 Steps to Buying
  Better Software." ELECTRONIC EDUCATION 2 (March
  1984): 46-51.

  Provides practical suggestions to follow before
  purchasing computer software programs.

Lathrop, Ann, and Bobby Goodson. COURSEWARE IN THE
  CLASSROOM: SELECTING, ORGANIZING AND USING
  EDUCATIONAL SOFTWARE. Reading, Mass.:
  Addison-Wesley, 1983.

Outlines techniques used to evaluate computer software. Includes an extensive software directory.

Miller, Steven E. "Evaluating Software." COMPUTER UPDATE (September/October 1984): 16-18.

Offers a set of questions user should ask before purchasing computer software.

Myers, Glenford J. THE ART OF SOFTWARE TESTING. New York: John Wiley and Sons, 1979.

Offers practical and theoretical ideas to explore when testing and debugging computer software.

Riordon, Tim. "How to Select Software You Can Trust." CLASSROOM COMPUTER NEWS 3 (March 1983): 56-60.

Discusses several issues relating to program effectiveness that can be used when selecting educational software.

Rosenzweig, Laura. "Teaming up Social Studies and Computer Teachers." ELECTRONIC LEARNING 7 (April 1985): 16, 21.

Demonstrates how database management software can be used as a curriculum aid in the social studies classroom.

Rossman, Michael. "How to Use the Computer in Science Class (And How Not To)." CLASSROOM COMPUTER LEARNING 4 (February 1984): 12-21.

Outlines strengths and weaknesses of the computer as used in science curricula.

Schantz, Letty M. "The Computer as Tutor and Tutee in Composition." THE COMPUTING TEACHER 11 (October 1983): 60-63.

Considers applications of the computer and computer software as tool for writing. Treats writing as developmental act according to Piagetian theory.

Southwell, Michael G. "Computers and Developmental
    Writing." THE COMPUTING TEACHER 10 (November
    1982): 34-35.

    Descibes how computers are used in an English
    writing lab. Considers implementation of Computer
    Assisted Instruction (CAI).

Sterling Swift Publishing Company. SWIFT'S
    EDUCATIONAL SOFTWARE DIRECTORT. Austin, Tex.:
    Sterling Swift Publishing Company, 1984.

    Gives a listing of educational software with
    descriptions. Editions available for several types
    of computers.

Tandy Corporation. TRS-80 EDUCATIONAL SOFTWARE
    SOURCEBOOK. Fort Worth, Tex., 1983.

    Provides a comprehensive listing of educational
    software available for TRS-80 computers.
    Descriptions and analyses included.

Tinker, Robert. "New Dimensions in Math and Science
    Software." CLASSROOM COMPUTER NEWS 3 (March
    1983): 36-39.

    A report for the U.S. Department of Education
    reviewing available software. Describes what is
    needed in the future.

CHAPTER SEVEN

UTILITY PROGRAMS

There is one collection of programs for the computer that was not discussed in Chapter Six. These programs encompass more than what we generally call educational computer software programs and for the sake of convenience and clarity have been designated as Utility Programs.

Many of these programs can be used directly with children in elementary classrooms while others are more appropriately used by older children and adults. Several of these software routines are efficiently used by teachers to carry out administrative functions or to create interesting signs and posters for display purposes in the school. In general these programs are not related to a particular academic discipline.

The software in this section covers a wide range of content areas as well as some very practical routines. Word processing software constitutes an important component as do related programs used for creative writing activities for young children. Database management software programs are discussed, showing how they can be used to create files and records, as are spread sheet programs that permit numeric analyses.

Programs that let the user easily construct signs and posters are introduced as well as software that develops and enhances typing skills. These and other programs included here have applications for children, teachers, and individuals who wish to make their personal and professional work less complex and tedious.

Word processing software has been available for several years. These programs are designed to make writing a simpler task by allowing the user to easily edit, modify, correct, and print material

that has been written. In the past large computers
were needed to run this software, but today there
is a multitude of word processing programs designed
for use on the microcomputer. Word processing
programs usually have many features in common, but
there are many differences in how they operate and
handle information.

In this section we will consider the most
important features to look for when purchasing a
word processing program. Your first question may be,
why do I need one when my typewriter functions well
as I carry out my writing tasks? The answer is
simple. You really do not need a word processor.
However, if a word processor is used, the quality of
written documents inevitably improves and the time
required to produce the final copy is dramatically
reduced.

As with a typewriter, the word processor allows
you to compose text at the keyboard, but this is
where the similarity between the two systems ends.
To make corrections, additions, and modifications
when using a typewriter you must retype the entire
document, use correcting fluid or tape, or cut and
paste the document together. Using a word processor
makes this task entirely unnecessary.

With this system you can easily correct
typographical errors, insert and delete information,
and easily move words, sentences, and paragraphs to
new positions. Information you have written can be
stored on cassette tape or floppy disk and retrieved
at a later time. After retrieving your document you
can make changes and additions and resave the text
file. A computer printer is used to get a hard copy
of your document. Many word processing programs give
the option of structuring the printout in almost any
form you wish. Retyping documents is entirely
unnecessary, giving the user more time to make sure
the final product is exactly what is wanted.
Students using this system are more motivated to
produce quality work.

Word processing can be used to write or edit
documents that already have been written. The most
convenient word processors to use are those that let
you make editorial changes while in the write mode.
Of course, you will have to master several
procedures to perform editorial functions. Some word
processing software requires the user to enter the

edit mode to make changes in the document. This
method works well, but can be cumbersome when making
modifications to a long document.

Word processors are provided with a rectangular
square that lets you know where the characters will
be entered. This is called the cursor, and can be
moved left and right across the monitor screen or up
and down over lines of text without erasing what it
passes over. High quality word processing programs
allow you to easily move the cursor from paragraph
to paragraph, from page to page, and from the
beginning to the end of the document.

Cursor movements are essential when making
editorial changes in the text you are writing. The
simplest changes in text are made by typing over
what you have written. In this case the original
characters are erased and replaced by the new
characters you have typed. By using the proper
commands you can readily delete text, add new
material, and move sections of the manuscript from
one location to another. The best word processing
programs automatically compensate for these changes
and restructure sentences and paragraphs so they are
properly spaced.

One decided advantage to using the word
processing system is the built-in word wraparound
feature. This becomes immediately apparent if you
watch the monitor screen as you enter several lines
of text. When using an electric typewriter you must
press the carriage return at the end of each typed
line. Word processing does not require the user to
press the return key at the end of each line. If the
word is too long to fit on the line, the entire word
is automatically moved to the beginning of the next
line.

As a matter of fact, pressing the return key
while word processing can cause problems, as this
tells the computer you have completed a paragraph.
Your printout may not be in the expected form if the
return key is accidentally pressed. There are
several additional screen display features that are
important when using a word processor. Many programs
display 24 lines of text on the monitor screen at
one time. As more information is entered the screen
automatically moves up material that has been
written, to accommodate the new information.

The number of vertical columns of text
displayed on the monitor screen at one time varies

depending on the word processor you are using. Some
word processors provide a 40-column screen while
others offer up to 70 or 80 columns. The standard
electric typewriter provides 80 columns of text and
most users find it convenient to use a word
processor having a similar arrangement. In some
cases you must purchase an 80-column printed circuit
board to achieve an 80-column monitor screen.

Most word processors will allow you to print
exactly what you have entered in the form that is
displayed on the screen. The better word processors
have a print menu that allows for modifications.
This means you can set margins to different
positions, use double or single spacing between
lines, and make other modifications as needed. The
best word processors also allow you to underline
text, center titles, use subscripts and
superscripts, as well as have the ability to use
running heads and footnotes. Whether or not all of
these features can be used depends on the type of
printer you have provided.

Many word processing programs have additional
features that are very useful but not necessary for
the functioning of the program itself. For example,
your word processor should include a manual that
explains in a clear and concise fashion how to use
the program. The manual should be structured so that
it is simple to find answers to questions that arise
while using the program.

Many programs have a built-in help menu showing
how to use commands and make use of options within
the program. Some word processing software is
provided with a built-in tutorial program on
cassette tape or floppy disk. This is very useful as
it lets you practice writing and modifying text
while using the many features the program offers.

Most word processing programs try to prevent
the accidental loss of text material or entire files
you have saved. Before making textual changes or
file deletions the program asks if you are really
sure you wish to make the change. Your response is
typically yes or no. The most sophisticated systems
also permit you to use your word processor in
conjunction with other designated software programs.

For example, some programs have a compatible
spelling checker that is used to examine words you
have typed. Other programs let you merge text from
other files into what you have written using the

word processor. These are good features, but are not
necessary when using the word processing system.

Word processing programs have been used
successfully with elementary aged children for the
last few years, although their use has not been
widespread. I believe that this will change in the
next few years as many word processing programs such
as Largewriter and Magic Slate have been
specifically written for use by children. These
programs are very easy to use and offer help and
command menus on the monitor screen. Their operating
instructions are written at a level which young
children can readily understand, but they still
provide many sophisticated functions for editing,
printing, and formatting documents the child has
composed.

I am not suggesting that word processing
software will replace paper, pens, and pencils,
rather it represents a new technology that can be
put to good use by the teacher. As with other
technologies, how it is introduced to children and
the strategies for use developed by the teacher will
determine how effective word processing can be as a
learning tool. I do not believe that this software
should be introduced before the third or fourth
grade, although some programs have been written for
younger children.

A word procesor can be a very useful tool
to help children improve their writing. Before
beginning to use a word processor for writing
activities, children should be familiarized with the
microcomputer and have had several experiences
working with computer software programs. They must
understand the differences between editing, saving,
and retrieving documents as well as knowing how a
computer printer can be used to generate hard copy
of what has been written.

There are many techniques to learn and
procedures to master before the elementary aged
child can truly benefit from using a word
processing program. The teacher must develop a
timetable that can be used to bring the child to a
state of readiness so that this software can be
meaningfully incorporated into the curriculum.

The best way to start is for the teacher to
demonstrate that the computer keyboard is very
similar to a typewriter. Ask several children to

type their names, or write simple sentences using the word processor. If the children have used other computer software programs, they will want to press the RETURN or ENTER key after each word or sentence they have typed. They must be shown that pressing these keys is only done at the completion of a paragraph. Otherwise the hard copy produced by the printer will not be in the form the child or teacher wants. This is a difficult concept for both children and adults to learn.

After learning to properly enter information, the students should then be taught how to save and retrieve information on computer disk or cassette tape, depending on the type of information storage and retrieval system you are using. Children soon learn that each text file must be named before it can be used. Using the storage capabilities of the word processor is an excellent classroom exercise as information written one day can be retrieved at a later time.

Once the children master these tasks, they can begin to use the edit features of the word processor. Each word processing program has its own procedures for using edit functions that are generally easy to use. The final steps in gaining mastery of a word processor is learning to select print formats and to use the computer printer. These processes are program and machine specific, but can be quickly learned by the child.

Soon, children will be able to write, edit, save, and retrieve documents using the word processor. Using a computer printer with the software will let the child produce written documents having a wide selection of formats. The speed of data entry will not be great, as the children will still lack typing skills. However, they will be able to modify and expand upon stories they have written, and make modifications suggested by the teacher. Using a word processor to best advantage requires a great deal of classroom preparation by the teacher. For this reason I believe that the introduction of word processing to children should take place during February or March of the school year.

Included below are several examples of word processing programs and spelling checkers that are in common use today. Information such as title, producer, age group for which the program is

intended, compatible computer equipment, and cost
is included. A summary discussion of the important
features of each system is also provided. The word
processing programs themselves offer a wide range of
features and applications. Some are designed for use
by children while others are intended to be used by
adults.

Appleworks
        Producer: Apple Computer, Inc.
        Availability: Apple 64K with 2 disk drives and
                      80-column text card
        Cost: $195.00
        Ages: Adult

        A versatile word processing program that
is easy to use and includes features one
expects in a quality word processing program.
Also includes a database program and a spread
sheet program that have good format and
structure. Can use these for professional
applications. An excellent value. Manual
provided and back-up disks can be made from the
master disk.

Apple Writer II, IIe
        Producer: Apple Computer, Inc.
        Availability: Apple 48K, 64K
        Cost: $125.00
        Ages: Adult

        An excellent word processor provided with
a quality reference manual. Has help and print
menus and disk based tutorial. Includes a word
processing language manual for doing
sophisticated work. Offers all advanced word
processing features. Can use a single disk
drive, but two disk drives work more easily.

Atari Writer
        Producer: Atari, Inc.
        Availability: Atari 16K
        Cost: $100.00
        Ages: 12-adult
        A menu driven word processing program that
is very easy to use. Offers good editing
features. Provides a variety of formats for
printouts. Manual includes a tutorial program
and well-written documentation.

Bank Street Speller
        Producer: Broderbund Software
        Availability: Apple 48K
        Cost: $64.95
        Ages: 11 and older

        A spelling checker for use with Bank
Street Writer. Has a 30,000-word vocabulary.
Can add more words if your system has two disk
drives. Easy-to-make corrections for misspelled
words in text. Provides back-up disk and
manual.

Bank Street Writer
        Producer: Broderbund Software
        Availability: Apple 48K, Atari disk, Commodore-
                      64 disk, IBM PC, IBM PCjr
        Cost: $69.95, IBM $79.95
        Ages: 11 and older

        Easy-to-use word processing system
designed for children and adults. Enters text
in the write mode and has transfer menu for
loading, storing, and printing. Offers good
screen prompts and a disk based tutorial. Has a
clearly written and well-organized manual.

Circascript, The Student Writer
        Producer: Intellectual Software
        Availability: Apple 64K, Commodore-64 disk
        Cost: $49.95
        Ages: 12 and older

        Well-designed, easy-to-use program having
many sophisticated features such as tab
settings and underlining capability. Offers
good print feature options and a tutorial.
Provides back-up disk and excellent
documentation.

CorrectStar
        Producer: MicroPro International
        Availability: IBM PC, IBM PCjr
        Cost: $195.00
        Ages: Adult

A well-designed spelling checker used with
the WordStar word processing program. Provides
an extensive dictionary and allows user to add
additional words. Uses a two-disk drive system.

Cut and Paste
    Producer: Electronic Arts
    Availability: Apple 64K, Atari 48K, Commodore-
                  64, IBM PC, IBM PCjr
    Cost: $50.00
    Ages: 10 and older

    User friendly program that can be employed
with children. Editing is done in the write
mode with prompts provided at the bottom of the
screen. Final form for printout not shown on
screen. A versatile program with excellent
documentation including several writing samples
on disk.

Homeword
    Producer: Sierra On-Line, Inc.
    Availability: Apple 48K, Commodore-64
    Cost: $69.95
    Ages: 10-adult

    Uses pictures on the screen to give
program instructions and options. No need to
learn commands. Can write, edit, store, and
print text. Gives tutorial on audiocassetts and
includes instruction manual. An easy-to-use
word processing program.

Home Word Speller
    Producer: Sierra On-Line, Inc.
    Availability: Apple 48K, Commodore-64
    Cost: $49.95
    Ages: 10-adult

    A spelling checker used with Homeword
word processor. Has 20,000-word dictionary.
Uses pictures to give program instructions.
Documentation provided.

Largewriter
    Producer: Intellectual Software
    Availability: Apple 64K
    Cost: $49.95
    Ages: 8 and older

A word processor designed for use with young children and the visually impaired. Gives large letters on the monitor screen. Provides three options for printout of written material.

Lets Explore Word Processing
    Producer: Milton Bradley
    Availability: Apple 48K
    Cost: $39.95
    Ages: 10-adult

    A highly interactive tutorial program that introduces children to the word processing system. Easy to use with clearly written instructions provided.

Magic Slate
    Producer: Sunburst Communications
    Availability: Apple 48K
    Cost: $65.00
    Ages: 7-adult

    An excellent, easy-to-use word processor for very young children. Provides 20, 40, or 80 columns of screen text. Has a wide range of features including: large letters, bold print, italics, underlining, centering, and typical editing functions. Has back-up disk and teacher's guide.

Magic Window II
    Producer: Artsci, Inc.
    Availability: Apple 64K
    Cost: $149.95
    Ages: Adult

    An easy-to-learn menu driven program. Subsystems for formatting, printing, maintenance of files, and editing are very well structured. Monitor screen shows how printed copy will appear. Manual is well written but a little hard to use for finding answers to questions.

Magic Words
    Producer: Artsci, Inc.
    Availability: Apple 48K

Cost: $69.95
Ages: Adult

A spelling checker designed for use with
Magic Window and many other word processors.
Has a 14,000-word dictionary and you can add
your own words. Spelling errors are easily
corrected and program can print spelling error
list. An excellent value with documentation
provided.

Milliken Word Processor
Producer: Milliken Pub. Co.
Availability: Apple 48K
Cost: $69.95
Ages: 8-10

A menu driven program offering picture
reminders on the screen for functions and
options. Has an editor, but does not provide
sophisticated word processing features.
Excellent for classroom use. Has back-up disk,
teacher's manual with related classroom
activities.

Screen Writer II Plus Dictionary
Producer: Sierra On-Line, Inc.
Availability: Apple 48K
Cost: $129.95
Ages: Adult

A comprehensive word processor with
spelling checker provided. Has 28,000-word
dictionary with user able to add up to 2500 new
words. Has easy-to-use editor and a good print
option menu. Extensive manual provided.

Scripsit
Producer: Tandy Corporation
Availability: TRS-80 models III and IV
Cost: $149.00
Ages: Adult

An excellent word processing program
having features of professional word
processors. A well-written and easy-to-use
manual is provided. Offers a variety of print
features.

Scripsit Dictionary
    Producer: Tandy Corporation
    Availability: TRS-80 Models III and IV
    Cost: $149.00
    Ages: Adult

        An excellent dictionary program offering
    an extensive word base and capacity to add user
    selected words. Easy to use and provided with
    good documentation.

Sensible Speller
    Producer: Sensible Software
    Availability: Apple 48K
    Cost: $125.00
    Ages: Adult

        A spelling checker with 80,000-word
    dictionary. With a second disk drive user can
    add up to 10,000 additional words. Program can
    work with many word processors including Bank
    Street Writer, Apple Writer, Screen Writer and
    WordStar. Back-up disk and dictionary disk
    provided.

Spellstar
    Producer: Micropro International
    Availability: Apple 48K
    Cost: $250.00
    Ages: Adult

        Spelling checker compatible with the
    WordStar word processor. Has a 20,000-word
    dictionary. Requires two disk drives to add new
    words. Works by dissecting the document and
    sorting and removing duplicate words before
    comparing to words in dictionary. An excellent
    program but requires a lot of disk space.
    Documentation provided.

Super-Text Professional
    Producer: Muse Software
    Availability: Commodore-64
    Cost: $99.00
    Ages: Adult

        A sophisticated word processor having
    professional format features that can
    accommodate a 40- or 80-column screen display.

Offers built-in calculator functions. Has good
formatting and editing features. Screen display
gives print format. Has back-up disk and user
guide.

The Electric Pencil
        Producer: ING, Inc.
        Availability: TRS-80
        Cost: $89.95
        Ages: Adult

        A very well constructed and easy-to-use
program. It is not menu driven. Lacks screen
display prompt lines but offers a very well
written manual that shows good organization.
Includes a reference card giving commonly used
commands.

The Writer's Assistant
        Producer: Interlearn, Inc.
        Availability: Apple 64K
        Cost: $59.95
        Ages: 8 and older

        Lets user write and edit in one mode using
single key commands. Offers built-in spelling
checker using 100-word dictionary. Has
sophisticated but easy-to-use features. Offers
a disk based tutorial and reference card for
commonly used commands. Offers help menus for
three different age groups. Manual itself is
somewhat cumbersome to use.

Thor
        Producer: Fastware
        Availability: IBM PC, IBM PCjr 128K RAM memory
        Cost: $295.00
        Ages: Adult

        Combination software offering both word
processing and database management. Works very
well with multiple sets of files. Very good for
administrative applications.

WordStar
        Producer: Micropro International
        Availability: Apple 64K

Cost: $495.00
Ages: Adult

A very sophisticated but complex program
that takes a long time to learn. Offers
multiple sets of help menus. User can readily
change format for each paragraph of text.
Screen shows print format. Gives wide variety
of print formats. Can be used with several
other software programs, including Spellstar
and Mail Merge. Offers virtually all text
features and has comprehensive manual.

We have now entered what might be called the
second generation of word processors. Many of the
new programs are clearly geared to learning and
teaching rather than simply to perform secretarial
and administrative functions. Today's software is
user friendly, interesting to use, and easy to
operate. Programs are available for use on most
microcomputers with versions available for virtually
every age group. The cost of word processing
programs has been greatly reduced in the past two
years.
    Using a word processor helps students produce
quality written work. Spelling, grammatical, and
syntactical errors are lessened because of the
easy-to-use edit features available. Similarly,
reports and papers can be restructured and material
added and deleted with relative ease.
    Using a word processor allows students to
freely and creatively express their ideas when they
learn they can easily make changes. They can
concentrate more closely on the content of the
document, knowing the form in which it is presented
can be finalized later. Word processors are becoming
an increasingly important part of language arts
development, as they can help students become better
writers.
    There is a collection of software designed to
help young children learn how to express ideas and
logically develop concepts. These computer programs
interact with the child in creative ways in helping
them learn to write short stories. In most cases
they provide story starters for the children.
Color graphics are used to create interesting scenes

that can be varied each time the program is run.
Children may be asked to construct stories about
these scenes from a series of questions and
statements made by the computer.
Many of these programs are very cleverly
designed, with sound educational principles clearly
evident. Often the stories can be printed using a
computer printer. The stories can be stored on
cassette tape or floppy disk, retrieved and edited.
Children frequently work together when constructing
stories, deciding the direction the plot will take.
Interactive group learning as well as individual
skill development are among the advantages of using
this software. These writing programs represent a
valuable learning resource when teaching language
development.

Adventuwrite
        Producer: Developmental Learning Materials
        Availability: Apple 48K
        Cost: $59.95
        Ages: 7 and older

        Is a unique writing program offering
        excellent color graphics. Children use words to
        describe scenes and the responses are stored on
        a set of nine note files. Students can also
        compose their own stories. An excellent
        program, including a utilities disk and a
        teacher's guide.

Kid Writer
        Producer: Spinnaker Software Corporation
        Availability: Apple 64K, Commodore-64
        Cost: $34.95
        Ages: 6-12

        The computer generates colorful scenes
        and children write corresponding stories. Has
        64 scenes in the memory bank. Teaches the
        fundamentals of word processing. A very good
        program for use with young children.
        Documentation provided.

Story Maker
        Producer: Bolt, Beranek and Newman Inc.
        Availability: Apple 48K

Cost: $30.00
Ages: 7-12

An interactive program that uses story
starters to help children write stories. Has a
very useful help menu and excellent
documentation. Very young children may need
assistance when first using the program.

Story Maker: A Fact and Fiction Tool Kit
Producer: Bolt, Beranek and Newman, Inc.
Availability: Apple 64K and Joystick
Cost: $95.00
Ages: 8 and older

A very well designed program that helps
children write stories, illustrate them using
pictures, and print the results. Offers eight
different type faces. The school version has a
picture bank of over 200 scenes. Very good
documentation provided.

Story Starter
Producer: Random House School Division
Availability: TRS-80 Model III Computer,
                cassette or disk
Cost: $49.50
Ages: 7-13

Provides an excellent screen display and
print features. An interactive program where
children start stories and the computer
provides helpful prompts to let them continue.
Uses four cause/effect relations, offering
levels of difficulty for each. Good
documentation provided.

Story Tree
Producer: Scholastic Software
Availability: Apple 48K, Commodore-64, IBM PC,
                IBM PCjr
Cost: $59.95
Ages: 9 and older

Lets children write and read interactive
stories. Provides story starters or you can
construct your own compositions. Can save,
edit, and print documents. A good introduction
to word processing containing a tutorial, two
sample stories, and a teacher's guide.

That's My Story
    Producer: Learning Well
    Availability: Apple 48K
    Cost: $59.95
    Ages: 8 and older

        An interactive program that offers story
    starters. Teachers can add new story starters.
    Has a printout feature and uses a branching
    questioning technique for story development.
    Comes with a back-up disk and teacher's guide
    giving suggested activities.

        There is also a collection of software that
    teaches and further develops typing skills. Until
    the user learns how to use the keyboard to enter
    information in a reasonably efficient manner, data
    entry for many software programs can be exceedingly
    slow and tedious. This is particularly true if you
    are writing computer programs or using a word
    processor.
        The majority of these programs use a unique
    format to help develop touch typing skills. Many
    provide an arcade type game simulation where the
    user shoots falling letters or words by pressing
    specific computer keys. In other cases you are asked
    to type letters, words, or phrases that are shown on
    the monitor screen.
        The design of these programs is excellent, as
    they require the learner to use standard finger
    positions on the keyboard. They are developmental,
    for they gradually take the user through a set of
    typing lessons using different sets of keys. They
    also offer varying levels of difficulty and some
    allow the user to select required response times
    from slow to fast. The most advanced programs print
    progress reports at the end of the lesson and will
    let teachers design their own assignments.
        Both children and adults find this approach to
    enhancing touch typing skills useful, fun, and
    interesting. You are quite literally learning while
    playing a game. Today and in future years mastering
    typing skills will become an increasingly important
    aspect of learning to maximize efficiency and
    practical applications of the computer. Not that
    taking a course in typing is not the best way to

learn these skills, rather that for some of us,
computer programs like these provide a good starting
point or offer ways to further develop skills. I
highly recommend the addition of a typing program to
your software collection.

Hi-Res Mastertype
    Producer: Lightning Software
    Availability: Apple 48K
    Cost: $40.00
    Ages: All age levels

        Uses an invader game format. Space ship
    gives user commands at the center of the
    screen. Letters and numbers appear at the
    corners of the screen and the user must type
    them to prevent them from descending. Offers 17
    lessons. Can correct mistakes and design own
    lessons. Excellent program that gives your
    score and typing speed.

Mastertype
    Producer: Scarboro Systems
    Availability: Apple 48K, Atari, Commodore-64,
                  IBM PC, IBM PCjr
    Cost: $39.95
    Ages: All age levels

        Players learn to type using a space
    invader game format. Teaches standard keyboard
    finger positions using an easy-to-learn format.
    Teacher can create individualized lessons.
    Documentation provided.

Typing Tutor II
    Producer: Microsoft
    Availability: Apple 48K
    Cost: $24.95
    Ages: All age levels

        Teaches typing and helps increase typing
    speed and accuracy. Computer monitors speed of
    response for each key. Provides a menu and lets
    user choose level of difficulty. Gives reports
    and evaluations. A unique and useful program
    providing good documentation.

Type Attack
    Producer: Sirus Software

Availability: Apple 48K
Cost: $39.95
Ages: All age levels

Uses an arcade game format letting user
choose speed and type of lesson. Can create
your own game. Gives practice with individual
characters and sets of them. User types letters
or words to keep them from landing. Includes
instruction manual.

A very practical application of microcomputer
technology is to use computer software to create and
save information typically contained in files and
records. Database computer software is the name
given to programs that perform this function. There
are many programs of this type in use today, ranging
from simple programs that keep mailing label
information to those that can perform a multitude of
functions.

In general a database can be thought of as a
collection of information that has been organized to
meet a particular need. Quality database software
programs allow you to search for records based on
user defined characteristics and print results in a
variety of formats. For example, suppose you had
entered data about computer manufacturers from
across the country. You could then use the database
to print an alphabetical list of all monitor
manufacturers from California whose machines have a
retail cost of less than $300.00 and have color
capabilities. The computer will do this in a matter
of minutes whereas a hand search through a file
system could very well take hours.

Database software makes working with files and
records a simpler, more efficient process. There are
several features to look for before purchasing a
database management software program. The key is to
obtain a program that meets your particular needs
today and is sophisticated enough to meet your
future requirements.

Quality database management software provides
an easy method by which files can be designed and
information added. They should provide convenient
ways to add new records and edit existing ones, and
should offer a multiple set of printing options.
Menu driven programs that have sets of default
values that can be changed are the most convenient

to use. Many of these programs offer mathematics
options that can be performed on numeric data as
well as being able to carry out simple statistical
analyses. The most advanced programs also allow the
user to merge data files created with the system and
to use data that has been saved in conjunction with
other computer software programs.

There are examples of two types of database
management programs included in this section. Some
of the programs are designed for use by adults to
perform a variety of relatively complex tasks, while
others are structured so that they can be used by
young children. These database programs provide a
meaningful way to teach children how to save and
retrieve information.

Teachers are beginning to find applications for
database software for creating files in a variety of
subject areas so that information can be sorted and
arranged in a number of ways based on criteria
established by the children. Information pertinent
to peoples of the world can be collected. Students
can then find ways in which they are similar and
different using sort routines provided by the
database. Data related to science such as habitats
and characteristics of animals, and geographical
information about parts of the United States or the
world can be stored and sorted using a database
management program. The possibilities are endless.

Programs that have been written for children
such as Friendly Filer and Secret Filer, have given
database software their recent popularity. As was
true for word processors, the teacher must carefully
orchestrate the preparation for use of databases
with elementary aged children. Before using the
database, children must first learn how to manually
sort information based on criteria that have been
established. They must also learn how to structure
fields so that sorting is possible. Once these
techniques have been learned, children quickly find
that database software lets them gather useful
information in a quick, easy, and reliable manner.

This section also includes programs that are
very similar to database software in design, but are
intended to help teachers maintain individual
student data. These can best be described as
electric gradebooks and are very similar to
gradebooks used by teachers everywhere. They offer a

wide range of options, including the ability to compute student grades and print reports. They provide an innovative way to keep student records and record their academic development.

Apple Grade Book
    Producer: J & S Software
    Availability: Apple 48K
    Cost: $49.50
    Age: Adults

        Handles 80 students per class with up to 35 grades per student. Easy to make corrections and add and delete student names. Can assign weighted values to grades. Offers a good format for printouts. Documentation provided.

Appleworks
    Producer: Apple Computer, Inc.
    Availability: Apple IIe with two disk drives
                  and extended 80-column card
    Cost: $195.00
    Ages: Adult

        See word processing reference for description.

Class Records
    Producer: Educational Systems Software
    Availability: Apple 48K
    Cost: $89.95
    Ages: Adult

        A superb easy-to-use record keeping program having the flexibility of being able to be used with other compatible modular programs. Can record attendance and grade information and store them on a duplicatable data disk. User can code attendance values and utilize a variety of forms for grades. Excellent report format produced. Documentation provided.

Data Handler
    Producer: MECC
    Availability: Apple 48K, IBM PC, IBM PCjr
    Cost: $49.00
    Ages: Adult

A simple easy-to-use menu driven database program. Offers search and sort routines and can generate mailing labels. Holds up to 1050 records. Provides a good selection of print formats and you can design your own. Provided with a back-up disk and manual.

Electric Grade Book
    Producer: Intellectual Software
    Availability: Apple 48K
    Cost: $79.95
    Ages: Adult

    Holds up to 40 students per file with 40 student marks per grading period. Can use letter or numeric grades or a mixture. Can assign weighted values to grades and add or delete names at any time. Computes averages and provides a selection of print formats.

Friendly Filer
    Producer: Grolier Electronic Publications, Inc.
    Availability: Apple 48K
    Cost: $39.95
    Ages: 4-12

    Introduces young users to concepts of structuring and creating database files. Children can design up to seven fields and perform search and sort operations on them. Several data disks can be purchased for use with this program. Includes instruction manual.

Master Type's Filer
    Producer: Scarborough Systems
    Availability: Apple 48K, Commodore-64, IBM PC,
                 IBM PCjr
    Cost: $40.00
    Ages: 10-adult

    An easy-to-use database program that makes excellent use of sound and color. Easy to enter data, perform sort routines, and print results in a variety of formats. Documentation included.

PFS File/PFS Report
    Producer: Software Publishing Corp.

Availability: Apple 48K, IBM PC, IBM PCjr
Cost: $250.00 Apple, IBM $280.00
Ages: Adult

   A sophisticated database program and
report generator. Allows you to design your own
form for input and output. Has excellent
documentation. An excellent program having most
desirable features.

Practifile
   Producer: Computer Software Associates
   Availability: Commodore-64 disk
   Cost: $54.95
   Ages: Adult

   An inexpensive database program offering
excellent potential for storing, writing, and
printing data records in a variety of forms.
Can also handle up to 10 math functions for use
in math equations. Has a very well written and
structured manual.

Quickfile II
   Producer: Apple Computer, Inc.
   Availability: Apple 64K with two disk drives
   Cost $100.00
   Ages: Older children and adults

   An easy-to-use database management program
with good documentation. Provides good format
for sorts and printouts. Convenient to edit,
add, and delete files. Designed for the
non-technically oriented user.

Secret Filer
   Producer: Information Technology Design
              Associates
   Availability: Apple 64K, Commodore-64 disk, IBM
                 PC, IBM PCjr
   Cost: $29.95
   Ages: 9-12

   Teaches children about the use of filing
systems and the use of search commands. Can
create their own databases and arrange data in

a variety of ways. Has save, edit, and erase commands. Has back-up disk and student handbook.

Teachers Record Book
    Producer: Successful Software
    Availability: Apple 48K
    Cost: $60.00
    Ages: Adult

    Can handle 120 students per class and up to 10 classses on a data disk. Can use predefined categories or define your own. Excellent output format including bar graphs. Can include customized messages for students.

The TC Filer
    Producer: The Teaching Company
    Availability: Apple 48K
    Cost: $20.00
    Ages: Young adults

    An easy-to-use but sophisticated database program created for teachers. Has a clearly and well-written 36-page manual. Written for non-technically oriented people. Offers multiple search and sort routines and a variety of print formats. An excellent value.

Thor
    Producer: Fastware
    Availability: IBM PC, IBM PCjr 128K RAM memory
    Cost: $295.00
    Ages: Adult

    See word processing section for program description.

    Another category of computer software programs includes software that permits the user to easily make numerical calculations and analyses as well as represent data in graphical form. Programs that let you perform extensive numerical calculations are called spread sheet software. Using a spread sheet program facilitates decision making and lets you perform countless operations on numeric data. A

quality spread sheet is designed to let the user
define mathematical relationships by writing
formulas.

In the past, use of spread sheet software has
been restricted to business and administrative
functions such as cost and inventory controls and
development of budget projections. More recently,
applications of this tool have become more diverse
in scope. Secondary schools are beginning to use
these programs with students in courses in the
field of business administration. Some elementary
schools have tried electronic spread sheets in fifth
and sixth grade classrooms. Given proper teacher
assistance, both applications of spread sheet
software have met with considerable success.

There is also a wide variety of statistics
packages available today that lets the user perform
any number of statistical operations on numeric
data. These software programs quickly compute values
for means, chi-squared, standard deviation, and many
other tests on paired and unpaired data. In most
cases they are of little direct use with young
children, but teachers may find these useful. These
programs are applicable to provide statistical
validity for data with which they may be working.

Finally, there are programs written which allow
one to easily construct charts and graphs which
provide graphic illustrations of information that
have been collected. Many provide colorful displays
of results on the monitor screen and offer hard copy
capabilities using a computer printer. Several of
these programs can be effectively used with young
children in the classroom, while others are designed
for use by adults. These offer many applications
that are useful, making this software worthy of your
consideration for adoption.

AceCalc
    Producer: Artsci Software
    Availability: Apple 64K, Franklin 64K
    Cost: $30.00
    Ages: Adult

        An easy-to-use spread sheet program
    provided with a well-documented manual. Offers
    70- or 80-column displays and adjustable column

widths. Maximum of 254 rows per file. An
excellent program having a tutorial and command
summary card.

Appleworks
    Producer: Apple Computer, Inc.
    Availability: Apple IIe with two disk drives
                  and extended 80-column card
    Cost: $195.00
    Ages: Adult

        See word processing section for program
    description.

Easy Graph
    Producer: Grolier Electronic Pub. Inc.
    Availability: Apple 48K
    Cost: $29.95
    Ages: 10-adult

        Teaches reading, creating, and
    understanding of graphs. User can create
    pictographs, bar graphs, and pie charts. Easy
    to use and includes well-organized and clearly
    written resource book.

EdSci Statisitcs
    Producer: Eduware Software
    Availability: Apple 64K
    Cost: $99.95
    Ages: Adult

        A professional statistics package that
    offers data and entry manipulation, statistical
    testing, and extensive use of data files.
    Performs most commonly used statistical
    calculations and tests.

Exploring Tables and Graphs
    Producer: Xerox Corporation
    Availability: Apple 64K
    Cost: $34.95
    Ages: 8-10

        Children work with picture graphs, tables,
    bar and area graphs. Provides excellent
    selection of topics. Teacher's guide and 12
    ditto masters included.

Exploring Tables and Graphs
     Producer: Xerox Corporation
     Availability: Apple 64K
     Cost: $34.95
     Ages: 10-12

          Students work with tables, picture, line,
     bar, and area graphs. Topics are well
     illustrated and interesting. Teacher's guide
     and 12 ditto masters included.

FlashCalc
     Producer: Visicorp
     Availability: Apple 64K
     Cost: $99.00
     Ages: Adult

          A fast operating system designed to
     perform all calculating functions. Has advanced
     print features. Can be used for professional
     applications.

Key-Stat
     Producer: Oakleaf Systems
     Availability: Apple 48K
     Cost: $29.95
     Ages: 15-adult

          Performs a series of frequently used
     statistical calculations. Can save and edit
     files and print out results. An easy-to-use
     program assuming no technical expertise.

Magicalc
     Producer: Artsci Software
     Availability: Apple 48K
     Cost: $149.95
     Ages: Adult

          A sophisticated spread sheet program
     offering 40- or 80-column display. User can
     define column sizes and values. Performs
     mathematical operations. Is compatible with
     Visicalc. Documentation provided.

Multiplan
     Producer: Microsoft
     Availability: Apple 64K, IBM PC, IBM PCjr

Cost: $275.00
Ages: Adult

A highly advanced spread sheet offering
40- or 80-column screen display. Performs many
mathematical functions. An excellent print
menu. Takes several hours to learn to use, but
is worth the effort.

PlannerCalc
    Producer: IBM
    Availability: IBM PC, IBM PCjr
    Cost: $79.95
    Ages: Older children to adults

A spread sheet program including 25 sample
spread sheet models covering a wide range of
subject areas. A well-constructed program that
is easy to use and provided with a good
reference manual written in non-technical
English.

PractiCalc II
    Producer: PractiCorp
    Availability: Apple 48K, Commodore-64, IBM PC,
                  IBM PCjr
    Cost: Apple $49.95, Commodore-64 $54.95, IBM
          $99.95
    Ages: Older children and adults

An easy-to-use spread sheet and word
processing program. Lacks extensive spread
sheet features but good for teaching purposes.
Manual lacks detailed information.

Statistics 3.0
    Producer: Eduware
    Availability: Apple 64K
    Cost: $39.95
    Ages: Adult

Carries out six statistical analysis
routines based on data entered by the user,
including mean, median, chi-squared, and
standard deviation. An easy-to-use program
providing quick results.

Survey Taker
    Producer: Information Technology Design
              Associates
    Availability: Apple 64K, Commodore-64
    Cost: $29.95
    Ages: 9-15

        Teaches statistical methods and how bar
    graphs are constructed. Children learn how to
    compile and present information. Can print
    survey questions and save, edit, and erase
    information. Includes back-up disk and student
    handbook.

Visicalc
    Producer: Visicorp
    Availability: Apple 48K, IBM PC, IBM PCjr
    Cost: $99.00
    Ages: Adult

        An electronic spread sheet that lets the
    user generate financial reports and make
    projections. Performs numerous user defined
    computations. A professional package offering
    many format options. Has good documentation.

    The last section includes a variety of computer
software programs that are of definite value to the
teacher. These programs range from routines that
easily let you create signs and posters to those
that produce crossword puzzles from word lists.
There are programs that serve the function of
gradebooks and others that let you develop
interesting puzzles and games. One or more of these
types of software programs have definite classroom
applications. To learn more about the wide range of
teacher utility programs on the market today, visit
a computer software store, or read information
presented in software catalogues and directories.

Clock
    Producer: Hartley Software
    Availability: Apple 48K, IBM PC, IBM PCjr
    Cost: $39.95
    Ages: 6-9

Children learn to convert from digital to
clock time. Has three lessons with multiple
levels of difficulty for each. Keeps student
records and provides a tutorial.

Create Lessons
    Producer: Hartley Software
    Availability: Apple 48K, IBM PC, IBM PCjr
    Cost: $29.95, IBM $39.95
    Ages: Adult

        Used for writing lessons, drill sequences,
    or tutorials. Teachers provide the questions.
    Can give hints and explanations and allow for
    many attempts per question. Has built-in math
    symbols and gives percent scores. Grade use: 1
    to 6. Has good documentation.

Create-Spell It
    Producer: Hartley Courseware
    Availability: Apple 48K
    Cost: $26.95
    Ages: Adult

        Teacher generates spelling lists that can
    be saved on disk. Can provide correct responses
    and keep student records. Has option to provide
    words orally by using cassette recorder and
    cassette control device ($79.95).

Crossword Magic
    Producer: HLS Duplication
    Availability: Apple 64K, Atari disk
    Cost: $49.95
    Ages: 8-adult

        Can create crossword puzzles using your
    words for any topic. Capable of adding across
    and down clues. Can save and print puzzles. A
    very easy to use program.

Data Plot
    Producer: MUSE Software
    Availability: Apple 48K
    Cost: $59.95
    Ages: 12-adult

User can create graphs and charts in color
including bar, line, and circle graphs. Offers
good detail and can print copies. Easy-to-use
program having good documentation.

Fact Sheets
    Producer: Hartley Courseware
    Availability: Apple 48K, IBM PC, IBM PCjr
    Cost: $49.95
    Ages: Adult

    A menu driven program that lets the
teacher create math fact sheets for addition,
subtraction, multiplication, and division. Can
choose level of difficulty. Produces random
problems each time. Good format for printout.

Learning System
    Producer: Microlab Learning Center
    Availability: Apple 48K
    Cost: $75.00
    Ages: Adult

    Teacher types in text information and can
ask questions based on it. An easy-to-use
routine that requires no knowledge of computer
programming.

Poster
    Producer: Scholastic
    Availability: Apple 48K, Commodore-64, IBM PC,
                  IBM PCjr
    Cost: $39.95
    Ages: 9-adult

    Creates colorful posters on screen using a
a variety of shapes and patterns. Uses a simple
programming language. Can edit, save, and
control size and speed of poster formation. Has
back-up disk, student manual, and reference
card.

Puzzles and Posters
    Producer: MECC
    Availability: Apple 64K, Commodore-64, IBM PC,
                  IBM PCjr, TRS-80 Model III
                  Computer

Cost: $44.00
Ages: 12-adult

Contains a menu offering several options:
make word puzzles, crossword puzzles, mazes,
posters, and banners. Computer automatically
designs puzzles for words you enter. Very
useful program having back-up disk and manual.

Snake
Producer: Burgmeier Software
Availability: TRS-80 Model III Computer
Cost: $50.00
Ages: 7-adult

An easy-to-use graphics language that lets
the user create pictures. Pictures can be
saved, edited, and printed and animation can be
provided for them. Teaches computer programming
concepts.

Test Generator Program
Producer: Educational Audio Visuals, Inc.
Availability: Apple 48K, TRS-80 48K Computer
Cost: $35.00
Ages: Adult

Stores up to 100 questions written by the
teacher, including multiple choice and short
answer questions. Can edit questions. Test
questions are randomly generated, with answer
sheets provided.

Testmaster
Producer: Intellectual Software
Availability: Apple 48K, Commodore-64 disk
Cost: $35.00
Ages: Adult

Creates multiple choice and short answer
questions. User can make up tests having up to
100 questions by selecting questions or letting
the computer randomly select them. Produces
answer keys.

The Complete Graphics System
Producer: Sunburst Communications
Availability: Apple 48K

Cost: $79.95
Ages: Adult

A sophisticated graphics program written
for the non-technical user. Can use over 100
colors to create shapes and characters.
Provides very good detail.

The Print Shop
Producer: Broderbund Software
Availability: Apple 48K, Commodore-64
Cost: $49.95
Ages: 10-adult

Lets user make flyers, letterheads, logos,
and cards. Offers a selection of type styles,
borders, and background patterns. Requires the
use of a computer printer.

The Professional Sign Maker
Producer: Sunburst Communications
Availability: Apple 48K
Cost: $59.00
Ages: 12-adult

Gives excellent quality graphic letters
for signs and posters. Can produce borders and
save work on disk. Recommends use with Epson
printer or others with proper interface card.

TRS-80 Author I
Producer: Tandy Corp./Radio Shack
Availability: TRS-80 Model III Computer
Cost: $149.95
Ages: Adult

Teachers create lessons on monitor screen.
Has editing features, graphics, branching, and
score keeping capability. Can provide hints,
glossary, and feedback comments. Has good print
options.

Using a Calendar
Producer: Hartley Courseware
Availability: Apple 48K
Cost: $39.95
Ages: 6-10

Shows children how to read and interpret a
calendar. Offers three lessons with multiple
levels of difficulty for each. Teacher can
modify and create lessons. Computer keeps
student records. Good graphics provided.

Wordsearch
     Producer: Hartley Courseware
     Availabiltiy: Apple 48K
     Cost: $29.95
     Ages: Adult

          Lets teacher create word puzzles using up
     to 22 words. Program requires a printer. Can
     choose from a set of options how you want the
     words to be hidden.

SOFTWARE DIRECTORY

Apple Computer, Inc.
  20525 Mariani Ave.
  Cupertino, CA 95014

Artsci, Inc.
  5547 Satsumma Ave.
  North Hollywood, CA 91601

Atari, Inc.
  1265 Borregas Ave.
  Sunnyvale, CA 94086

Bolt, Beranek and Newman, Inc.
  10 Moulton St.
  Cambridge, MA 02238

Broderbund Software
  17 Paul St.
  San Rafael, CA 94903

Developmental Learning Materials
  1 DLM Park
  Allen, TX 75002

Educational Audio Visuals, Inc.
  Pleasantville, NY 10570

Educational Systems Software
    23720 El Toro Rd.
    El Toro, CA 92630

Electronic Arts
    2755 Campus Drive
    San Mateo, CA 94403

Fastware
    200 Freeway Drive East
    East Orange, NJ 07018

Grolier Electronic Pub. Co.
    Sherman Turnpike
    Danbury, CT 06816

Hartley Courseware
    P.O. Box 419
    Dimondale, MO 48821

HLS Duplication
    1008 Stewart Drive
    Sunnyvale, CA 94086

International Business Machines, Inc.
    P.O. Box 1328-W
    Boca Raton, FL 33432

IJG, Inc.
    1953 W. 11th St.
    Upland, CA 91786

Intellectual Software
    798 North Ave.
    Bridgeport, CT 06606

J & S Software
    140 Reid Ave.
    Port Washington, NY 11050

Learning Well
    200 South Service Road
    Roslyn Heights, NY 11577

Lightning Software
    P.O. Box 11725
    Palo Alto, CA 94306

Minnesota Educational Computing Corporation
3490 Lexington Ave.
N. St. Paul, MN 55112

MicroPro International
33 San Pablo Ave.
San Rafael, CA 94903

Milliken Publishing Company
1100 Research Blvd.
St. Louis, MO 63132

Milton Bradley
443 Shaker Rd.
East Longmeadow, MA 01028

Microsoft
10700 Northrup Way
Bellevue, WA 98004

Muse Software
347 N. Charles St.
Baltimore, MD 21201

Oakleaf Systems
P.O. Box 472
Decorah, IA 52101

PractiCorp
The Silk Mill
44 Oak St.
Newton Upper Falls, MA 02164

Random House School Division
7307 S. Yale St.
Tulsa, OK 74136

Scarboro Systems
25 North Broadway
Tarrytown, NY 10591

Scholastic Inc.
2931 E McCarty St.
P.O. Box 7502
Jefferson City, MO 65102

Sensible Software
66619 Perham Dr.
W. Bloomfield, MI 48033

Sierra On-Line, Inc.
36575 Mudge Ranch Rd.
Coarsegold, CA 93614

Sirus Software
10364 Rockingham St.
Sacramento, CA 95827

Software Publishing Corporation
1901 Landings Dr.
Mountain View, CA 94043

Spinnaker Software Corporation
215 First St.
Cambridge, MA 02142

Sunburst Communications
39 Washington St.
Pleasantville, NY 10570

Tandy Corporation/Radio Shack
1400 One Tandy Center
Fort Worth, TX 76102

The Teaching Company
P.O. Box E
Lexington, MA 02173

Visicorp
2895 Zonker Rd.
San Jose, CA 95134

BIBLIOGRAPHY

Allen, Vaikko. "Software Side by Side." ELECTRONIC
LEARNING 4 (April 1985): 52-53.

   Provides detailed comparisons of six spread sheet
   software programs using a convenient chart form.

Anderson, John J. "Commodore 128: Capability and
Compatability in Commodore's New Flagship."
CREATIVE COMPUTING 11 (July 1985): 30-35.

Outlines the physical characteristics and
technical capabilities of this new machine.

Arrants, Steve. "Appleworks. Apple's Own Integrated
Software Package." CREATIVE COMPUTING 10 (June
1984): 43-47.

Provides a sequenced description of the steps
followed when using the Appleworks program for
word processing, database management, and spread
sheet analysis.

Arrays, Inc. BOOK OF APPLE SOFTWARE, BOOK OF IBM
SOFTWARE, BOOK OF ATARI SOFTWARE. Los Angeles,
Calif. The Book Division, 1984.

Three software directories that provide excellent
reviews of computer programs. Gives graded
evaluations of each program.

Bardige, Art. "Word Processing. How Will It Shape
the Student as a Writer?" CLASSROOM COMPUTER NEWS
3 (November/December 1982): 24-27, 74-76.

Gives a roundtable discussion of computer
educators on the impact of word processing and how
children write.

Blank, Deborah E. "Stepping Through Fast-Food Land:
A Spread Sheet Tutorial." THE COMPUTING TEACHER
12 (June 1985): 26-28.

Illustrates in a clear and concise fashion how to
use the Visicalc spread sheet using fast-food
orders as examples.

Boyle, James P. "Software: Side by Side."
ELECTRONIC LEARNING 3 (March 1984): 64-65.

Outlines salient characteristics of seven typing
programs in tabular form. Provides very useful
comparisons.

Consumer Reports. "The Computer as
Super-Typewriter." CONSUMER REPORTS 48 (October
1983): 540-548.

Provides a well-written discussion of
characteristics of good word processing programs
and includes a wealth of examples.

Dauite, Colette. "Writing, Creativity and Change."
CHILDHOOD EDUCATION 59 (March/April 1983):
227-231.

Outlines how word processing can greatly simplify
and shorten many writing tasks.

Degnan, Sarah C. "Word Processing for Special
Education Students: Worth the Effort." T.H.E.
JOURNAL 12 (February 1985): 80-82.

Considers impact word processing software has had
on teaching writing to children with special
needs.

Dewey, Patrick R. "Searching for Software."
POPULAR COMPUTING 3 (Mid-October 1984):
137-141.

Excellent article describing many computer
software directories available for several types
of computers.

Garvey, Ian. "Spelling Checkers. Can They Actually
Teach Spelling?" CLASSROOM COMPUTER LEARNING
5 (November/December 1984): 62-65.

Outlines in tabular form characteristics of
several spelling checker programs and their
educational implications.

Honeyman, David S. "Data Bases and Special
Education IEP Reports." ELECTRONIC LEARNING
(March 1985): 26.

Shows how database software can be used to create
files that generate a wide range of reports.

Jarchow, Elaine McNally. "Computers and Composing:
The Pros and Cons." ELECTRONIC EDUCATION 3
(May/June 1984): 38.

Charts ten positive and negative conclusions
summarizing the effects of using word processing
software in the classroom.

Kaplan, Howard. "Thor." POPULAR COMPUTING
(February 1985): 158-159.

Outlines how this program can be used to help
organize your thoughts and work.

Kay, Alan. "Computer Software." SCIENTIFIC
AMERICAN 251 (September 1984): 53-59.

Outlines practical functions for database
management and spread sheet software.

Knapp, Linda. "Word Processors." ELECTRONIC
LEARNING 3 (March 1984): 54-58.

Well-written article providing useful descriptions
of what to look for when purchasing a word
processing program and how to test a word
processing program in a computer store.

Miller, Michael J. "Making Sense of Database
Software." POPULAR COMPUTING 3 (June 1984):
106-109.

Defines terms used to describe different types of
database management software and reviews several
programs.

Ohanian, Susan. "How Today's Reading Software Can
Zap Kid's Desire to Read." CLASSROOM COMPUTER
LEARNING 5 (November/December 1984): 26-31.

Addresses pedagogical issues related to teaching
children reading, using computer software.

Pollitt, Alyce Hunt. "Warming to the Wonders of the
Word Processor: An English Teacher's Introduction
to the Computer." THE COMPUTING TEACHER 11 (May
1984): 48-49.

Describes how word processing was used by
skeptical teachers to write the manuscript for an
English classroom newspaper.

Sacks, Jonathan. "Appleworks." POPULAR COMPUTING
(February 1985): 152-157.

Provides a detailed discussion of the structure
and uses of the Appleworks software program.

Solomon, Gwen, and Al Stuttles. "Software: Side by
    Side." ELECTRONIC LEARNING 3 (March 1984):
    54-58.

Compares features of five word processing programs
and six writing programs in table form. A very
useful article.

Staples, Betsy. "Electric Pencil PC." CREATIVE
    COMPUTING 10 (March 1984): 126-135.

Gives descriptions and operating instructions to
be used with this word processing program.

Sterling Swift Publishing Company. SWIFT'S
    EDUCATIONAL SOFTWARE DIRECTORY. Austin, Tex.:
    Sterling Swift Publishing Company, 1984.

A directory providing descriptions of computer
software programs. Has editions giving available
software for several types of computers.

Tandy/Radio Shack. EDUCATIONAL SOFTWARE DIRECTORY
    3rd ed. Fort Worth, Tex., 1984.

A directory of software for TRS-80 computers
including indices, descriptions, and grade levels.

Watt, Daniel. "Word Processing and Writing."
    POPULAR COMPUTING (June 1982): 124-126.

Presents a case study to illustrate how word
processing can be used to improve writing by
children.

White, Ron. "PFS:File and PFS:Report." POPULAR
    COMPUTING 3 (June 1984): 155-163.

Clearly outlines many database management
functions that can be done with this software.

Wilson, Jean W. "VisiCalc in the Elementary
    School." THE COMPUTING TEACHER 12 (June 1985):
    29-30.

Outlines how VisiCalc can be used as part of the
elementary academic curriculum in science, social
studies, mathematics, and as a management tool.

CHAPTER EIGHT

SPECIAL EDUCATION

During the past three or four years classroom microcomputers have played an increasingly important role in the education of children having special needs. Recent software and hardware developments • have made it possible for visually and hearing impaired children to have educational experiences that were far too frequently impossible in the past. Similarly, children having severe physical disabilities are now able to explore their world in ways that were not possible until the advent of the microcomputer.

Other children having psychologically based learning disabilities have used the classroom microcomputer to enhance their learning and develop patterns of logical thinking strategies and skills. Each month educational journals report new and innovative ways that the computer has been used as an effective tool to facilitate the learning process of children with special needs. Significant expenditures of time, energy, and money by educators, the computer industry, and governmental agencies have made it possible for the application of computer technology to meet the needs of many of our special citizens.

. Today we are at the forefront of the development of new technologies that will assist us as teachers in the education of children having special educational requirements. Children who were unable to communicate effectively in the past are now able to express their views and feelings to others using the microcomputer. Specialized adaptive computer hardware and software have played an important role in this process. As educators our challenge is to keep abreast of the latest developments in computer technology and find ways to

incorporate them into the individualized educational
plans that are designed when working with children
having special needs.

Before exploring specific examples of how
computers can be used in special education, we
should first examine characteristics of computer
based instruction as it applies to children having
special educational needs. Many of these
characteristics logically overlap with those
previously discussed for use with children in
traditional classrooms, but there are many important
distinctions. In virtually all cases it is how the
teacher incorporates the microcomputer into the
learning environment that will determine the
effectiveness of computer based instruction.

Computer based instruction can provide an
individualized learning environment for the child
with the computer playing the role of a tutor. Well-
written software programs can be tailored to meet an
individual student's needs so that the emphasis is
placed on learning ideas and information rather than
on simply getting the correct answer. Children are
encouraged to experiment and take risks without fear
of negative reactions from the teacher or from other
children in the classroom.

Children can repeat activities as often as they
wish, thereby developing a sense of independence and
personal responsibility for their learning. Well-
written programs have built-in loops that let
children review material as often as necessary
without conveying the attitude that they may be slow
learners. The best software programs also allow the
user to choose from multiple levels of program
difficulty while children test new ideas and develop
new problem solving strategies. Children having
special needs can begin to perceive themselves as
active learners.

Computer software programs require children to
make judgments and decisions so they are inherently
involved in the learning process. They must make
their own decisions and not wait for another student
to answer a question as is frequently the case in
traditional classroom environments. The computer
provides immediate feedback to the child, without
making overt or subtle value judgments about the
quality of the child's responses. Students begin to
correct conceptual errors they are making when they
work with the microcomputer.

Computer based instructional programs require that the user enter responses to questions or provide information to the computer. This can be done in a variety of ways, including using the computer keyboard or computer joysticks or game paddles. Many programs allow for input using light pens or graphics tablets. Still other input devices designed specifically for physicaly disabled individuals provide for input by voice or by pressure sensitive devices that require blowing puffs of air into a mouthpiece. Regardless of the type of device used to provide information to the computer, use of this machine encourages children to be precise and accurate. Hand-to-eye coordination is frequently improved when a computer based learning program is regularly used.

Children are also able to begin to manipulate letters, words, and numbers in ways that were not previously possible. They can begin to see new patterns and explore relationships in new and exciting ways. The frustration level often observed when children with special needs are learning in the classroom is often greatly reduced. The multisensory learning environment that the computer provides plays an important role in this process.

Many people believe that using computers with children having special needs is not appropriate in classroom settings. They feel that these children will not be able to manipulate the computer as the machine itself is too complex. Children having learning disabilities will experience high levels of frustration if they attempt to use the computer to solve mathematical problems or work with computer programs dealing with linguistics.

Furthermore, educators arguing against computer based education suggest that working with software programs will tend to further isolate children having special needs from their classmates. If this occurs, social skill development and the development of communications skills will be retarded. Educational traditionalists contend that special education teachers are extremely busy and do not have time to explore applications of this new technology to the classroom. Teachers need extensive periods of time to learn to use the computer themselves and develop sound educational protocol for use with children. Time and resources are simply not available.

Most children, regardless of whether or not they have learning disabilities, will soon adjust to working with the computer if appropriate input and output devices are provided. Children are excited by computers and do not find them to be intimidating. Computers seem to bring forth a quality of persistence in children, as they are almost universally willing and anxious to try a software program over and over again. Providing that the software program is age and ability level appropriate, children seldom become overly frustrated or want to leave the computer environment.

A child having problems with fine motor control can frequently manipulate the computer more effectively than other educational materials like pencils, crayons, clay, and paper. Children with special needs typically require the teacher to repeatedly give instructions on how to complete a lesson. They may have to wait until the teacher is able to provide them with individual help, thus increasing the dependence on others. Computer software demonstrates infinite patience and provides immediate reinforcement, giving the learner a greater feeling of independence.

Teachers find that it takes far less time than expected for children to learn to use the computer. Well-designed and documented software programs are easy to master and give children a feeling of self-esteem and personal accomplishment. If computer based activities are carefully planned children begin to learn from their classmates, giving the teacher time to work with individual students and do other things. The better software programs can reduce teacher workload by recording student progress and keeping records of their responses.

The computer has had a radical impact on our society at all levels. Our changing world has seen increased levels of automation in homes, offices, business, and industry. The computer has had an impact on our communication, educational, and transportation systems. Our challenge as educators is to provide children with special educational needs with the tools and experiences they need so they can function as useful citizens in tomorrow's world. To do this we must begin today.

The microcomputer can be used as a tool to help us develop new strategies and approaches to learning that will make the education of the physically and

psychologically disabled more productive. Software
programs are available today that help the teacher
assess and evaluate the educational strengths and
weaknesses of the learner. These programs can help
develop individualized educational plans, keep
ongoing student records, measure progress, and test
what the children have learned. If the teacher has
pedagogically well-founded goals, using the
microcomputer can help prepare children for the
world beyond the classroom.

The microcomputer has provided children having
extreme communication difficulties with a means of
reaching others that was unheard of a few years ago.
Word and pictorial screen commands have been used
effectively with dyslexic and hearing impaired
children. Children having speech and vision
difficulties have used word processors and speech
synthesizers to receive and communicate ideas and
information. As the microcomputer increases the
speed of communication children are able to spend
less time receiving and giving information and more
time in the analysis of its content.

Hearing impaired individuals have significantly
benefited from microcomputer technology. There are
several excellent computer software programs
available that teach lipreading, using cleverly
designed graphics that clearly convey ideas and
terminology. One of the newest technologies is the
development of computer hardware and software that
can translate speech into words on the monitor
screen. These devices will undergo refinements in
the years to come. Computer printers can be used to
generate paper copies of conversations that have
taken place.

Speech synthesizers used for both computer
input and output have greatly improved the ability
of the vision impaired to work with the
microcomputer. There are also programs available
that let the user type instructions on the computer
keyboard as input and have output generated by
speech synthesizers. Only the best speech
synthesizers have a true human quality for sounds
and speech patterns but these are quite expensive.
The future should bring inexpensive speech
synthesizers that will be indistinguishable from the
spoken word.

Many computer programs can produce very large
letters and characters on the monitor screen that
can be of definite value to the visually impaired.

Similarly, most computer printers can be easily
programmed to give extra large dark characters.
Braille keyboards are available for some computers
with braille templates easily provided for most
machines. There are several printers on the market
today that give text output in braille. Other
software programs can convert type to braille and
braille to type. These are exciting developments
that can help the visually impaired student
communicate more effectively with the microcomputer.

There are many types of adapted hardware that
can let the physically disabled person work
efficiently with the microcomputer. Keyboard
templates are very useful when individuals lacking
fine motor coordination use the microcomputer. These
devices literally provide holes over each key so
that keys are not accidentally pressed. Perhaps the
most exciting development has been the adaptive
firmware card. These cards are placed in an internal
accessory slot within the computer simply by
plugging them in. They now allow computer input to
be achieved by a variety of ways to meet the needs
of the severely physically disabled. For example,
with the adaptive firmware card computer keys can be
redefined so that instructions for input can be
simplified to single keystroke entries. Head
controlled pointers and mouth directed puff switches
can then be used. Tremendous strides have been made
in making microcomputer hardware and software
accessible to individuals having a variety of
physical limitations.

There are also many educational advantages to
having gifted children work with microcomputers in
the classrom setting. There are very many software
programs available that can be used effectively with
gifted children. These are easily identified as good
software if they provide age or grade levels for
which the program is designed. Although these
programs can be used to great advantage, what must
first be defined are educational goals and carefully
conceptualized teaching strategies. Only then can
gifted children achieve the maximum benefit from
working with a microcomputer.

As educators our goal should be to provide
computer experiences for gifted children so they can
utilize the full potential of the computer. We
should develop a multitude of ways to stimulate

their intellectual interest and curiosity so they will become highly motivated to learn more about these machines. Only then will gifted children be able to maximize their learning from the many excellent computer software programs available today.

When working with gifted children teachers should carefully plan computer based activities so that they are coordinated and integrated with other kinds of learning that occur in the classroom. Computer based learning can provide logical extensions of ideas and concepts that are difficult to duplicate in other ways and these can be of great educational value to gifted children.

Teachers should also plan group activities using the computer so that student interactions are encouraged and provided for. When planning computer activities teachers should concentrate on ideas, principles, and concepts about which they are very well versed whether or not they are well acclimated to using the computer. As with any other learning experience, computer based learning entails careful planning, incorporating a clearly defined set of educational goals.

There are many types of computer experiences that have been used effectively with young gifted children. In many cases word processing software has been found to improve the quality of students' writing. Using it children are easily able to explore and experiment with word usage, as well as with sentence and paragraph structure. Logic programs and educationally designed adventure games have also been used successfully with gifted children.

Computer simulation programs are almost universally successful, as they provide an ongoing challenge to students to improve their score by developing and implementing new problem solving strategies. Writing programs in computer languages such as BASIC or Logo has been found to present a stimulating educational opportunity for the gifted child. Computer programming provides the opportunity for gifted children to use their creativity and logic skills to build structures and effect solutions to problems that are difficult to simulate in other ways. We do not yet know the long-term impact microcomputer technology will have on gifted children as this technology is too new.

There are several characteristics that teachers should identify when choosing computer software programs for use with children having special psychological or physical requirements. Information presented on the monitor screen should be given in small amounts at a time with liberal spacing provided between successive lines of text. Useless characters and graphics should not be part of the screen display, but relevant information should be reinforced by graphics, color, and sound.

Ideally, the speed at which the software program presents information should be regulated by the teacher with the child being given ample time and opportunity to respond correctly. Children should be given immediate and appropriate feedback if they respond incorrectly and be offered multiple levels of program difficulty from which to choose. Quality computer software should always be designed with clearly articulated educational goals and depict real life situations, thus giving children the opportunity to learn how to form generalizations. Educational computer software programs written for children with special needs must always address the needs of the group for whom they were designed.

Well-conceptualized computer software have clearly written instructions that are age appropriate and congruent with the ability levels of the children for whom they are intended. Children should need a minimum amount of teacher supervision when working with the software. Computer feedback should be immediate for both correct and incorrect user responses with the child being given a reasonable number of attempts to answer questions before the correct response is provided. Multisensory computer responses using sound, color, and graphics enhance the learning experience.

Finally, the best software designed for use with special needs children let users save and later edit program results. These programs help the teacher monitor student progress by keeping records of results, frequently measuring progress against standardized or teacher defined norms. The most effective computer software programs allow for multiple types of user input, including such devices as game paddles, joysticks, graphics tablets, and light pens.

The next section of this chapter provides a catalogue of many computer hardware and software products that have been used effectively with

children having special educational needs. This
listing is not all-inclusive, rather it provides a
general sampling of what is available. The best
advice is to go to a computer store and work with
these devices before considering purchase, as these
materials must be seen and worked with before their
effectiveness can be measured. The future will bring
many more innovative devices that can be used with
children when they are working in the computer
environment.

Academic Skill Builders in Language Arts
        Producer: DLM Teaching Resources
        Availability: Apple IIe
        Cost: $44.00 per program
        Ages: 6-10

        A series of six disks containing programs
        including: Spelling Wiz, Verb Viper, Word
        Invasion, Word Man, Word Master, and Word
        Radar. Drill and practice programs using
        keyboard or game paddle input. Has sound
        effects and provides speed and time
        variability. Includes an instruction manual.

Academics with Scanning
        Producer: Computers to Help People Inc.
        Availability: Apple 48K
        Cost: $10.00
        Ages: 8-12

        Helps children with severe physical
        disabilities do math class work. Teacher types
        in questions, problems, or worksheet
        information and the child uses switches to
        generate video and hard copy output.

Adaptive Firmware Card
        Producer: Adaptive Peripherals
        Availability: Apple 48K
        Cost: $350.00
        Ages: All ages

        An excellent device that allows physically
        disabled individuals to input data into the
        computer by a variety of means. Can be used
        with software programs.

Baudot ASCII Porta Printer Plus
Producer: Krown Research, Inc.
Availability: Apple 48K, IBM PC, IBM PCjr
Cost: $699.00
Ages: All ages

A telecommunication system for the hearing impaired. Lets user communicate with others via the telephone. Gives screen printout of what is typed. Has a built-in printer to record what was communicated.

Body Awareness
Producer: Learning Well
Availability: Apple 48K
Cost: $49.95
Ages: 5-7

A software program offering one key input that helps children locate and identify parts of the body. Seasons of year and apparel of screen characters vary. Teacher can set game options. Includes a guide giving suggested activities.

Braille Edit
Producer: Raised Dot Computing
Availability: Apple 48K
Cost: $250.00
Ages: All ages

A word processor that converts print into Contracted Braille and Contracted Braille into print. Allows visually impaired and sighted people to work together.

Challenge Math
Producer: Sunburst Communications
Availability: Apple 48K, Commodore-64
Cost: $55.00
Ages: 7-12

Uses sound and color graphics to teach math estimation skills for whole numbers and decimals. Teacher can modify levels of difficulty. Includes three games, back-up disk, and a teacher's manual.

Code Quest: Strategies in Problem Solving
    Producer: Sunburst Communications
    Availability: Apple 48K, Atari disk, TRS-80
                  Color Computer
    Cost: $55.00
    Ages: 9-13

    User tries to break a series of codes that
reveal the identity of mystery objects. User
can enter own codes and clues from any subject
area. Helps develop discrimination,
classification, and pattern identification
skills. Includes back-up disk and teacher's
guide.

Compudapter
    Producer: R/M Systems
    Availability: Apple 48K, IBM PC, IBM PCjr
    Cost: $1500.00
    Ages: All ages

    A sophisticated system that uses an
easy-to-install adaptive keyboard that allows
for several modes of alternative input to the
computer, including touch and mechanical
switches as well as sip and puff switches.

Cybertalker 2
    Producer: Cyberon Corporation
    Availability: Most computers
    Cost: $5000.00
    Ages: All ages

    A sophisticated speech synthesizer
offering good quality sound reproduction. Has a
4000-character built-in memory that can be
expanded to 20,000 characters.

Deafsign
    Producer: Advanced Computer Services
    Availability: TRS-80 Model III Computers
    Cost: $69.95
    Ages: All ages

    A software program that teaches sign
language to the hearing impaired. Provides
review exercises and includes a teacher's
manual.

Echo II Speech Synthesizer
    Producer: Street Electronics Corporation
    Availability: Most computers
    Cost: $149.95
    Ages: All ages

        An inexpensive speech synthesizer that
    converts ASCII text into speech. Voice output
    sounds mechanical but can be understood with
    practice.

Expanded Keyboard for Apple Computers
    Producer: EKEG Electronics Company, Ltd.
    Availability: Apple computers
    Cost: $695.00
    Ages: All ages

        A specialized keyboard designed to meet
    the needs of individuals having a wide range of
    physical handicaps. Replaces the standard Apple
    keyboard.

First Categories
    Producer: Laureate Learning Systems
    Availability: Acorn, Apple 48K
    Cost: $120.00
    Ages: 8-12

        User can utilize single key input, game
    paddles, or joysticks for input. Teaches
    categorization of nouns. Teacher can tailor
    program to meet individual needs and ability
    levels. Echo II speech synthesizer can be used
    with this program.

First Words
    Producer: Laureate Learning Systems
    Availability: Apple 48K
    Cost: $185.00
    Ages: 7-adult

        Teaches vocabulary using 100 pictures with
    animation and speech that show the meaning of
    50 nouns. Has varying levels of difficulty and
    requires the use of an Echo II speech
    synthesizer.

Fun House Maze: Strategies in Problem Solving
      Producer: Sunburst Communications
      Availability: Apple 48K
      Cost: $55.00
      Ages: 9-adult

          Takes the user through a three-dimensional
      maze that provides practice in developing
      problem solving strategies. Gives good practice
      in developing pattern recognition skills.
      Includes back-up disk and teacher's manual.

Getting Ready to Read and Add
      Producer: Sunburst Communications
      Availability: Apple 48K, Atari 16K,
                    Commodore-64
      Cost: $55.00
      Ages: 5-7

          Reinforces letter and number recognition
      and teaches shape discrimination. Sound, color,
      and animation are used to identify and match
      shapes, upper and lower case letters, and
      numbers. Teacher can control selection of
      numbers and letters. Manual and back-up disk
      included.

I-COM
      Producer: Intex Micro Systems Corporation
      Availability: Most computers
      Cost: $2500.00
      Ages: All ages

          Lets the physically disabled user press a
      single switch for input to the computer.
      Includes a speech synthesizer.

K-Guard
      Producer: Prentke Romich Company
      Availability: Apple, Epson, IBM, Texas
                    Instruments Computers
      Cost: $100.00
      Ages: All ages

          This device fits over the keyboard,
      increasing typing accuracy for individuals
      having difficulties with fine motor control.
      Offers several modes for user input.

Keyswapper 1,4
    Producer: Vertex Systems
    Availability: Apple 48K
    Cost: $45.00
    Ages: All ages

        A software program that lets the user
    reconfigure the keyboard keys and set up single
    key-strokes to replace multiple keystroke
    entries.

Koala Pad
    Producer: Koala Technologies
    Availability: Apple 64K, Atari disk, IBM PC,
                IBM PCjr, Commodore-64 disk
    Cost: $125.00 Apple, $110.00 Atari, $149.95
                IBM, $110.00 Commodore-64
    Ages: All ages

        Teaches drawing and sketching using a
    video sketch pad. Drawings can be saved,
    edited, recalled, and combined. Computer
    keyboard not used. Teaches logical thinking
    skills.

Microcommunicator
    Producer: Grover and Associates
    Availability: Apple 48K
    Cost: $45.00
    Ages: 8-adult

        A software program that uses single
    keystroke entries or a mouthstick to display a
    wide variety of sentences. User can construct
    individualized sentences from a large built-in
    vocabulary list.

Micro-Maestro
    Producer: Chalkboard, Inc.
    Availability: Atari cartridge, Commodore-64
                cartridge
    Cost: $24.95
    Ages: 5-adult

        Converts the Power Pad to a piano
    keyboard. User can hear what is played and see
    the notes on the monitor screen. Has a range of
    two octaves.

Model SYS 300
Producer: Interstate Electronics Corporation
Availability: Most computers
Cost: $1995.00
Ages: All ages

An excellent speech recognition system
that lets the user give input by voice
commands. Has a 200-word vocabulary potential.

Odd One Out
Producer: Sunburst Communications
Availability: Apple 48K
Cost: $55.00
Ages: 5-12

Offers five programs including: Pictures,
Words, Letters, Numbers, and Word Problems that
help develop classification skills. Teacher can
customize items and choose varying levels of
difficulty. Excellent color graphics and sound.

PC-Orator
Producer: ARTS Computer Products
Availability: IBM PC, IBM PCjr
Cost: $495.00
Ages: All ages

A software program that lets all input to
the computer be given orally. A good speech
recognition system.

Peachy Writer
Producer: Cross Educational Software
Availability: Apple 48K
Cost: $24.95
Ages: All ages

A text editing system software program
that generates double sized screen characters.
Can interface with some Epson printers to
produce large sized printed text.

Picturewriter
Producer: Scarborough Systems
Availability: Apple 64K, Atari disk, IBM PC,
                  IBM PCjr

Cost: $39.95
Ages: 8-adult

Uses a joystick to let user draw lines,
shapes, and pictures. Areas can be filled in
with colors. Pictures can be saved and edited
and shapes set to music.

Power Pad
     Producer: Chalkboard, Inc.
     Availability: Apple 64K, Atari cartridge,
                   Commodore-64 cartridge, IBM PC,
                   IBM PCjr
     Cost: $99.95
     Ages: 5-adult

     A 12-inch by 12-inch touch sensitive pad
that communicates information to the computer.
Serves as a drawing pad, colored painting
canvas, piano keyboard, and more.

Rocky's Boots
     Producer: The Learning Company
     Availability: Apple 48K
     Cost: $75.00
     Ages: 10-14

     An excellent software program that helps
develop logic skills in children by having them
build animated machines to score game points.
Has excellent graphics and provides increasing
levels of difficulty.

Shadow/Vet
     Producer: Prentke Romich Company
     Availability: Most computers
     Cost: $599.00
     Ages: All ages

     A voice input device that lets severely
disabled children program a computer. Has a
40-word vocabulary, with additional 40-word
overlays available.

Speak Up
     Producer: Laureate Learning Systems, Inc.
     Availability: Apple 48K
     Cost: $95.00
     Ages: 8-adult

Used with the Echo II speech synthesizer.
A word and phrase maker and editor that
generates sounded words using a 300-word
dictionary.

Special Needs Volume 1: Spelling
    Producer: MECC
    Availability: Apple 64K
    Cost: $44.00
    Ages: 7-12

Contains 24 drill and practice spelling
and word recognition programs. Motor impaired
children can use keyboard or game paddles for
input. Includes back-up disk and teacher's
guide. Teacher can modify words and sentences.

Special Needs Volume 2: Simulations and Drills
    Producer: MECC
    Availability: Apple 48K
    Cost: $44.00
    Ages: 7-12

Includes two simulation and three drill
and practice programs teaching basic arithmetic
concepts. Back-up disk and teacher's manual
provided.

Starter Kit
    Producer: Chalkboard, Inc.
    Availabiltiy: Apple 48K, IBM PC, IBM PCjr
    Cost: $49.95 Apple, $79.95 IBM
    Ages: All ages

Required to connect the Power Pad to IBM
and Apple computers.

Target #2410
    Producer: Technical Aids and Systems for the
              Handicapped
    Availability: Most computers
    Cost: $1229.00
    Ages: All ages

A mouth operated keyboard input device.
Puffs of air are used to input commands to the
49 keys. A well-designed system.

The Communicator
        Producer: Prometheus Software
        Availability: Apple 48K
        Cost: $130.00
        Ages: All ages

            Lets individuals with severe physical
        disabilities use a single switch input device.

The Factory: Strategies in Problem Solving
        Producer: Sunburst Communications
        Availability: Acorn, Apple 48K, Atari,
                      Commodore-64, IBM PC, IBM PCjr,
                      TRS-80 Computers
        Cost: $55.00
        Ages: 9-adult

            A three-part program using color graphics
        and animation that lets students create
        geometric products on a simulated machine
        assembly line. Helps develop deductive thinking
        and integrative skills. Back-up disk and
        teacher's guide included.

The Incredible Laboratory: Strategies in Problem
Solving
        Producer: Sunburst Communications
        Availability: Apple 48K, Atari disk,
                      Commodore-64
        Cost: $55.00
        Ages: 8-adult

            Students experiment to see cause/effect
        relations of mixing chemicals. Provides
        discovery learning through trial and error
        while children practice refining information
        through research and implementation. Offers
        varying levels of difficulty and excellent
        color graphics. Back-up disk and teacher's
        guide provided.

The Pond: Strategies in Problem Solving
        Producer: Sunburst Communications
        Availability: Apple 48K, Atari, Commodore-64,
                      IBM PC, IBM PCjr, TRS-80
                      Computers
        Cost: $55.00
        Ages: 8-adult

Students are presented with a frog lost in a pond of lily pads. In freeing the frog students learn to recognize patterns generated from data. Practice and game options provided. Has varying levels of difficulty. Game points are awarded on efficiency of patterns. Includes back-up disk and teacher's manual.

Voice Input Module
    Producer: Voice Machines Communications, Inc.
    Availability: Apple Computers
    Cost: $995.00
    Ages: All ages

A voice input system for the computer where the user can program up to 172 words at one time. Has a built-in vocabulary for several programs, including WordStar and Visicalc. Can do graphics with this system.

Vortrax Personal Speech Synthesizer
    Producer: Vortrax, Inc.
    Availability: Most computers
    Cost: $295.00
    Ages: All ages

An inexpensive speech synthesizer that converts ASCII text into speech. Provides fairly crisp speech patterns.

Computer Products Manufacturers

Adaptive Peripherals
4529 Bagley Ave. North
Seattle, WA 98103

Advanced Computer Services
14 Lynne Lane
Frostproof, FL 33843

ARTS Computer Products
145 Tremont Street #407
Boston, MA 02111

Computers to Help People, Inc.
1221 West Johnson Street
Madison, WI 53715

Cross Educational Software
P.O. Box 1536
Ruston, LA 71270

Cyberon Corporation
1175 Wendy Road
Ann Arbor, MI 48103

Developmental Learning Materials
One DLM Park
Allen, TX 75002

EKEG Electonics Co., Ltd.
P.O. Box 46199, Station G
Vancouver, British Columbia
Canada V6R 4G5

Grover and Associates
7 Mt. Lassen Drive D116
San Rafael, CA 94703

Interstate Electronics Corporation
1001 East Ball Road
Anaheim, CA 92803

Intex Micro Systems Corporation
755 West Big Beaver Road
Suite 1717
Troy, MI 48084

Krown Research, Inc.
6300 Arizona Circle
Los Angeles, CA 90045

Laureate Learning Systems
1 Mill Street
Burlington, VT 05401

Learning Well
200 S. Service Road
Roslyn Heights, NY 11577

Minnesota Educational Computer Consortium
2520 Broadway Drive
St. Paul, MN 55113

Prentke Romich Company
8769 Township Road 513
Shreve, OH 44676-9421

Prometheus Software
5 Devon Street
Lynbrook, NY 11563

R/M Systems
22903 Fern Avenue
Torrance, CA 90505

Raised Dot Computing
408 South Baldwin
Madison, WI 53703

Scarborough Systems
25 N. Broadway
Tarrytown, NY 10591

Street Electronics Corporation
1140 Mark Avenue
Capinteria, CA 93013

Sunburst Communications
Washington Avenue
Pleasantville, NY 10570

Technical Aids and Systems for the Handicapped
70 Gibson Drive #1
Markham, Ontario
Canada L3R 2Z3

The Learning Company
4370 Alpine Road
Portola Valley, CA 94025

Vertex Systems
7950 West 4th Street
Los Angeles, CA 90048

Voice Machine Communications, Inc.
1000 South Grand Avenue
Santa Ana, CA 92705

Vortrax, Inc.
1394 Rankin
Troy, NY 48083

BIBIOGRAPHY

Bennett, Randy Elliot. "Applications of
    Microcomputer Technology to Special Education."
    EXCEPTIONAL CHILDREN 49 (October 1982):
    106-113.

    Gives a comprehensive discussion of how
    computers can be used to assist in classroom
    instruction and administration, ranging from
    developing individualized instructional plans
    to special services that can be provided using
    the microcomputer.

Boehcher, J. "Computer-Based Education: Classroom
    Applications and Benefits for the Learning
    Disabled." ANNALS OF DYSLEXIA 33 (1983).

    Outlines characteristics of computer based
    education and benefits for learning disabled
    students.

Bowe, Frank. "Micros and Special Education."
    POPULAR COMPUTING (November 1984):   121-128.

    Discusses characteristics and uses of speech
    recognition hardware. Includes excellent
    product descriptions.

Browning, Phillip, and Gary Nave. "Computer
    Technology for the Handicapped." THE COMPUTING
    TEACHER 6 (September 1983):   56-59.

    Reviews adaptive hardware and software and how
    they can be used with disabled individuals.

Cain, Edward J. "The Challenge of Technology:
    Educating the Exceptional Child for the World
    of Tommorrow." TEACHING EXCEPTIONAL CHILDREN
    16 (Summer 1984):   239-241.

    Shows how computer technology can be used in
    the education of children with special needs.

Clements, Douglas H. COMPUTERS IN EARLY AND
    PRIMARY EDUCATION. Englewood Cliffs, N.J.:
    Prentice-Hall,   1985.

Contains a chapter with helpful information on how computers can be used to meet the needs of disabled children.

Goldberg, E. Paul. SPECIAL TECHNOLOGY FOR SPECIAL CHILDREN. Baltimore: University Park Press, 1983.

Demonstrates how the computer can be used with children having a wide range of physical and psychological disabilities.

Goldberg, E. Paul, et al. COMPUTERS, EDUCATION AND SPECIAL NEEDS. Reading, Mass.: Addison-Wesley, 1984.

Shows how the computer can be incorporated into a variety of curricular areas for use with disabled children.

Hamlett, Carol L. "Microcomputer Activities for Gifted Elementary Children: Alternatives to Programming." TEACHING EXCEPTIONAL CHILDREN 16 (September 1984): 253-257.

Gives a well-thought-out treatment of computer activities that can be used with gifted children.

Hannaford, Alonzo E., and Florence M. Taber. "Microcomputer Software for the Handicapped: Development and Evaluation." EXCEPTIONAL CHILDREN 49 (October 1982): 137-142.

Discusses positive aspects as well as potential problems using computer hardware and software with disabled individuals.

Harvey, William J., and Dean W. Ginther. "Lowering the Barriers to Computer Use." THE COMPUTING TEACHER 11 (April 1984): 45-47.

Describes how the classroom can be modified to meet the needs of the disabled as well as how to select and modify computer hardware and software.

Hasselbring, Ted S., and Carol L. Hamlett.
"Planning and Managing Instruction: Computer-
Based Decision Making." TEACHING EXCEPTIONAL
CHILDREN 16 (Summer 1984): 248-252.

Outlines how the software program AIMSTAR can
be used by teachers having little computer
experience to develop and maintain records of
students' achievements and progress.

Kleinman, Glenn M. "Computers Make Special
Education More Effective and Fun." CREATIVE
COMPUTING 10 (October 1984).

Presents positive and negative arguments for
using microcomputers with children having
special needs.

McWilliams, Peter A. PERSONAL COMPUTERS AND THE
DISABLED. Garden City, N.Y.: Doubleday and
Company, 1984.

Contains several directories of products,
services, and software that are helpful when
using the microcomputer with the disabled.
Outlines how computers can be used with people
having different disabilities.

Pollard, James P. "Adaptive Devices for Special
Education." ELECTRONIC LEARNING 3 (February
1984): 44-46.

Describes how three input/output devices can be
used with physically and visually impaired
students. Includes good product descriptions.

Pournelle, Jerry. "Micro Revolution." POPULAR
COMPUTING 4 (June 1985): 46-51.

Provides a useful discussion of how computer
hardware and software can be used in teaching
children with special needs.

Rotenberg, Leslie. "Learning Disabilities Guide."
TEACHING AND COMPUTERS 2 (May/June 1985):
39-45.

Illustrates how several types of computer
hardware and software can be used with children

having learning disabilities. Includes a
listing of resource agencies and publications.

Talmy, Shel. "Computing for the Handicapped."
CREATIVE COMPUTING 10 (February 1984):
222-235.

Provides a comprehensive review of the voice
module method for entering data into an Apple
computer for use with disabled users.

CHAPTER NINE

HIGHLIGHT TOPIC
PROGRAMMING ... TO TEACH OR NOT TO TEACH

One issue immediately arises when children use
a computer in the classroom: Should the child be
taught a computer language to be able to write a
program, or simply learn to use existing software?
Of course, there are countless programs already
written that cover a wide range of subjects.
Furthermore, these programs are usually superior to
what the beginning programmer can produce. Writing a
computer program is often very time-consuming.
Should the child engage in other, seemingly more
productive activities?
    The issue is easily resolved. Learning to
program a computer to perform user defined tasks
frequently involves several learning experiences
that are not otherwise attainable. In today's world
of high technology, both children and adults fear
that the computer may begin to control their lives. At
school, children learn that the computer is easy to
manipulate and, thus, understand that they are in
control of the machine. The child soon learns that a
properly functioning computer doesn't make mistakes,
and that errors are inevitably the fault of the
operator or writer of the program. The machine can
only perform operations that the human programmer
designates. This sense of control over a product of
the technological revolution is a valuable lesson
for the young child to learn.
    By writing computer programs, children develop
a familiarity with the computer learning environment
that they do not get from working with a prepared
software program. A computer language and the
computer keyboard are tools to be used to
communicate with the machine. The monitor lets the
children see what they have done and how the

computer responds to commands. Program storage via
disk or tape demonstrates that information can be
saved and at a later time retrieved at the request
of the user. Programs that have been retrieved can
then be edited, added to, or combined with other
routines written by the programmer. By programming,
a child begins to appreciate the intricacies and
interrelationships of the computer.

Perhaps a more important result of learning to
write computer programs is the development of
thought processes necessary to formulate a logical
set of problem solving strategies. Teaching problem
solving strategies has always been difficult because
of the variety of knowledge and skills involved.
With a computer, children can define problems such
as how to make and save a picture or how to
incorporate several small figures into a single
scene. Creation of games, music, and animated
pictures requires problem solving skills. This act
of creating is an invaluable lesson that is
difficult to evaluate by traditional means.

Computer programming also lets a child divide a
complex problem into its component parts and then
attack each one individually. The solution to one
part of the total problem may involve a unique
problem solving strategy. The final product involves
assimilating these solutions into an interrelated
scheme which teaches the child about
interrelationships and the concept of integration.

Use of programming techniques also allows the
user to ask "What if" types of questions. In any
discipline one must consider the effects of changing
a variable or parameter on the final solution.
Computer programming offers a tool by which this
lesson can be taught. Children frequently, and
rightly so, work together on computer programs, thus
encouraging the natural exchange of ideas. This
cooperation and joint labor on a project is a
typical part of the computer learning environment.

In order to write a computer program, one must
have a clear understanding of the nature of the
problem to be solved and develop an explicit method
of solution. The user has to think clearly and
logically and to develop a plan of attack. All
computer languages offer flexible methods of
solution, allowing for creativity and individuality.
However, programming languages have a definite
vocabulary and grammar that comprise the syntax of

that language. The importance of rules for structure
and usage must be learned by the user.

One of the most meaningful experiences for a
programmer is trying to identify errors and make
corrections in existing programs. Debugging a
program is often a frustrating but extremely
worthwhile activity. The child must rethink the
method of solution that was chosen to solve the
problem and be able to articulate the particular
problem solving stategy that was utilized. Answers
to the question: "What is wrong with my program?"
are often of greater value than the results of the
program.

If children are to be taught computer
programming in elementary school, one must ask where
this will take place and who will do the teaching.
Should the school relegate the teaching of computer
programming to the "expert" who comes into the
classroom once or twice a week or have programming
taught as one of the activities in the resource
room. Or should you, the classroom teacher, become
familiar enough with a computer programming language
to teach it to your students?

All three models for teaching computer
programming to young children have been used with
varying degrees of success in schools throughout the
United States. The computer should be another
learning tool available in the regular classroom.
The teacher can easily learn the fundamental
commands of a computer language. Practicing at the
machine after reading an introductory manual and
possibly participating in a computer workshop is the
best way to start. By learning to program a
computer, you can readily assimilate the computer
into your educational program. This will further
help to show children that the computer is not a
mysterious, magical machine, but simply another of
many experiences that the teacher offers to enhance
learning.

The specific language you choose is not
important although the language must be compatible
with your computer. Learning Logo would be an
excellent choice, providing your school has a Logo
disk or easy access to one. BASIC is another option
chosen by most schools across the country. Once the
child can make the computer carry out user defined
tasks, you and the children will find ways to
further enhance learning.

The experiences provided by the computer
environment constitute valid reasons why children
should be taught to program a computer, although
many of the advantages are not easily measured and
evaluated. We have not yet developed the tools
necessary to measure the impact that the computer
has had on children, nor undertaken longitudinal
studies of its impact on them and society at large.
However, it is clear that the computer is playing an
increasingly significant role in our daily lives and
will continue to do so in the future. This is a
valid reason why children should learn how this
machine functions and, more importantly, how they
can control it.

CHOOSING A COMPUTER LANGUAGE

There is a wide variety of computer languages
that have been developed in the past 25 years. Most
of the over 150 languages have been created to meet
specific user needs, although there are several
all-purpose computer languages available. But what
really constitutes a computer language? A computer
language is a set of systematized instructions that
allow the user to control the multitude of
operations that the computer can perform. We call
these sets of instructions a language because they
let us communicate with the computer in a manner
that the machine understands. Each language has its
own format and structure that comprise the syntax of
that language. People who design computer languages
try to make them very similar to real languages in
order to simplify mastery of them by users.
Most microcomputers have the computer language
BASIC, meaning Beginners All-Purpose Symbolic
Instruction Code, built into the internal software
that is a part of the computer system. If users
master BASIC, they can communicate with the computer
asking it to perform many tasks. Microcomputers do
not have to be modified to use this language, nor
does additional hardware or software have to be
purchased. BASIC is easy for teachers to learn and
is structured in a way that makes it easy to teach
children. For these reasons the majority of public
and private schools that use microcomputers choose
BASIC as their primary teaching language.

There are two other ways that additional computer languages can be introduced to the microcomputer. The first method involves using a computer disk or tape that teaches the computer the language. The computer language Logo is introduced to the computer by this method. This method has the drawback that language disks and tapes are machine specific, and that they are not available for all computer systems. Language disks and tapes are often costly, especially if multiple copies are needed for use in several classrooms. Many microcomputers providing fewer than 48K random access memory cannot use some language disks as these disks or tapes, themselves take up a great deal of computer memory leaving little for the programmer to use.

The second method involves the placement of a printed circuit board within the computer. This is easily done by the non-expert, but circuit boards are costly and they too are machine specific. The computer language Pascal is introduced to many microcomputers by this method. Some microcomputers cannot accommodate additional languages introduced in this way.

Mainframe and some minicomputers frequently have several computer languages such as COBOL, BASIC, FORTRAN, and Pascal available to the user. These powerful computer systems can perform a multitude of functions and are often used in secondary school and college settings. Use of these computer systems in elementary schools has been limited because of cost and the lack of availability of appropriate software.

An issue that must be addressed when one considers using a computer in the elementary classroom is whether or not the teacher must learn a computer language. You must also evaluate possible educational advantages and drawbacks in the teaching of computer languages to young children. Your initial reaction might be that the presence of a computer in the classroom implies that the teacher and/or the children should be able to write computer programs for it. This is not the case.

Effective use of the computer in the classroom does not imply that the user can write computer programs any more than being able to drive an automobile implies that you can design and build one of your own. Knowing how to assign the computer tasks to perform in a manner in which the machine understands is a very useful, productive educational

activity at which relatively few computer users are
proficient. It is not necessary for everyone to
become a computer programmer.

A more realistic first step for you, the
teacher of young children, might be to discover ways
that the computer can be used as a valuable
educatonal tool. Attending workshops, lectures,
seminars, and demonstrations is a good way to start.
The next step might be to experiment with several of
the educational programs that have been prepared, as
well as teacher utility programs that have been
written.

For those of you who wish to explore the world
of computer languages, this section includes a brief
look into several of the most commonly used ways by
which you can communicate with the computer. These
descriptions are not intended to serve as
programming manuals, but do offer insight into the
design, structure, and application of selected
computer languages.

Consider first that learning to write computer
programs helps children further develop logical
thinking skills. The programmer must clearly define
a problem and develop strategies through which a
solution can be effected. The computer offers a
valuable experience for children to further develop
hand-eye coordination and fine motor control. Group
interactions among students offer a means for each
child to contribute toward the solution of a
problem. Children almost universally perceive the
microcomputer as an interesting and exciting
addition to the classroom learning environment.

It is not that the computer gives "the answers"
to all questions we, as educators, are asking about
the future education of our youth. Rather the
computer is another tool which, if used properly,
can open up horizens for the child explore in
sometimes new and innovative ways. We do not know
how these machines will be used in classrooms of the
future. Predictions can be made, but the educational
use of computer technology is continuously expanding
into every aspect of the curriculum. Hardware and
software developments and innovations will bring us
a multitude of possibilities for incorporation of
microcomputer technology into the education of our
youth.

Delta Drawing

Delta Drawing is a computer graphics program that was formulated as an outgrowth of Logo. Delta Drawing is not a true computer language as it only offers the graphics mode and cannot perform mathematical operations, word manipulations, or other tasks inherent to true computer programming languages. It can, however, be a valuable tool as it lets children make colorful drawings on the monitor screen. Drawings created by students can be saved on a computer disk or tape and later combined with other pictures to create a more complex scene.

This program enables the child to develop a fundamental understanding of the sequential step-by-step thinking that is a requisite for problem solving when using the computer. To work with Delta Drawing effectively, the user does not have to know computer programming or have typing skills, nor does the user have to be proficient in reading and writing. This program encourages planning and creative thinking, while at the same time allows for trial and error learning. For these reasons Delta Drawing is included in this section.

Delta Drawing is available from Spinnaker Software Corporation and is designed for children ages 4 to 12. The cost of the program is $49.95, with versions available for Apple, Atari, Commodore-64, and IBM PC computers. If a graphics printer is available, drawings can be printed on computer paper.

An important feature of this program is the way it lets children give instructions to the computer using single keystroke commands. Typing words or inputing complex sequences of instructions is not a realistic possibility for the child who is just developing reading readiness or basic reading skills. Cards are provided with the program that define key input functions. There are also cards that offer instruction, telling the user how to construct simple drawings. Many teachers choose to make their own cards that are tailored to specific lessons. Delta Drawing commands are easy to use and soon allow children to create interesting shapes, pictures, and scenes. Learning with this program is cumulative, at the same time encouraging experimentation and creative approaches to the formulation of graphic designs.

Delta Drawing is a good way to introduce the
microcomputer to five- or six-year-old children.
There are several reasons why I believe this
software represents a good starting point. Delta
Drawing almost always fascinates children and it is
very easy to use. With this software children
familiarize themselves with many important features
of the computer system, as they will save
information within the computer, print text and
graphics thay have created, save and retrieve
programs from computer disk. Delta Drawing also
allows for creativity for the children decide what
will be drawn. It is also an introduction to how a
structured computer language operates.

If possible, a color monitor should be used
with Delta Drawing to take advantage of the color
options it provides, although a black and white
monitor can be used. If a printer is used with this
program to get paper copies of the pictures children
have created on the monitor screen, a Grapple
printer interface card produced by Orange Micro,
Inc., must be used in place of the printer interface
card that was provided with the printer. Text
commands can be made using the standard printer
interface card that is provided with the printer.

Introducing this program to children is quite
simple. After the program has been loaded, the
children can then begin to create drawings using
single key stroke commands. The set of commands used
with Delta Drawing is included in this chapter.
There is also a set of "Fast Start" cards provided
with the program that illustrate how to draw
squares, circles, triangles, as well as a collection
of pictures.

After learning to use Delta Drawing to create
shapes, the teacher should next show the children
how to save their pictures within the memory of the
computer. This is accomplished by typing the number
1 at the completion of the drawing. The child can
then erase the drawing from the screen, later press
the number 1 and the drawing and instructions that
were given will reappear on the monitor screen.
Drawings can be easily combined to create more
complex scenes and interesting designs.

You are now ready to introduce color for use in
the drawings. The interior of a closed structure can
have color added to it, or the background for the

drawing can be colored. Examples of how to select a color from the Delta Drawing color menu are given on subsequent pages. The most important point to remember when selecting a color is to make sure that the cursor is positioned within the portion of the picture to which you wish to add color.

The last task to be taught to the children is how they can save their programming instructions on a computer disk in order to retrieve them at a later time. When a drawing has been completed, depress the CONTROL key, then type the letter S. Now type the letter T and press the RETURN key to save your text file. Give the file a name of up to 27 characters in length and press the RETURN key once more. Your text file is now saved on your computer data disk.

To load the previously saved file, press the CONTROL key and the S key simultaneously to tell the computer you wish to use a disk system procedure. Press L to load the file, then T telling the computer it is a text file you wish to load. After pressing the RETURN key, as many as 15 files stored on the computer disk will be displayed on the monitor screen. The left and right arrow keys are used to point to the file you wish to load. After pressing the RETURN key, the file you have chosen will be loaded into the computer. The program you have loaded can then be modified, printed, or combined with other pictures to create a more complex drawing.

To create drawings, you must learn the appropriate Delta Drawing commands. A detailed outline of how to use Delta Drawing is included with the programming disk or tape. The accompanying chart lists some commands which let the user immmediately start to create drawings.

Commands Used With Delta Drawing

Key	Command	Functions
D	Draw	Cursor goes forward one step and draws a line.
M	Move	Cursor moves one step without drawing a line.
R	Right Turn	Cursor turns right 30 degrees.
L	Left Turn	Cursor turns left 30 degrees.

U	U-Turn	Cursor turns 180 degrees.
CTRL-D	Half Draw	Cursor moves 1/2 step and draws a line.
CTRL-M	Half Move	Cursor moves 1/2 step without drawing a line.
CTRL-R	Half Right Turn	Cursor turns right 15 degrees.
CTRL-L	Half Left Turn	Cursor turns left 15 degrees.
SHIFT ?	Random	Next drawing command is randomly generated (except U-Turn).
E	Erase	Erases last command entered.
CTRL-E	Erase	Erases entire drawing.

CTRL-D or similar statements given above tell the user to hold down the control key on the keyboard while pressing the letter D. Keyboard commands are always given using upper case letters. Many computers have a cap lock key that can be set to make this process easy.

The procedure outlined below shows how to use a Delta Drawing disk with a computer having a disk operating system. Cassette tape or cartridge versions of Delta Drawing are also used in this fashion. All versions of this software program are as easy to use.

Now you are ready to use Delta Drawing. First, place the master disk in the disk drive of your computer, label side up, and close the door. Turn on your computer and monitor. The disk drive will whir and clatter for several seconds while the program is being loaded. When the light to the disk drive goes off and a prompt appears on the monitor screen, you are ready to begin. The documentation provided with Delta Drawing includes an operations manual and a set of cards that show in a clear, concise fashion how to use this program.

The two sample programs given here illustrate how you can use Delta Drawing to create pictures. Be sure that you press CTRL-E when you have completed each picture to erase it from the computer's memory.

1   Drawing a Square

Press D D D D D (or 5D if you wish)
Press R R R
Press D D D D D
Press R R R
Press D D D D D
Press R R R
Press D D D D D

2   Drawing an Equilateral Triangle

Press D D D D
Press L L
Press D D D D
Press L L
Press D D D D

If you are using a color monitor, Delta Drawing lets you select colors for the lines you draw, fill in the figures created with color, or select a background color for your drawing. The chart below gives the commands necessary to add color to your drawing.

Adding Color to Your Picture

Key	Command	Function
C**	Select Color	Used to choose color for the drawing, fill in, or background. ** requires a color input number that is selected from a menu on the screen when C is pressed.
CTRL-F	Fill Shape	Causes the shape you have drawn to be filled in with the last color selected. Fill Shape works in the black/white mode only if you are drawing using a white line on a black background.
SHIFT +	Add Background	Causes the background to be filled in with the last color selected.

The sample program below is used to draw a
square using a colored pen. The square is then
filled in with a color, and a background color
chosen for the drawing.

Press C
Select and enter a color number from the menu.
Press 5D 3R 5D 3R 5D 3R 5D
Place the cursor in the square, using Move and
Turn functions but not touching a line.
Press C
Select and enter a color number from the menu.
Press CTRL-F
Place the cursor in the background area of your
picture using Move and Turn functions.
Press C
Select and enter a color number from the menu.
Press SHIFT +

Your drawing is now complete. It is difficult
to convey the excitement and sense of personal
accomplishment a child feels when the first drawing
has been completed. This type of learning is not
finished in a single session at the computer.
However, teachers are inevitably surprised at the
rate at which young children learn to use this
program.
The obvious advantage of this software is that
it is designed to let children experiment with
lines, shapes, and colors. Children can immediately
change background colors or the colors of objects
that have been drawn. Soon they will learn that
individual pictures they have drawn can be
incorporated into a single scene. Teachers have
found endless ways to incorporate Delta Drawing into
their curriculum.
There are many additional features of Delta
Drawing that we have not explored. These aspects are
treated in detail in the manual that accompanies the
program. The teacher learns more about the
capabilities of Delta Drawing while working with
students. In general, children find this program
easy to use as well as being interesting and fun.
Frequently groups of children working together to
create a picture also create a sense of teamwork and
develop qualities of cooperation in group
activities.

Logo

Logo is a computer language that lets children and adults communicate with the computer to solve a wide range of problems. As was true with Delta Drawing, Logo has a powerful graphics component that is particularly useful when used in the elementary classroom. In addition to its graphic component called Turtle Graphics, Logo offers a computer world that can solve mathematical problems, work with words and lists, and perform countless other useful tasks.

Children and adults of all ages find many aspects of Logo that are interesting and useful. There are several versions of Logo currently available, with Apple Logo, Krell Logo, and Terrapin Logo being the most commonly used. Versions of Logo are available for use with several computer systems including Apple, Atari, Commodore, Franklin, IBM, Texas Instruments, and TRS-80 Radio Shack computers at a cost of between $125.00 and $150.00.

Logo is different from most computer languages in that it is conceptualized to enhance learning in a general sense, for it was formulated in part on the research of Jean Piaget into how children develop thinking skills. It was developed by Seymour Papert in the mid-1960's to present an environment in which children can learn and begin to build and create.

Developed from the notion that children learn most efficiently from examples and models, Logo strives to create for the child a world in which mathematics (geometry in particular) becomes second nature to the child. This language is very understandable; it uses familiar words. The graphics and color capabilities make it particularly attractive. The nature of the language itself lets children use their conceptual knowledge to create individualized procedures that are taught to the computer. Children realize that they are teaching the computer rather than being taught by it.

Learning to become proficient in using Logo is more time consuming than mastering Delta Drawing, but the extra time and effort are well spent. Logo is designed so that children and adults can learn together. It is an easy language to learn and simplifies the task of making the computer do many exciting and educationally valuable things.

In a very friendly, informal way, Logo can introduce to a child the concept of variables as well as the notion of a defined procedure. With Logo the user can save designed and drawn graphics when written as procedures. These pictures can later be edited, expanded, and used as part of a construct that the child may create at some later time.

To communicate with Logo, you must understand that it has a very limited but powerful vocabulary. It is a very "fussy" language, so your instructions must be input in the precise manner that Logo expects. Below you will find some simple commands that will let you start making Logo drawings.

Commands Used in Logo

Abbrev.	Command	Example	Function
FD	Forward	Fd 10	Moves turtle 10 units in direction it is pointing.
BK	Backward	Bk 5	Turtle moves in opposite direction 5 units.
LT	Left	LT 60	Turtle turns 60 degrees left.
RT	Right	RT 90	Turns turtle 90 degrees right.
DRAW	Draw	DRAW	Erases drawing and brings turtle home.
HOME	Home	HOME	Turtle goes to center of screen.
CS	Clearscreen	CS	Erases screen leaving turtle where it is.
NODRAW	NoDraw	NODRAW	Logo enters text mode.
HT	Hide Turtle	HT	Makes turtle invisible.
ST	Show Turtle	ST	Makes turtle visible.
PU	Pen Up	PU	When turtle moves no no line is drawn.
PD	Pen Down	PD	Turtle draws line when it moves.
BG	Background	BG 2	Background color set as green.
PC	Pen Color	PC 4	Pen color set as orange.

Before we examine a Logo program, there are some things about using the computer keyboard with Logo that you should know. For example, simply typing a keyboard character does not actually communicate with the computer. You must press the RETURN key after typing a command to tell the computer you have entered information. The location on the monitor screen where the next character will be positioned is indicated by a blinking light called a cursor in the text mode, and by a triangular shaped cursor called a turtle in the graphics mode.

When using Terrapin Logo, the ESC (escape) key makes the cursor move backward and erase the character you have just typed. The CTRL (control) key is used in conjunction with other keys to perform special functions. For example, pressing the CTRL and G key combination makes Logo stop whatever it is doing. Whenever you use the CTRL key, hold it down while pressing the other key. In any case, the RETURN key does not have to be pressed when using ESC or CTRL functions.

If you wish to use symbols located above the number keys and punctuation marks, press the SHIFT key and the appropriate character as you would on any typewriter. A REPT (repeat) key is found on many computer keyboards. If you press a character and simultaneously press the REPT key, you will type that character as long as you keep the REPT key depressed. Some computer keyboards such as the Apple IIe keyboard have a built-in repeat function. This means that if you hold a key down, that character will continue to be typed.

The commands used in all versions of Logo are essentially identical, but there are subtle differences in the use of special keys. For example, when using Apple Logo, to erase what you have just typed, use the left arrow key instead of the ESC key used in Terrapin Logo. In general, all versions of Logo are similar, and differences are easily found by examining the programming manual.

We are now ready to see how Logo works. Versions of Logo are available on floppy disk, cassette tape, or cartridge for use with different computers. The illustration provided here demonstrates how Logo is loaded using a computer disk system. Place Logo in the disk drive,

close the door to the disk drive, and turn on your
computer. Soon a message like "Welcome to Logo" will
appear on the monitor screen. The message varies
according to the type of Logo you are using. To
prevent possible damage to Logo, remove it from the
disk drive after use. A question mark will appear on
the screen followed by the blinking cursor. The
question mark is a prompt indicating that Logo is
waiting for you to type something.
     To create a Logo picture, you must tell Logo
that you wish to draw. Each version of Logo has a
method to do this. In Apple Logo the command
CLEARSCREEN or CS is used, while in Krell and
Terrapin Logo the command DRAW must be typed. In
either case, you must press the RETURN key after
typing the command.
     A triangle called a Turtle will now appear in
the center of the monitor screen. When you tell Logo
to draw a line, the Turtle moves, leaving a line
behind it. The Turtle shows the direction in which
you are pointing. The Logo commands provided in the
previous table tell the Turtle what to do and how to
do it. For example, the command FD 12 tells the
Turtle to take 12 steps forward. LT 90 indicates to
Logo that the Turtle should turn to the left 90
degrees from the direction in which it is now
pointing.
     Now we can create a picture using Logo. The
sample programs included cause Logo to draw various
shapes. Be sure to press the RETURN key after typing
each command. More complex and interesting programs
can be written once you have become familiar with
the language.

     Drawing a Rectangle   Drawing a Triangle

             FD 30   FD 65
             LT 90   RT 120
             FD 50   FD 65
             LT 90   RT 120
             FD 30   FD 65
             LT 90
             FD 50

Drawing a Window

```
FD 50      FD 50      FD 25
RT 90      RT 90      RT 90
FD 50      FD 25      FD 25
RT 90      RT 90      RT 90
FD 50      FD 50      FD 50
RT 90      RT 90
```

There are commands which reduce the number of steps required to construct a Logo drawing. For example, REPEAT 4[FD 50 RT 90] will cause Logo to draw a square using one instruction. There are other commands that allow you to use Logo to perform a wide variety of operations, from doing problems in mathematics to working in creative ways with words and lists. These are explored in any good Logo programming manual.

Young children soon find that the world of Logo provides a stimulating and exciting learning environment. In a very natural, intuitive way they begin to explore and define geometric relationships. Formal rules for the construction of shapes are not necessary as the child learns by doing. Children perceive Logo as a friend and partner in learning. "How I can make Logo ..." is a statement almost universally heard in classrooms where this computer language is used.

The user can also teach Logo new commands called procedures. A procedure can be saved on a disk or cassette tape, printed using a printer having graphics capabilities, and combined with other procedures to make a composite drawing. This capability has broad educational connotations as it lets a child discover relationships and exercise creativity. Frequently, children learn procedures from classmates and incorporate them into their own store of knowledge.

The examples shown below illustrate how the user can teach the computer user defined procedures called SQUARE and TRIANGLE. These procedures are then incorporated into a new procedure called HOUSE. If these procedures are saved on disk or tape, they can then be used as part of any future construction. Clearly, this is an important and powerful aspect of Logo.

```
TO SQUARE                              TO HOUSE
   REPEAT 4 [FD 50 RT 90]                 SQUARE
END                                       RT 90
                                          FD 50
TO TRIANGLE                               TRIANGLE
   REPEAT 3 [RT 120 FD 30]             END
END
```

If you have a color monitor, Logo can draw
lines in color and let you choose from several
background colors. Your color choices depend on the
type of computer you are using. For example,
Commodore Logo offers 16 color choices, while Logo
used on Apple computer provides 6. The tables given
on the next page show how you can choose pen colors
and background colors using Apple and Terrapin Logo.
     Logo is not only for young children. People of
all ages can use Logo in a variety of ways. Logo
procedures can be written to solve a variety of
mathematics problems as well as to provide users
with interactive programs on a wide range of
subjects. The possibilities and applications of this
language in education are almost endless. Elementary
school age children, middle and high school
students, and adults attending colleges and
universities can benefit from learning Logo. It is a
developmental language designed to help the learner
learn.
     As seen from the Logo programming examples
illustrated here, Logo is much more sophisticated
than Delta Drawing. The tasks that can be performed
with this language are almost limitless. A good
starting point is to have children make simple
drawings using the immediate execution mode. After a
few sessions children easily learn to manipulate the
turtle to create interesting drawings. Children
experiment with lines and soon learn many
fundamental rules used to form geometric shapes like
squares, triangles, and rectangles. This is
accomplished without formal instruction being given
in the rules of geometry.
     The immediate execution mode scenes that have
been drawn cannot be saved on computer disk or
cassette tape. Soon children will want to save
structures they devised so that they can edit and
expand upon them at a later time. Now is the time to
show them how to write permanent instructions in the

form of Logo procedures. Several examples of Logo
procedures are given in this chapter. Saving a Logo
procedure on computer disk or cassette tape is easy
to do. Type the word SAVE "(Program Name) and press
the RETURN or ENTER key. The procedure will then be
saved using the program name that was chosen.
     The teaching of Logo is a never ending process
as there are always additional techniques to learn.
In many school systems Logo is used each year in all
of the elementary grades. Often when children reach
secondary schools they are taught other computer
languages such as BASIC or Pascal, although Logo
could be used to perform any of the tasks that older
children and adults might wish to do. It is very
likely that older users believe that since Logo was
written for young children, this language cannot
meet their more advanced needs. This is not the
case.
     Logo is an interesting, useful, and valuable
language that has direct application for children in
elementary classrooms. The language is easy to
learn, but meant to be learned at the computer. It
is worth your time to learn more about Logo.

Selecting Background Colors

Apple Logo	Terrapin Logo	Effect
SETBG 0	BG 0	background is black
SETBG 1	BG 1	background is white
SETBG 2	BG 2	background is green
SETBG 3	BG 3	background is violet
SETBG 4	BG 4	background is orange
SETBG 5	BG 5	background is blue

Drawing Lines in Color

Apple Logo	Terrapin Logo	Effect
SETPC 0	PC 0	draws in black
SETPC 1	PC 1	draws in white
SETPC 2	PC 2	draws in green
SETPC 3	PC 3	draws in violet
SETPC 4	PC 4	draws in orange
SETPC 5	PC 5	draws in blue

BASIC

During the mid 1960's John Kemeny and Thomas
Kurtz created the computer language BASIC. Their
goal was to develop a computer language that
undergraduate students at Dartmouth College could
use on existing computer time-sharing equipment. The
reason for this was simple. Up to this time most
computer languages were designed with specific
applications in mind. What was needed was an
easy-to-learn language designed for general
applications for use by the non-technically oriented
person. It was seen as a modification of the more
technical language FORTRAN that was in common use at
the time. BASIC offered additional advantages over
other languages that were being used.

BASIC was designed to be used as an interactive
computer language. This means that BASIC is
structured to easily accommodate input from the user
as part of the execution of the program. Getting the
computer to print your programming results is also
simple using this language. Writing computer
programs in BASIC to solve simple to moderately
complex problems is relatively easy for the
beginning programmer to learn. This had not been
true for many other computer languages that were in
common use.

With the advent of the microcomputer in the
mid-1970's, BASIC assumed a more important role.
Almost universally, BASIC was chosen as the primary
computer language for these systems. There are
several reasons why this choice was made. Early
microcomputers had a very limited amount of memory
available. These machines could not accommodate a
language like Pascal or Logo. In fact, even today
the majority of the microcomputer's internal memory
is taken up by interpreters for languages like
Pascal or COBOL.

BASIC is also very easy to learn and has
instructions that very closely resemble English.
Programs can be written in BASIC using only a few
instructions. BASIC has a set of mathematical
functions built into it, and offers a simple way to
handle word variables.

When microcomputers were first used in
educational settings, teachers began using BASIC as
the instructional language. Also, many
microcomputers could not accommodate a language

other than BASIC. For these reasons it is the
primary computer language taught to children in over
90% of the schools across the country.
     As with other computer languages, BASIC has its
own vocabulary. A partial listing of words used when
programming in BASIC is included in the accompanying
table. Many microcomputers offer a graphics mode as
part of its BASIC interpreter, as well as color and
sound capabilities. This makes BASIC a very useful
language for use in the classroom.

COMMANDS USED IN BASIC

NEW	Tells the computer to erase what is currently in memory.
PRINT	Used to get information displayed on the monitor screen.
INPUT	Lets the user communicate directly with the computer.
GOTO	Tells the computer to move to another section of the program.
IF ... THEN	A logic statement that lets the computer make comparisons.
END	Tells the computer the program is completed.
RUN	Causes the computer to execute the program in memory.
GET	Lets the user communicate directly with the computer.
RETURN/ENTER	Is pressed after giving the computer an instruction.
LIST	Causes programming lines to be displayed on the monitor screen.
<>	Means is not equal to.
REM	Lets the user add remarks that are not part of the executable part of the computer program.
FOR ... NEXT	Used as a loop structure to do repeated operations.
C=C+1	A counter used to keep track of how many times an operation has been done.

     We will now examine a computer program written
in BASIC. This program shows how a multiple choice
quiz can be designed using this language. The syntax
may seem confusing and redundant, but any good
programming manual explains how programs can be
designed and written.

BASIC Program 1

```
10  PRINT "HI, MY NAME IS MICRO THE COMPUTER. WHAT'S
    YOUR NAME?"
11  PRINT "TYPE IN YOUR NAME AND PRESS THE RETURN OR
    ENTER KEY."
30  INPUT NAME$
40  PRINT "WELL ";NAME$;" LET'S PLAY GUESS MY
    SHAPE."
50  PRINT "    *********"
60  PRINT "    *       *"
70  PRINT "    *       *"
80  PRINT "    *       *"
90  PRINT "    *********"
95  PRINT:PRINT
100 PRINT "AM I  1) A CIRCLE  2) A RECTANGLE  3) A
    SQUARE?"
110 PRINT "TYPE IN THE NUMBER YOU CHOOSE."
120 GET CHOICE
130 IF CHOICE=2 THEN PRINT "GREAT ";NAME$;" YOU GOT
    IT."
140 IF CHOICE<>2 THEN PRINT "SORRY, TRY AGAIN.":GOTO
    50
150 END
```

By examining this program, you may be able to predict what will appear on the monitor screen when the program is run. The following table shows what appears on the monitor screen for the user to see.

Computer Output for BASIC Program 1

HI, MY NAME IS MICRO THE COMPUTER. WHAT'S YOURS?
TYPE IN YOUR NAME AND PRESS THE RETURN OR ENTER
KEY.
(USER TYPES IN OWN NAME.)
WELL (USER'S NAME) LET'S PLAY GUESS MY SHAPE.

```
    *********
    *       *
    *       *
    *       *
    *********
```

AM I 1) A CIRCLE 2) A RECTANGLE 3) A SQUARE?
TYPE IN THE NUMBER YOU CHOOSE
2 (USER TYPED A 2)
GREAT, (USER'S NAME), YOU GOT IT.

To try this program on a microcomputer, turn on the computer in the manner prescribed by the manufacturer, type the word NEW, and press the RETURN/ENTER key after you type each line of the program. Type the word RUN and press the RETURN/ENTER key to see how the program works. Notice that each statement in BASIC has a line number. This is necessary as the computer follows programming instruction in a linear manner going from lower to higher numbered lines. This uses logic in writing programs in BASIC.

The second sample program shows how a typical number guessing game is structured. Included in the program are REM (remarks) statements. These are not actually part of the program as it is run, rather they tell the programmer useful information.

BASIC Program 2

```
1     LET COUNT=0
10    PRINT "I'M THINKING OF A NUMBER BETWEEN 1 AND
      100."
20    PRINT "TRY TO GUESS MY NUMBER."
30    REM LINE 40 PICKS A RANDOM NUMBER BETWEEN 1 AND
      100
40    LET NUM=INT(100*RND(1))+1
45    REM HOW TO PICK A RANDOM NUMBER IS MACHINE
      SPECIFIC
50    INPUT "YOUR GUESS IS ";S
55    REM LINE 60 KEEPS TRACK OF THE NUMBER OF
      GUESSES
60    LET T=T+1
70    IF G=NUM THEN GOTO 200
80    IF G<NUM THEN PRINT "TOO LOW, TRY AGAIN.":GOTO
      50
90    IF G>NUM THEN PRINT "TOO HIGH, TRY AGAIN.":GOTO
      50
100   REM LINES 70-90 EXAMINE THE USER'S GUESSES
200   PRINT "YOU GOT IT! ";NUM;" WAS MY NUMBER."
210   PRINT "IT TOOK YOU ";T;" GUESSES."
220   REM NOTICE THAT PRINT STATEMENTS CAN INCLUDE
      QUOTATIONS AND VARIABLES.
230   PRINT "BYE FOR NOW."
250   END
```

BASIC programs 1 and 2 will run on any microcomputer as the commands used are universal and are not machine specific. There are subtle variations in BASIC from one manufacturer to another that are called dialects of the language. These are usually minor variations that are easily learned.

To show graphics and sound capabilities using BASIC is difficult, as each manufacturer has a unique method for handling computer graphics. BASIC program 3 shown below will run on any Franklin or Apple computer.

BASIC Program 3

```
10   INVERSE:FLASH
20   PRINT "COMPUTER GRAPHICS DEMO"
30   NORMAL
40   REM LINE 10 CAUSES THE WORDS COMPUTER GRAPHICS
     DEMO TO BLINK ON THE MONITOR SCREEN.
50   PRINT "WE ARE ABOUT TO BEGIN."
55   SPEED=150
56   LET X$=CHR$(7)
60   FOR X=1 TO 20
70   PRINT X$
80   NEXT X
85   SPEED=255
90   REM LINES 55-80 CAUSE 20 BEEPS TO BE SOUNDED.
95   REM LINE 100 TELLS THE COMPUTER TO ENTER THE
     GRAPHICS MODE.
100  GR
110  REM LINES 120-180 DRAW A MOVING CAR.
120  FOR M=1 TO 30
140  COLOR=3
150  HLIN M,M+2 AT 10
155  HLIN M,M+2 AT 11
160  HLIN M,M+2 AT 12
165  COLOR=6
166  HLIN M,M+5 AT 13
170  HLIN M,M+5 AT 14
175  HLIN M,M+5 AT 15
176  FOR X=1 TO 100:NEXT X
177  COLOR=0
178  HLIN M,M+2 AT 10
179  HLIN M,M+2 AT 11
180  HLIN M,M+2 AT 12
181  HLIN M,M+5 AT 13
182  HLIN M,M+5 AT 14
183  HLIN M,M+5 AT 15
```

```
185 NEXT M
195 LET S=-16336
200 FOR C=1 TO 50
205 LET X=PEEK(S)-PEEK(S)+PEEK(S)-PEEK(S)
210 NEXT C
215 TEXT:HOME
220 REM LINES 200-210 GIVE A BUZZ SOUND.
250 PRINT "END OF GRAPHICS DEMO."
260 END
```

Terms for Graphics Demo Program

INVERSE	Reverses the screen from black on white to white on black.
FLASH	Causes next words on monitor screen to blink.
NORMAL	Returns computer to normal mode of screen display.
SPEED	Sets speed at which characters are presented on monitor screen. (1-255, slow to fast.)
GR	Tells computer to enter low resolution graphics mode.
COLOR	Lets you choose from among 16 colors for monitor display. A color number must be included.
HLIN	Tells the computer to plot a horizontal line.
HOME	Clears the monitor screen of all characters.
TEXT	Tells the computer to leave graphics mode.
PEEK	Tells computer to activate a memory location.

COLOR MENU

0	black	8	brown
1	magenta	9	orange
2	dark blue	10	grey
3	purple	11	pink
4	dark green	12	green
5	grey	13	yellow
6	medium blue	14	aqua
7	light blue	15	white

As you can see, BASIC offers a wide range of options. You can also work with words, called strings in computer jargon, in a variety of ways. BASIC can be used to create charts and tables and perform a variety of mathematical and manipulative functions. Many versions of BASIC offer a high resolution graphics mode that lets you draw lines. These are additional reasons why BASIC is the most frequently used computer language in classrooms today.

The programming examples given here illustrate how the teacher might write computer programs in BASIC to meet educational needs. You can see by the structure of these programs that they are almost written in a conversational way. As with all computer languages, BASIC has its own unique syntax, meaning vocabulary and programming format. It is simple to learn and through the learning process shows the user how the computer functions.

Quite obviously, programs of this complexity cannot be written by very young children. Young children often find the immediate execution mode of this language to be a useful starting point. Simply stated, the immediate execution mode does not require use of line numbers and gives immediate computer response to user input statements.

Consider what would happen if you typed "3+4" and pressed the RETURN or ENTER key. The computer would respond by printing a "7" on the monitor screen. If the user typed PRINT "MICRO" the computer response would be the word "MICRO." Many elementary teachers have found that using the immediate execution mode is a good way to introduce BASIC to young children. Journals written for use by classroom teachers contain articles in each issue showing how teachers have found interesting and educationally valuable ways to use this language.

BASIC is most effectively used with children who are at least nine years old. Some reading and writing skills are necessary as well as a fundamental grasp of the concepts of sequencing and formulation of interrelationships. When properly presented, BASIC can enhance and broaden the classroom learning experience.

Pascal

The computer language Pascal has come into recent prominence in the United States for use in business, industry, and education. It is named after the famous seventeenth-century French mathematician Blaise Pascal and was developed in the late 1960's. Philosophically, Pascal is designed as a language to teach computer programming as a systematic discipline founded on fundamental concepts that are clearly and naturally reflected by the language. Another aim is to discover uses and applications of the language that are both reliable and efficient on today's computers. In computer circles Pascal is viewed as a good all-purpose computer language.

Instructions given in Pascal are divided into sentences which are referred to as statements. The language has a limited vocabulary, and commands seem very similar to, but not quite like, English sentences. Pascal is a structured computer language, therefore its format is rigid and all information must be entered in a prescribed fashion. Teachers of Pascal see this as a strength, as it clearly demonstrates to the learner the importance of good form, structure, and organization.

The chart below illustrates in general terms how all Pascal programs are structured. These sections must be included in all programs, but there is considerable flexibility within each section so that the user has a variety of techniques to solve a problem.

Program Title
    Includes the name of the program.

Program Declaration Section
    Includes definitions of such things
    as variables and constants.

Program Execution Section
    Must start with a BEGIN statement
    and terminate with an END. Includes
    all programming statements required
    in order that the programs function
    properly.

Pascal has a set of words that it knows, called reserved words. A student writing a Pascal program cannot use these words for any purposes other than those for which they are intended. For example, PROGRAM is a reserved word used to define the title of the program and cannot be the name given to a variable. The listing below gives some of the more commonly used reserved words.

Reserved Word	Function
AND	A conjunction indicating that two or more conditions must be true.
ARRAY	A family of related variables.
BEGIN	Tells the computer you have started an executable section of the program.
DIV	Gives the integer quotient when one number is divided by another.
END	Tells the computer you have completed an executable section of the program.
IF ... THEN ... ELSE	Lets the computer choose between appropriate options based on stated conditions.
OR	A conjunction indicating that either of two conditions must be met for a condition to be true.
REPEAT ... UNTIL	Defines conditions that must be met before the program can enter an exit controlled loop.
WHILE ... DO	Defines conditions that must be met if the program is to enter a loop.

Suppose we examine a Pascal program that will print out your name and address. The RETURN/ENTER key must be pressed after completing each program line.

Pascal Program 1

```
PROGRAM NAMEADDRESS(OUTPUT);
BEGIN
     WRITELN ('NAME: JANE AND JOHN DOE');
     WRITELN ('ADDRESS: 100 MAIN STREET');
     WRITELN ('          HOMETOWN, USA')
END
```

After you type the word END and press the
RETURN/ENTER key, the computer will immediately
print the name and address in the form shown below.

```
          NAME: JANE AND JOHN DOE
          ADDRESS: 100 MAIN STREET
          HOMETOWN, USA
```

Even a cursory examination of this program
gives insight into how this language is structured
and how the user communicates with the machine. The
first line tells the computer that the title of the
program is NAMEADDRESS and that the machine is
directed to generate output to the user. Notice that
the title NAMEADDRESS is written as a single word.
This is necessitated because program names in Pascal
must be a single word. The BEGIN statement in line 2
indicates to the computer that we are starting the
program execution section of the program. As no
variables have been used, a declaration section is
not required. Lines 3-5 tell the computer what is to
be printed. The parentheses serve to group the
information, while the single quotation marks tell
the machine to print the information exactly as it
appears between the single quotation marks. Finally,
the END statement at line 6 tells the computer we
have finished the executable section of the program.
    As you can see, Pascal has a syntax that is
different from Logo or BASIC. It is another "fussy"
language, as the structure, format, and punctuation
used must be exact. But, it is very readable and the
logic is easy to follow. The next program better
illustrates the potential and capabilities of this
language.
    This program will compute the circumference and
area of a rectangle based on the length and width
values given by the user.

Pascal Program 2

```
PROGRAM RECAREAPER (INPUT,OUTPUT);
VAR
      LENGTH,WIDTH,PERIMETER,AREA:REAL;
BEGIN
      READ (WIDTH,LENGTH);
      WRITELN ('RECTANGLE WIDTH: ',WIDTH);
      WRITELN ('RECTANGLE LENGTH: ',LENGTH);
      AREA:=WIDTH*LENGTH;
      PERIMETER:=2.0*(WIDTH + LENGTH);
      WRITELN;
      WRITELN ('THE AREA OF THE RECTANGLE IS
      ',AREA);
      WRITELN ('THE PERIMETER OF THE RECTANGLE
      IS ',PERIMETER)
END
```

The output from a run of this program is illustrated below. If you try this program on your computer using Pascal, the numbers printed may look a little strange to you. This is because Pascal prints calculated values using exponential notation. Pascal can be told to print results in the more common form, but for simplicity's sake these instructions were not included. Let us suppose that the user types in 5 and 15 for width and length respectively.

Output for Pascal Program 2

```
RECTANGLE WIDTH: 5
RECTANGLE LENGTH: 15
THE AREA OF THE RECTANGLE IS 75
THE PERIMETER OF THE RECTANGLE IS 40
```

As you have seen, Pascal is a structured computer language that makes use of English words and has a very logical format. Most microcomputers cannot do Pascal unless a Pascal Language Card has be added. At present it is taught in many colleges and universities, and to some extent in public and private high schools. This trend will continue, as the Educational Testing Service that administers the College Board examinations has chosen Pascal as the computer language to be used on that test. Undoubtedly, use of this language will filter down to the junior high school level, and possibly even to the upper elementary grades.

As it is a compiled language having a rigid
structure and syntax, its applicability to the lower
elementary and preschool classrooms will, however,
be minimal. The manner in which Pascal handles
computed number values and to some extent commands
may also present a barrier for use with very young
children. Still, Pascal will come into increasing
prominence in the years to come.

Pilot

Pilot is a computer language that was developed
in the 1970's as an outgrowth of Pascal. It is
designed for teachers who know little about
computers or computer programming, but wish to use
the computer to help tailor an academic program to
meet specific and individualized student needs. Use
of Pilot for Computer-Assisted Instruction (CAI) has
been effective for tutorial purposes as well as for
developing tests and measuring student progress. It
has not been included as a computer language that
teachers would use with young children, but as a
utility language that can be easily learned and used
by teachers.

The dialects of Pilot that are available today
are much more extensive than earlier versions and
frequently make use of today's microcomputer sound
and graphics capabilities. The principal advantage
of Pilot as a programming language is that it was
designed to be interactive and can be easily learned
by anyone regardless of prior experience using the
computer. A drawback is that a Pilot language disk
must be purchased for use on a microcomputer. Many
microcomputers cannot accommodate Pilot as a
computer language.

Each part of a Pilot program begins with a
label that serves to identify that section of the
program so that it can be referred to at a later
time. A label cannot be more than six characters in
length and, when typed, is always preceded by an
asterisk (*).

An instruction name of one or two letters
typically follows the label section of a Pilot
program. A summary of sample instruction names is
given below. The colon (:) is an essential part of
an instruction line that is frequently preceded by

the instruction name and any modifiers or
conditioners that have been used.

Sample Pilot Instructions

Name	Abbrev.	Function
REMARK	R	Comments for the teacher but not the student.
TYPE	T	Prints text on monitor screen.
ACCEPT	A	Accepts student responses to questions.
MATCH	M	Compares student response to correct one.
JUMP	J	Moves to another section of the program.
END	E	Ends a section of the program.
COMPUTE	C	Performs computations and stores results.
GRAPHICS	G	Draws dots and lines on the monitor screen.

Pilot also offers the use of modifiers which
can alter the manner in which an instruction works.
One common use of modifiers is to accept a response
as correct even if the response was spelled
incorrectly by the child.

Conditioners are used in Pilot programs to test
if the student's response to a question was the
correct one. These are not required in a Pilot
program, but are often found to be helpful.

Expressions are non-essential parts of the
program that serve to test the student's response to
see if it is the correct one. If an expression is
tested and found to be true, the instruction is
executed. An evaluation of false causes the
instruction to be skipped.

The Pilot program shown here illustrates how
you can construct a set of review questions based on
a short story.

Pilot Program 1

R: Sample Pilot Program. Remarks (R) are used
    to explain how the program functions.

*   Begin

T: One day, Missy took a walk in a park./She
    found a quarter lying on the/ground. Soon
    she saw a rabbit eating/grass near a
    tree. Missy ran to the/store and bought
    some popcorn for the/rabbit. When she
    returned to the park/the rabbit was gone,
    so she fed the/popcorn to the pigeons.
R: The Text (T) section will appear on the
    monitor screen.

T: What did Missy see eating grass?
A:
R: Pilot is waiting for the child's/response.

M: Rabbit!Rabit!a Rabbit!a Rabit
R: Allows for variations including
    misspellings.

TY: Great, you got it!
R: Gives this response for correct answer.

JY: Continue
R: If answer is correct go to the next
    question.

T2: You missed it. Missy saw a rabbit/eating
    grass.
R: The student has two chances to answer the
    question. If both answers are incorrect,
    the correct answer is given.

J2: Continue
R: If the second answer is correct jump to
    the label Continue.

T: Sorry, that's not right. Try again.
R: Gives the student a second chance.

J: Begin
R: Sends Pilot to the Begin label to ask the
    question again.
*   Continue

R: This could start another question.
.
.
.

J: End
R: Program jumps to the label End.

* End
R: The closing routine for a Pilot Program.

E: End
R: Signifies the end of the program.

    As you can see, Pilot is a very simple computer language. This demonstration program does not do justice to the language, rather it is intended to show how the language can be used. Pilot offers many additional features that are useful and rewarding to the teacher and student. Depending on the type of computer you have, it offers an extensive graphics capability, including the use of color and sound.

    Pilot can perform mathematical operations and a variety of manipulative functions. It can be used to test the child's knowledge of math operations, as well as keep track of student progress and test scores. Materials you have written can be stored on disk and are readily retrievable.

    Pilot also offers an easy-to-use and effective structure for what are termed Teacher Utilities. As with all computer languages, it has its own unique syntax, although in this case the syntax bears a close resemblance to English. The advantage of using this language lies in its ability to personalize instruction for each child. CAI does not substitute for the teacher, instead Pilot can be used as one more remedial and enrichment tool. It can be effectively used for any grade level in almost all subject areas. Writing Pilot programs is easy, and they are easy to use by people of all ages. Pilot is worth exploring for use in your classroom.

Lisp

Lisp is a computer language that was developed in the 1950's by John McCarthy at the Massachusetts Institute of Technology. It is one of the oldest computer languages that is still used today. Lisp is a list processing language that was created for computerized studies of artificial intelligence. It was originally designed to be used with large mainframe computer systems, but there are versions today that are used with microcomputers.

Lisp is not a complex computer language. Its structure is designed to maximize interactions between the computer and the user. Lisp is one of the most effective interactive computer languages. It has a regular and consistent syntax, and is particularly interesting to use when devising computer games and puzzles.

Eliza is the most famous Lisp program that has been written. Joseph Weizenbaum developed the Eliza program to simulate a discussion between a patient and a non-directive psychiatrist. Eliza simulates artificial intelligence of the computer by matching patterns of user statements to programmed responses by the computer. This program has an extensive word list, making conversations between the machine and the human interesting and at times informative. One can almost believe that the machine is thinking.

List processing is the greatest strength of this computer language, although it can deal with mathematical expressions and calculations. Lisp has a very precise syntax that requires prescribed punctuation. The format this language requires is unique as is its word requirements. The accompanying chart shows how some mathematical operations are treated in Lisp.

Operation	Lisp Form	Lisp Response
Addition	:(ADD 7 16 3)	26
Subtraction	:(SUB 173 51)	122
Multiplication	:(MULT 2.3 5)	11.5

Notice that the syntax of Lisp requires that each statement begin with a colon (:), and that the statement itself is enclosed in parentheses. There must be a space between the name of each operation and the number that follows it. A space must also be placed between each number. Once the expression is

typed by the user and the RETURN or ENTER key
pressed, Lisp immediately responds with an answer.
    In Lisp programming, the first item following a
parenthesis is called a function and that which
follows is the argument for that function. For
example, ADD is a function and 7 16 3 is the
argument for the ADD function.
    Lisp can also treat more complex mathematical
functions and arguments. The Lisp expression :(MULT
3(ADD 4 2)) gives a computer response of 18. To get
this result, Lisp first evaluates the sub-expression
(ADD 4 2) as 6. It then treats 6 as the second
argument. Thus, :(MULT 3 6) is evaluated as 18.
    All mathematical and list expressions are
treated using the standard rules for evaluation when
terms are grouped by parentheses. The expression
:(MULT (MULT (ADD 1 0)(ADD 1 1))(MULT (ADD 2 1)
(ADD 1 3))) is evaluated by Lisp as 24.
    There are several other types of functions and
operations that are used in Lisp programming.
Predicates are Lisp functions that give a computer
response of true or false. In Lisp, true is written
as T and false as NIL. The table shown below gives
some frequently used predicates and how Lisp
evaluates their arguments.

Function	Lisp Response
:(GREATER 3 4)	NIL
:(GREATER 100 -100)	T
:(ZERO (ADD 3 -3))	T

    All Lisp functions must be in the form of
lists. Lists are always linear collections of
objects separated by blank spaces and surrounded by
parentheses. A list consists of atoms or other
lists. An atom is the name given to the fundamental
data unit in Lisp. Atoms can be numbers, letters, or
words. The Lisp expression (DOGS(LOVE)TO(CHEW
A)BONE) contains both atoms and lists. DOGS, TO and
BONE are atoms, while LOVE and CHEW A are lists.
    Lisp evaluates lists, but the first element of
a list must be a Lisp function. The remainder of the
list is the data to be acted on by the function and
is called an argument.
    If you wish an expression to be printed as
written and not evaluated, a single quote mark is
used. The Lisp expression :'(ADD 3 4) causes (ADD 3
4) to be displayed on the monitor screen.

There are several expressions that let the programmer perform operations on lists. The expression CAR causes the first element of a list to be displayed, while CDR gives all but the first element of the list. The example shown below demonstrates how these expressions can be used.

Lisp Expression

```
:(CAR'((I WANT)(TO LEARN)(PROGRAMMING)))
:(CDR'((I HAVE)(A COMPUTER)(NOW)))
```

Lisp Response

```
I WANT
A COMPUTER NOW
```

The expressions CONS and CONC are used to extend and join lists. CONS takes the first Lisp argument and places it at the beginning of the second argument. CONC joins two lists by placing the first list in front of the second. The expression below shows how we can perform additional operations on lists.

Lisp Expression

```
:(CONS(CAR'(I WANT TO LEARN PASCAL))(CDR'(THEY
HAVE LEARNED LISP)))
```

Lisp Response

```
(I HAVE LEARNED LISP)
```

The expression SETQ is used to define a function in terms of an atom and to substitute its value for that of the atom. The example included shows how easy SETQ is to use.

Lisp Expression

```
:(SETQ ATOM 1'FOUR SCORE)
:(CONS ATOM 1'(AND SEVEN YEARS AGO))
```

Lisp Response

```
FOUR SCORE
(FOUR SCORE AND SEVEN YEARS AGO)
```

As we have seen, Lisp is used to perform a variety of mathematical and word list manipulations. Additional expressions and applications are included in any good Lisp programming manual. Both Logo and Lisp are easy computer languages to learn, and are among the most effective to use when processing words and lists.

BIBLIOGRAPHY

Barnes, B.J., and Shirley Hill. "Should Young Children Work With Microcomputers--Logo Before Lego?" THE COMPUTING TEACHER 10 (May 1983): 11-14.

Suggests young children will not be harmed by early experiences with the computer. Contends computer experiences should not substitute for experiences with real things.

Becker, Henry. "How Schools Use Microcomputers." CLASSROOM COMPUTER LEARNING 4 (September 1983): 41-44

Considers classroom applications of the microcomputer, and how children use their time when working with them.

Beckerman, Judith. "You Don't Have to Learn the Language." THE COMPUTING TEACHER 10 (February 1983): 23-31.

Describes how computer programs can be used in elementary classrooms.

Elfring, Gary. "Choosing a Programming Language." BYTE 10 (June 1985): 235-240.

Provides criteria that help user make decisions about which programming language to use.

Gardner, David, and Marianne Gardner. APPLE BASIC MADE EASY. Englewood Cliffs, N.J.: Prentice-Hall, 1984.

Gives simple overview of BASIC. Excellent treatment of sound, color, and graphics on Apple computer.

Gnosis, Inc., ed. LEARNING LISP. Englewood Cliffs,
N.J.: Prentice-Hall, 1984.

Offers a good introduction to the language and its
applications. Contains numerous illustrations and
examples.

Harvey, Brian. "Why Logo?" BYTE (August 1982):
163-189.

Offers a good overview of applications for several
computer languages. Emphasizes Logo as a good
teaching language.

Hennefeld, Julien. USING BASIC. Boston: Prindle,
Weber & Schmidt, 1981.

Provides a systematic treatment of BASIC. Gives
many programming examples and sample programs.

Howe, Harold. "Computers the New Kick in the
Schools." THE COLLEGE BOARD REVIEW 128 (Summer
1983): 24-32.

Examines role computers have played in education
and role they will play in the future.

Miller, Samuel, and Ron Thorkildsen. GETTING
STARTED WITH LOGO. Allen, Tex.: Developmental
Learning Materials, 1983.

Provides an excellent introduction to the language
for the beginner. Includes a multitude of examples
and classroon applications.

Pantiel, Mindy, and Becky Petersen. KIDS TEACHERS
AND COMPUTERS. Englewood Cliffs, N.J.:
Prentice-Hall, 1984.

Offers a non-technical discussion of uses and
applications of computers in the elementary school
classroom.

Papert, Seymour. "Computers and Computer Cultures."
CREATIVE COMPUTING (March 1981): 83-92.

Suggests that computer programming enhances
thinking and exploration in the young child.
Advocates Logo as a language for use with
children.

Richards, James L. PASCAL. New York: Academic
Press, 1982.

Gives a comprehensive treatment of the language.
Contains little material for early education. Good
for the more technically oriented.

Tesler, Lawrence G. "Programming Languages."
SCIENTIFIC AMERICAN 251 (September 1984): 70-78.

Compares the structure and uses of selected
computer languages including: Logo, Pascal,
FORTRAN, Prolog, and Compel.

Watt, Daniel. "Should Children Be Computer
Programmers?" POPULAR COMPUTING (March 1981):
83-92.

Argues that programming helps children develop
logical thinking skills.

Willis, Jerry W., and D. LaMont Johnson. COMPUTERS,
TEACHING AND LEARNING. Beaverton, Ore.:
Dilithium Press, 1983.

Provides a good introduction to how computers and
computer languages can be used in education.
Written for the non-technically trained reader.

Wold, Allene. "What Is a Programming Language?"
CLASSROOM COMPUTER NEWS 3 (April 1983): 46-49.

Offers a good introduction to the nature of
computer languages.

CHAPTER TEN

WHAT THE FUTURE HOLDS

Since 1975 the microcomputer has exerted an
increasing impact on our daily lives in many obvious
as well as in subtle ways. Tasks performed by office
secretaries to architectual design projects have
seen the infiltration of this new technology. There
are many reasons for this, but the main factors have
been steadily decreasing costs of computer hardware
and the development of an excellent collection of
software programs to meet specialized needs. As new
hardware and software are developed there will be a
growth in the use of computer technology in almost
every human endeavor.

Our educational system has struggled to try to
identify the most appropriate ways to use computer
technology to enhance the education of our young
children. As with any new development there is
inertia that must be overcome before we can move
forward. Today's teachers are rapidly familiarizing
themselves with microcomputers and how they can be
most effectively used in the classroom. The growing
level of computer literacy among teachers and the
improved quality of computer software programs that
have been written have played an important role.

The future will bring additional applications
of computer technology to the classroom learning
environment. One reason for this is that the next
generation of teachers and children will have
personally experienced applications of computer
technology throughout their lives. They will have
have become as familiar with computers as today's
adults are with television and stereo component
systems. Both teachers and children will find new
and creative ways to use microcomputers that are
unthought of today.

The computer itself will likely undergo many
changes that will further the development of new

269

areas in which it can be used. Tomorrow's machines will be smaller and less expensive than the microcomputers on the market today. Computers are currently available that can fit into a large briefcase, but some future microcomputers will be smaller still. These machines will have the video display, external memory, and print features of computers we have today, but will have far greater internal memory capabilities and operate at much faster speeds. These machines will be able to use the spoken word as input and be able to give output in the form of synthesized speech patterns. Highly advanced computer simulated three-dimensional color graphics will be commonplace. These machines will have built-in telecommunication capabilities so that users can instantly give and receive input from other computer systems.

The future will bring further integration of computer technology into every aspect of our personal and professional lives. It has been estimated that by the year 1990 about 30% of the jobs in this country will require some level of computer literacy by the workers. Children in our schools will have a much higher level of computer literacy than the public at large. Estimates are that up to 70% of the school aged children will be computer literate before the year 2000. Being a computer literate person will be necessary for future generations.

Before considering specific applications of computer technology for the the future, we will examine how these machines are being used today. Now, computers and computer technology perform a tremendous number of diverse functions. In many cases we are not aware that the computer is impacting on our lives, as we cannot see these machines perform tasks. Considering the growth rate of the computer industry in the past 25 years, both in terms of hardware and software applications, some people feel that we have achieved the ultimate uses of this new technology. This is not the case, for without doubt many new applications of computers are yet to be developed. Before considering future uses of these machines, let us contemplate some of the ways they are being used today.

We have just begun to scratch the surface of home applications for the microcomputer. For most families computerized game systems have provided the initial introduction to computer technology. During

the last few years their cost has been dramatically
reduced and the quality and quantity of games
available has significantly grown, making them
readily available to many consumers. These
activities have shown the average person how easy
computer based hardware and software are to use and
the interesting graphics that are possible.

Microcomputers started to appear in homes when
users wanted to do more with this technology by
having personal control over what will be done and
how tasks will be accomplished. Home users are able
to play much more interesting and thought provoking
games than ever before. Both children and adults
have begun to find uses for the many educational
software programs that are available for home use.
Programs in the sciences, mathematics, language
arts, and computer design have come into prominence.
The microcomputer is not relegated to a position in
a closet or toy box after a period of time, instead
it remains in dens, studies, and family rooms.

Many home users have learned to write computer
programs in one or more computer languages. Children
and adults are learning that writing activities are
more easily accomplished using computer based word
processing programs. Some users have found that one
or more database management programs can be valuable
in keeping personal inventory records. Recipe files,
inventories of household appliances, and articles,
as well as information needed for income tax
purposes can be efficiently stored and updated using
the microcomputer.

The home computer is also often used to prepare
and maintain household budgets and make financial
projections through application of spread sheet
software. Home users have also found that many tasks
traditionally done at the office or job site can be
done at home using the microcomputer.

We have just begun to realize the potential of
microcomputer telecommunication applications using
the home computer. Many users currently subscribe to
computer bulletin boards and belong to networks that
allow for the two-way exchange of information and
ideas. Some home users have their computers linked
to office machines via modem connections, making
work at home more efficient and easy. The future
will bring many new advances in how we can use
computer technology for interpersonal
communications.

Computers are rapidly becoming a natural part of the school environment at all levels of our educational system. Teachers are using computer software programs to supplement classroom activities done in more traditional materials and in some cases are using microcomputer programs to teach new concepts and ideas to children and adults. Computer based tutorials and simulation programs are among the most commonly used software in educational settings.

The impact of the word processor on improving the quality of written work is just beginning to be realized. Teachers can now ask students to rewrite papers without forcing them to recopy what they have previously written. Applications of computer graphics hardware, such as graphics tablets, are now being explored for uses in the arts. Similarly the many music related hardware and software materials are just starting to be applied in classrooms.

Many teachers have found computer programming a stimulating and educationally valuable tool to use with young children. They have found that writing computer programs encourages creativity in children, encourages them to logically develop ideas and problem solving strategies. Students learn to ask their own questions and develop methods of solution either by working individually or with other students.

There are many ways that computers are used to carry out administrative functions in schools. They are used to keep individual student records for such things as attendance, health, and academic transcript data. Many school systems use computers for scheduling and room assignment purposes. Teachers have also begun to use computer software to administer tests and keep class records for students. Additional applications of computer technology for classroom uses will be developed in the future.

Computer technology is used extensively by the medical community to help meet administrative and patient needs. Computer software is used to keep, maintain, and update patient records. Computers are used to assign patients' rooms and for scheduling facilities for special purposes such as operations. Computer databases keep records and schedules for medications as well as for laboratory and test results.

Hospitals are beginning to store nurses' and doctors' notes on the computer as well as past medical histories of patients. In many cases the computer is used to assist the physician in making medical diagnoses and developing courses of treatment. Computer databases containing patient records about disease processes are an invaluable aid when research studies are conducted.

The medical community has made excellent use of this new technology. Uses ranging from business applications such as inventory control, accounts receivable, and payroll functions to health care prevention records and data for organ donor banks have become commonplace. In general, the larger medical facilities have made the most efficient use of computer based technology.

Almost every component of the transportation industry has been affected by the advent of computer technology. Structural designs for automobiles incorporating many safety features are developed using the computer to assist engineers. Many features built into the automobiles you drive, such as fuel injection systems and electronic ignitions are regulated by on-board small computer microprocessors. Many sophisticated automobiles offer computer generated voice comments to drivers, letting them know if the vehicle is turned off, the doors are closed, or if the lights have been left on. Computers are also used to test automobiles for pollutant emissions and other safety features during periodic automobile inspections.

The aircraft industry would not function well if it were not for the computers used to assist air traffic controllers to maintain air safety in keeping aircraft properly positioned in relation to one another. Computers on board planes help pilots with navigation and in flying the aircraft. The computer also plays an important role in training and updating pilots using cockpit flight simulators. The development of new aircraft design could hardly be accomplished without the application of this new technology. Other uses include keeping records of current passenger reservations. The computer performs many functions necessary for the operation of our space shuttle.

Railway systems use the computer to control and monitor the movement of trains as well as to regulate activities carried out in railway yards. The trucking industry often uses computers to perform similar functions as well as to plan and update delivery and shipping schedules. Ships frequently use computers to keep cargo and passenger records and to assist engineers in developing new structural designs for vessels.

The type of computer equipment used by the business community varies greatly and ranges from microcomputers to mini- and mainframe machines. What kind of computer is used depends on the size of the business and the tasks that the machine is assigned to perform.

Computer software for word processing, database management, and spread sheet analysis are frequently found to be indispensable. Software programs that keep accounting records, maintain updated inventories, and generate payrolls are examples of specific applications of computers used for business activities. They are also used to make budget projections and to assess material and labor needs. Many larger institutions use computer based telecommunication systems to interact with other agencies and of course compose countless letters and reports using word processing software. The computer has had a profound impact on the day-to-day operations within the business community.

Local, state, and federal governmental agencies have been using computer technology for several years to meet a variety of needs. The Census Bureau has been using computers to compile and tabulate data as well as to carry out statistical analyses. Census results are now available only months after the census has been completed compared to years in earlier times. Similarly, the Internal Revenue Service and state departments of taxation have found the computer to be invaluable for checking tax forms for accuracy and determining if tax refunds are in order. Virtually all of our state and federal tax information is now kept on computer.

The preparation of federal, state, county, and municipal budgets is inevitably done with the aid of a computer. Other agencies such as the Postal Service and the Department of the Treasury have found computer technology helpful in meeting their needs. Departments of criminal justice including the Federal Bureau of Investigation have databases that help them solve crimes and learn more about criminal activities. Each year governmental departments find new uses for computer technology.

Applications of computer technology to environmental issues have recently begun to come into prominence. Computers are universally used today to help develop weather predictions and long-range forecasts. They are also used to monitor air and water quality and to analyze them for contaminants and pollutants. The activity levels of volcanos such as Mount St. Helens are closely recorded by computers as are areas associated with high levels of earthquake activity.

Farmers have also felt the impact of computer technology as computers are used to help analyze terrain, soil, and the amount of rainfall expected in a given location. Farm products themselves are frequently tested using computer based equipment. We can fairly state that computers are used to manage and regulate food and water resources around the world.

Today's computers affect our personal lives in a variety of ways and have shown similar influences in the business, education, and industrial communities. It is difficult to accurately predict how computers will be used in the future, as the level of technological sophistication in the computer industry is growing at an unprecedented rate. Tomorrow will bring uses for microcomputers that are unthinkable in today's terms. We do have some clear indications of likely ways that these tools will be used to better our lives and make many of the tasks we perform easier and quicker. The following applications have been extrapolated from current research and by future indications.

The typical home owner will find the computer to be an invaluable asset in performing many time consuming and costly tasks. Microcomputers will have software available that can help diagnose electrical and plumbing problems. Heating and air conditioning needs can be tailored to meet changing structural requirements and to account for variations in climatic conditions. Additions to homes like sun decks as well as landscaping for yards will be planned and designed through computer simulation programs using a sophisticated level of computer graphics.

Computers of the future will have much greater internal and external memory capabilities. They will very likely be networked to larger machines giving home users access to databases containing tremendous amounts of information on a wide range of subjects. People will be able to access books and journals currently found in libraries and be able to read almost any newspaper through a datalink to a large mainframe computer. Computerized systems will be used to provide security against household theft as well as maintain surveillance against dangers from smoke and fire in all areas of the home. Dangers from natural gas and fuel oil leaks will be reduced as computers will monitor the quality and composition of the air we breathe.

In the future microcomputers will play an active role in household management and financial planning. Planning for food and clothing needs will be made easier by the home computer in the same way that computerized cash registers keep records of transactions and maintain inventory records for retail stores today. Families will be able to plan vacations easily as the computer can be used to plan routes to take, give listings of available motel accommodations, and provide graphics depicting places to see and things to do.

Children will use the computer for tutorials in a wide range of academic subjects. Family members will be able to take the equivalent of correspondence course on virtually any subject and be able to access an almost inexhaustible library of computer games and activities. The computer will help improve the quality of life for children and their families in a variety of ways.

Home computers will also be able to answer many legal questions that arise from time to time and play an active role in home financial management. They will keep individual health records and help in the detection and prevention of disease. Computers will be able to analyze patterns of food purchases, thereby letting the home computer continuously monitor nutrition patterns of families. Finally, citizens will be able to communicate with other people, agencies, and businesses using the telecommunication capabilities of tomorrow's computers. Electronic mail will become commonplace, reducing the time and expense associated with our daily communications. The microcomputer will have many capabilities that will make our lives simpler and increase the amount of free time for recreational purposes.

Most of the professions as well as many business and industrial complexes have yet to realize the full potential of the microcomputer. The future will bring a wide variety of new uses and applications. Banks and investment agencies will be able to provide services directly to consumers at their homes or offices. Computerized 24-hour tellers used today represent the first step in this direction. Grocery and clothing stores will be able to respond to customer requests given via the home computer to prepare orders for delivery or pick up. Long check-out lines and choosing merchandise from shelves may become a thing of the past.

Newspapers, magazines, and professional journals may have subscriptions available to consumers using the home computer as the transmission medium. This process is in its infancy today: some newspapers are available on modem telephone connections. Many cable television networks offer a 24-hour news station that provides a continuous updated set of local, national, and international events. Home and professional users will be able to trace stories that have been written over the span of weeks, months, or years as information will be stored on databases. Information will be able to be sorted and recalled at the user's discretion.

We have already begun to see the significant impact that computerization has had on the industrial and construction industries. Computer assisted maufacturing processes and computer aided design offer a valuable resource for the future. Products will be produced more quickly and efficiently having computer tested safety features that are unthought of today. Tomorrow will bring an industrial complex that makes better use of human and material resources and does not adversely affect our ecological environment.

There will be a profound impact on our educational system by computers of the future. Children will become much more independent learners able to handle more information with the aid of classroom microcomputers than they can today. Each classroom will contain several microcomputers giving each child virtually unlimited computer access. They will learn to synthesize and analyze information more efficiently and will develop a formidable repertory of problem solving strategies.

Children will have large databases available to
them containing information on virtually every
academic subject. Information in the fields of
history, sociology, and anthropology will literally
be at their fingertips. Much information now
relegated to the school library will be available
using the classroom microcomputer so that ideas can
be researched and questions answered almost
immediately. Classroom computers will be networked
so interclass communications will be possible as
well as telecommunication links between schools and
to large educational databases.

Children will have home computers connected to
those in school so assignments can be easily done
and updated. All written work as well as an
increasing number of mathematics assignments will be
done using word processing software. The computer
software elementary school aged children use will be
menu driven and offer extensive tutorial and review
options. Enhanced color graphics, animation, and
sound potentials for these programs are in the
offing, making learning fun and interesting.

Tomorrow's children will have no difficulty
adjusting to the involvement of computer technology
as part of their learning process. Children have
vivid imaginations and will have grown up during the
microelectronic revolution. Young people of all ages
are enthusiastic when they interact with a computer
and are not awestruck by its capabilities. The focus
will be on learning and not on this new computer
technology. Our task is to prepare tomorrow's
children for future applications of the computer in
education by helping them develop proper methods and
models for learning.

Future teachers will be stimulated and
challenged by the application of computer technology
to the classroom. They too will have grown up during
the microcomputer revolution, and will be much more
comfortable and secure working with computers than
we are today. Teachers will play an increasingly
important role as designers and developers of
computer software destined for classroom use. They
will be able to work much more closely with parents
toward enhancing skill development of children.
Home-to-school computer links will make this an
everyday occurrence.

Many administrative and academic burdens will
be lifted from teachers by classroom computerized
management systems. Student records, grades, and

records of academic and social development will be kept on the classroom computer. Papers written by children will be filed in the computer. The microcomputer could then check for spelling, grammar, and syntax errors and provide the children with comments suggesting alternative forms and structures. Increasing numbers of books will be provided with computer disks containing tutorial, remedial, and extension activities for children to do.

Teachers will find that children are less likely to be grouped by age or grade level, rather by their levels of academic progress and interests. This is a logical outgrowth of the individualized instruction provided using computer based technology. It is hoped that this will lead to an increased level of interest in learning and the willingness by the children to pursue an active role in that process.

Computer software that will be developed will address specific curricular needs that children must learn. These programs will be tailored to the children's cognitive development and what they are capable of learning at different age levels. Teachers will play an increasingly important role in this developmental process. Each classroom will have access to large collections of computer software programs on a wide range of subjects that have been field tested and evaluated by teachers.

As we look to the future, traditional experiences and activities provided in today's classrooms must not be forgotten or ignored. After all, the fundamental role of education and the teacher will still be the same. Our task still will be to provide young children with the personal and academic skills that will let them grow and develop in tomorrow's world. There will always be an important place in the classroom for drawing, painting, and working with clay. The value of working with blocks, creating music, and reading cannot be underestimated. Teachers and children will always find experimentation and playing games to be worthwhile educational pursuits.

No one can be certain what new and innovative developments will come forth from the microcomputer industry. As educators we must be aware of this new technology and learn to evaluate how it can best be used in the learning environment. Only then can we

insure that future generations of children will
receive the best possible education we can offer.
The challenge is yours.

BIBLIOGRAPHY

Bitter, Gary, and Ruth A. Camuse. USING A
    MICROCOMPUTER IN THE CLASSROOM.   Reston, Va.:
    Reston Publishing, 1984.

    Has a well-written chapter outlining
    characteristics and applications of computers
    in the future.

Carey, Peter.   "The Future of the Micro: Looking
    Ahead at the Next Decade." POPULAR COMPUTING
    2 (January 1985):   89-90, 178-179.

    Examines how future microcomputers might be
    used in a variety of professions.

Clark, Gary.   "Using Computers to Enhance Thinking."
    ELECTRONIC EDUCATION 4 (January 1985):   20, 27.

    Describes how children might use computers in
    the future.

Horn, Carin E., and James L. Poirot.   COMPUTER
    LITERACY: PROBLEM SOLVING WITH COMPUTERS.
    Austin, Tex.:   Sterling Swift, 1983.

    Has an excellent section on future applications
    of the computer to a variety of fields.

McNeil, Dan.   "Ten Years After: The Micro's Imprint
    on Society." POPULAR COMPUTING 2 (January
    1985):   72-88.

    Discusses how computers might impact on a
    variety of businesses and industries.

Pantiel, Mindy, and Becky Petersen.   KIDS, TEACHERS
    AND COMPUTERS: A GUIDE TO COMPUTERS IN THE
    ELEMENTARY SCHOOL.   Englewood Cliffs, N.J.:
    Prentice-Hall, 1984.

   Provides a good chapter describing how future
   computers might influence our educational
   system.

"Trying to Predict the Future." POPULAR COMPUTING
   3 (November 1984): 30-44.

   Has a series of interviews with experts
   outlining how computers may impact on our
   society.

CHAPTER ELEVEN

RESOURCES

This section includes a listing of resources
that are useful for the classroom teacher. This
collection has selected books that can be used with
children in the elementary classroom. These books
consider a wide range of issues from introducing
computer literacy to children to teaching concepts
of computer programming. In general these books are
very well illustrated with both pictures and
diagrams and written in a fashion that the young
reader can easily comprehend.

There are also materials listed that will be of
particular use for the teacher. These include a list
of books that discuss such issues as computer
literacy, how the computer functions, as well as
several texts on writing computer programs in
various languages. There are furthermore several
hardware and software directories that may be
especially useful to the teacher.

The last section provides a listing of computer
journals that will be especially useful to the
teacher. They offer a wide range of articles from
the technical to those intended for use by
elementary classroom teachers having little
background in computer technology. Most school and
public libraries subscribe to one or more of these
publications.

A brief, annotated description is included with
each of the books and journals. Including some of
these works as part of your reading list will
provide a good start toward rendering yourself
computer literate. In any case, you will learn a
great deal about how other teachers have used
computers as a classroom learning tool.

BOOKS FOR CHILDREN

Babcock, Eloise C. COMPUTER READINESS. Phoenix:
Think Ink Publications, 1981.

Provides a wide range of pre-computer
activities for young children.

Ball, Marion J., and Sylvia Charp. BE A COMPUTER
LITERATE. Morris Plains, N.J.: Creative
Computer Press, 1977.

A very well illustrated book for children
showing structure of computer systems and their
appplications.

Berger, Melvin. COMPUTER TALK. New York: Julian
Messner Pub. Co., 1984.

A dictionary of computer terminology written
for children.

Bitter, Gary G. EXPLORING WITH COMPUTERS. New
York: Julian Messner Pub. Co., 1981.

A well-illustrated 64-page book that introduces
computer literacy to children.

Bolognese, Dan, and Robert Thornton. DRAWING AND
PAINTING WITH THE COMPUTER. New York:
Franklin Watts, 1983.

A well-illustrated book for children
introducing computer graphics and telling how
to use computer hardware.

Cassidy, Pat, and Jim Close. BASIC PROGRAMMING FOR
KIDS. Englewood Cliffs, N.J.: Prentice-Hall,
1983.

Introduces computer programming in BASIC to
elementary aged children.

Cohen, Frances Lieberman. BASICALLY SPEAKING: A
YOUNG PERSON'S GUIDE TO COMPUTING. Reston,
Virginia: Reston Pub. Co., 1983.

A well-written text that considers how the
computer system works as well as providing an
introduction to programming.

COMPUTER PROGRAMMING FOR KIDS AND OTHER BEGINNERS.
Austin, Tex.: Sterling Swift, 1983.

A well-constructed volume showing how to write
computer programs. Versions available for
Apple, IBM, and Radio Shack computers.

Grauer, Robert T.; Judy Gordony; and Marsha Schemel.
BASIC IS CHILD'S PLAY. Englewood Cliffs, N.J.:
Prentice-Hall, 1984.

A workbook teaching BASIC to young children
having no prior experience. Gives sample
programs. Versions available for several types
of computers.

Hargrove, James. MICROCOMPUTERS AT WORK. Chicago:
Children's Press, 1984.

A very well illustrated volume depicting
functions and operations of the microcomputer.

Hawkes, Nigel. COMPUTERS IN ACTION. New York:
Franklin Watts, 1984.

Shows how computers handle data and their many
professional applications.

Horn, Carin E., and Carroll L. Collins. COM-LIT:
COMPUTER LITERACY FOR KIDS. Austin, Tex.:
Sterling Swift, 1983.

Considers a variety of issues and applications
of computer literacy for children. Introduces
BASIC and Logo programming.

Kohl, Rachel, et al. THE GENIE IN THE COMPUTER:
EASY BASIC THROUGH GRAPHICS. New York: John
Wiley and Sons, 1982.

Written for the upper elementary grades. Shows
children how to program in BASIC using computer
graphics as the vehicle.

Leskowitz, Barry. COMPUTING IN LOGOLAND.
    Lexington, Mass.: D.C. Heath, 1984.

    Logo tutorial written for grade 4-6 children.
    Well-written book for beginners showing many
    features of Logo in clear, concise fashion. Has
    multiple activity sheets at end of each
    chapter.

Lipscomb, S.D., and M.A. Zuanich. BASIC FUN:
    COMPUTER GAMES, PUZZLES AND PROGRAMS CHILDREN
    CAN WRITE. New York: Avon, 1982.

    Includes many programs written in BASIC with
    ideas suggesting how children can modify them.

Lipscomb, S.D., and M.A. Zuanich. BASIC BEGINNINGS.
    New York: Avon, 1983.

    Contains examples of computer programs to
    illustrate how this language is structured and
    used.

Maier, June M. SPOTLIGHT ON COMPUTERS. New York:
    Random House, 1984.

    Shows grade 1-3 children what computers can do
    and how they function. A well-structured
    workbook that includes activity pages at the
    end of each chapter. Teacher's guide available.

Marrapodi, Maryann. SPOTLIGHT ON LOGO. New York:
    Random House, 1984.

    A workbook for grade 3-6 children showing how
    Logo can be used to answer questions. A
    well-structured book that gives many Logo
    programming examples.

Moore, Margaret. LOGO DISCOVERIES. Palo Alto,
    Calif.: Creative Publications, 1984.

    A well-illustrated volume showing elementary
    school children how to use the Logo language.
    Includes many ideas for teachers.

Rice, Jean. MY FRIEND THE COMPUTER. Minneapolis:
    T.S. Denison and Company, 1981.

A well-illustrated volume for children showing
how computers are designed and function.
Includes section on programming in BASIC.

Rice, Jean, and Sandy O'Connor. COMPUTERS ARE FUN.
Minneapolis: T.S. Denison and Company, 1981.

Illustrates what a computer can do and how it
does it. Includes introduction to computer
programming.

Richard, Ian. COMPUTERS. New York: Franklin
Watts, 1983.

A well-illustrated book outlining functions of
computers and how they operate.

Rose, Ann. STEP BY STEP THROUGH LOGO TURTLE
GRAPHICS. Englewood Cliffs, N.J.:
Prentice-Hall, 1983.

Shows elementary children how to use Terrapin
Logo. Well illustrated with helpful programming
suggestions.

Stevens, Lawrence. COMPUTER PROGRAMMING BASICS.
Englewood Cliffs, N.J.: Prentice-Hall, 1984.

Offers an introduction to BASIC, including many
sample programs for children to try.

Sturvidge, Helena. MICROCOMPUTERS. New York:
Franklin Watts, 1984.

Considers computer technology as it relates to
software and hardware. Provides introduction to
programming.

Thornbug, David D. EVERY KID'S FIRST BOOK OF ROBOTS
AND COMPUTERS. Greensboro, N.C.: Compute!
Books, 1982.

Logo computer commands are related to Big Trax
programming in a way that is easy for children
to understand.

Van Horn, Royal. COMPUTER PROGRAMMING FOR KIDS AND
OTHER BEGINNERS. Austin, Tex.: Sterling Swift,
1983.

Written for middle elementary school children
using Apple or Radio Shack computers.
Introduces programming through examples.

Witte, Carol.   SIMPLE COMPUTER PROGRAMS.   Torrance,
Calif.:   Frank Schaffer Publications, 1984.

Provides duplicate masters that introduce BASIC
programming to young children. Do not have to
use a computer.

Yule, David A.   APPLE LOGO FOR KIDS.   Summit,
Pa.:   Tab Books, 1984.

Written as a Logo programming manual for upper
elementary school children. Includes sample
games and activities. Has a conversion chart so
can be used with other versions of Logo.

BOOKS FOR TEACHERS

Alesandri, K.L.   APPLE FOR THE TEACHER.   Santa
Monica: Microconnect, 1984.

Provides a computer based instruction program
for children ages 5 to 9.

Ball, Marion, and Sylvia Charp.   BE A COMPUTER
LITERATE.   Morristown, New Jersey: Creative
Computing Press, 1977.

Considers terminology and topics relating to
computer literacy.

Berden, Donna; Kathleen Martini; and Jim Muller.
THE TURTLE'S SOURCEBOOK.   Reston, Va.:   Reston
Pub. Co., 1983.

A well-illustrated book that shows how to learn
Logo and teach it to children.

Bitter, Gary, and Ruth Camuse.   USING A
MICROCOMPUTER IN THE CLASSROOM.   Reston,
Va.:   Reston Pub. Co., 1984.

A well-written book giving K-12 applications of
computers for classroom use. Has a useful

listing of computer hardware, software, and
books.

Bitter, Gary. COMPUTERS IN TODAY'S WORLD. New
York: John Wiley and Sons, 1984.

A paperback computer literacy book including
sections on programming in BASIC and Pascal.

Bowman, Sally, ed. ATARI SPECIAL ADDITIONS OF
SOFTWARE VENDORS. San Jose: Atari, Inc.,
1984.

Provides hardware and software descriptions for
materials for this computer.

Carlson, Edward H., KIDS AND THE APPLE.
Chatsworth, Calif.: Datamost, Inc., 1982.

A manual organized into easy-to-follow lessons,
excellent for classroom use. Versions available
for several types of computers.

Coburn, Peter, et al. PRACTICAL GUIDE TO COMPUTERS
IN EDUCATION. Reading, Mass.: Addison-Wesley,
1982.

Shows novice users how to select computer
hardware and software and how to incorporate
them into the curriculum.

COMMODORE SOFTWARE ENCYCLOPEDIA. King of Prussia,
Pa.: Commodore Business Machines Software
Group, 1984.

A directory providing information about
software available for Commodore computers.

COMPUTERS IN MATHEMATICS: A SOURCEBOOK OF IDEAS.
Morris Plains, N.J.: Creative Computing, 1979.

Shows how a computer can be used to build
mathematical skills.

EDUCATIONAL SOFTWARE DIRECTORY. Manchaca, Tex.:
Sterling Swift, 1984.

Has individual directories listing and
describing software for several types of
computers.

EDUCATIONAL SOFTWARE SOURCEBOOK. Fort Worth, Tex.:
Radio Shack Education Division, 1984.

Gives listing and descriptions of software for
use with TRS-80 computers.

Gardner, David, and Marianne Gardner. APPLE BASIC
MADE EASY. Englewood Cliffs, N.J.:
Prentice-Hall, 1984.

Provides a good overview of BASIC with an
excellent treatment of sound, color, and
graphics on the Apple computer.

Goldberg, E.P., et al. COMPUTERS, EDUCATION AND
SPECIAL NEEDS. Reading, Mass.: Addison-Wesley,
1984.

Provides useful information on using computers
with children having special needs. Has
directory of hardware and software.

Harper, Dennis O., and James H. Steward. RUN:
COMPUTERS IN EDUCATION. Belmont, California:
Wadsworth, 1983.

Gives examples of how computers and computer
technology has been applied to education.

Hunter, Beverly. MY STUDENTS USE COMPUTERS:
LEARNING ACTIVITIES FOR COMPUTER LITERACY.
Reston, Va.: Reston Publishing, 1983.

Offers a large collection of computer
activities for use with elementary school aged
children.

Johnson, Jerry. GRAPHICS DISCOVERIES BOOK I. Palo
Alto, Calif.: Creative Publications, 1984.

Introduces low resolution graphics using Apple
computers. Assumes a fundamental knowledge of
BASIC. Has over 100 sample programs. Computer
disk with solutions to problems is available.

Johnson, Jerry. GRAPHICS DISCOVERIES BOOK II. Palo
    Alto, Calif.: Creative Publications, 1984.

    A continuation of GRAPHICS DISCOVERIES BOOK I.
    Includes introduction to high resolution
    graphics on Apple computers. Has many
    programming examples with solutions available
    on disk.

Kelman, Peter, et al. COMPUTERS IN TEACHING
    MATHEMATICS. Reading, Mass.: Addison-Wesley,
    1983.

    Gives K-12 teachers examples of how the
    computer can be incorporated into the teaching
    of mathematics.

Kemeny, John, and Thomas Kurtz. BACK TO BASIC.
    Reading, Mass.: Addison-Wesley, 1985.

    Examines the history of this language and how
    it is currently used. Includes numerous
    examples.

Kute, Stan. PASCAL DISCOVERIES. Palo Alto,
    Calif.: Creative Publications, 1984.

    An 80-page book written for beginning
    programmers in Pascal. Well illustrated and
    contains many program examples. Computer disk
    supplement is available.

Landon, Ruth K. CREATING COURSEWARE. New York:
    Harper and Row, 1984.

    Has many examples of how to design computer
    programs for several academic disciplines.

Lathrop, Ann, and Bobby Goodson. COURSEWARE IN THE
    CLASSROOM: SELECTING, ORGANIZING AND USING
    EDUCATIONAL SOFTWARE. Menlo Park, Calif.:
    Addison-Wesley, 1983.

    Gives teachers clearly outlined criteria to use
    when evaluating educational software. Includes
    a listing of programs.

Ledyard, Henry E., and Patrick McQuaid. FROM BAKER
STREET TO BINARY. New York: McGraw-Hill,
1983.

Traces the history and concepts of the computer
in a unique storybook fashion using Sherlock
Holmes to solve mysteries.

Lombardi, John V. COMPUTER LITERACY: THE BASIC
CONCEPTS AND LANGUAGE. Bloomington, Ind.:
Indiana University Press, 1983.

Discusses computer literacy issues including
how a computer works, word processing, and
spread sheet software. Also speaks to computer
resources and programming.

Luehrmann, Arthur, and Herbert Peckham. APPLE
PASCAL: A HANDS-ON APPROACH. Wallingford,
Conn.: McGraw-Hill, 1981.

A well-written volume introducing programming
in this language. Gives much useful and
practical information.

MECC COMPUTERS IN THE CURRICULUM: A COMPUTER
LITERACY GUIDE. St. Paul, Minn.: MECC, 1984.

Provides a K-6 computer literacy curriculum.
Includes lesson plans incorporating computer
literacy into academic disciplines. A clearly
written book providing a comprehensive
treatment of computer literacy.

Malone, Linda, and Jerry Johnson. BASIC
DISCOVERIES. Palo Alto, Calif.: Creative
Publications, 1984.

An 80-page paperback for beginners introducing
BASIC programming. Well illustrated,
easy to use, with many sample programs.
Computer disk with solutions to problems is
available.

Malone, Linda, and Jerry Johnson. PROBLEMS FOR
BASIC DISCOVERIES. Palo Alto, Calif.: Creative
Publications, 1984.

A companion volume for use with BASIC
DISCOVERIES. Has sets of problems with many
solutions given. A computer disk suppement is
available.

Moore, Margaret L. GEOMETRY PROBLEMS FOR LOGO
DISCOVERIES. Palo Alto, Calif.: Creative
Publications, 1984.

Tells how Logo can be used to teach geometric
concepts. A well-written and clearly
illustrated book designed as a follow-up for
LOGO DISCOVERIES. Computer disk supplement
available.

Moore, Margaret L. LOGO DISCOVERIES. Palo Alto,
Calif.: Creative Publications, 1984.

An 80-page paperback for beginners introducing
Logo programming. Has many examples
illustrating good style and programming
technique. Computer disk supplement available.

Moore, Margaret L. LOGO DISCOVERIES: INVESTIGATING
NUMBERS, WORDS, AND LISTS. Palo Alto,
Calif.: Creative Publications, 1984.

Shows user having a familiarity with Logo
graphics how to construct interactive
procedures to solve problems. Clearly written
with many sample programs. A computer disk
giving solutions to problems is available.

Moore, Margaret L. LOGO DISCOVERIES: INVESTIGATING
RECURSION. Palo Alto, Calif.: Creative
Publications, 1984.

Introduces recursion to user having a
familiarity with Logo. Has many
well-illustrated sample procedures. A computer
disk supplement is available.

Myers, Glenford J. THE ART OF SOFTWARE TESTING.
New York: John Wiley and Sons, 1979.

Offers many useful, practical, and theoretical
ideas to explore when testing and debugging
computer software.

Osborn, Adam, and David Bunnell. AN INTRODUCTION TO
    MICROCOMPUTERS VOL O THE BEGINNERS BOOK.
    Berkeley, Calif.: Osborn/McGraw-Hill, 1982.

    A very well written treatment of how the
    components of a computer system function and
    how they are integrated.

Pantiel, Mindy, and Becky Peterson. KIDS, TEACHERS
    AND COMPUTERS. Englewood Cliffs, N.J.:
    Prentice-Hall, 1984.

    A well-written paperback outlining issues
    dealing with computers and education. A good
    classroom related treatment.

Papert, Seymour. MINDSTORMS: CHILDREN, COMPUTERS,
    AND POWERFUL IDEAS. New York: Basic Books,
    1980.

    Gives history of the Logo language and how it
    relates to the cognitive development of
    children.

PROGRAMS FOR THE HANDICAPPED. Shreve, Ohio:
    Prentke Romich Company, 1983.

    Lists and gives descriptions of software that
    can be used with the disabled.

Radin, Stephen, and Fayvian Lee. COMPUTERS IN THE
    CLASSROOM: A SURVIVAL GUIDE FOR TEACHERS. Palo
    Alto, Calif.: Science Research Associates,
    1984.

    Includes a discussion of computer hardware,
    software, and BASIC. Has a useful index of
    manufacturers, journals, and publishers.

Shank, Roger. THE COGNITIVE COMPUTER. Reading,
    Mass.: Addison-Wesley, 1984.

    Examines the relation between computer use and
    cognitive development and learning. Well
    written and easy to read.

Shelly, Gary B., and Thomas Cashman. COMPUTER
    FUNDAMENTALS FOR AN INFORMATION AGE. Brea,
    Calif.: Anaheim Press, 1984.

    Provides an excellent treatment of a variety of
    issues dealing with the structure and function
    of the computer system.

Suid, Murray. THE TEACHER-FRIENDLY COMPUTER BOOK.
    Palo Alto, Calif.: Monday Morning Books,
    1984.

    Shows teachers how to introduce computer
    literacy into the curriculum. Gives many ideas
    and activities teachers can carry out with
    children.

Taber, F. MICROCOMPUTERS IN SPECIAL EDUCATION:
    SELECTION AND DECISION MAKING PROCESS. Reston,
    Va.: The Council for Exceptional Children,
    1983.

    Introduces how computers are used in education
    with emphasis on special education.

TEXAS INSTRUMENTS PROGRAM DIRECTORY. Lubbock,
    Tex.: Texas Instruments, 1984.

    Gives a listing of hardware and software that
    can be used with Texas Instruments computers.

THE ADDISON-WESLEY BOOK OF APPLE COMPUTER SOFTWARE.
    Lawndale, Calif.: The Book Company, 1984.

    Lists and provides descriptions and evaluations
    of softwre for Apple computers. An Atari
    computer edition also available.

THE BASIC HANDBOOK: ENCYCLOPEDIA OF THE BASIC
    LANGUAGE. El Cajon, Calif.: Compusoft, 1981.

    An excellent reference book explaining how to
    use words in BASIC. Has good examples.

THE SOFTWARE DIECTORY. Columbus, Ohio: Linc
    Resources, 1984.

    Lists software for special education, including
    administration, educational, and professional
    applications.

TRS-80 SOFTWARE DIRECTORY.   Kansas City, Mo.: Vital
    Information, 1983.

    Gives listing and evaluation of software for
    TRS-80 computers.

Vockell, Edward L., and Robert H. Rivers.
    INSTRUCTIONAL COMPUTING FOR TODAY'S TEACHERS.
    Riverside, N.J.: Macmillan, 1984.

    Introduction to computing and how computers can
    be used for classroom applications with
    children.

Watt, Dan.   LEARNING WITH LOGO.   New York:
    McGraw-Hill, 1984.

    An excellent book with numerous examples of how
    to write programs in this language.
    Terrapin/Krell, Apple, and Commodore Logo
    versions available.

Way, Jacob.   COMPUTERS AND READING INSTRUCTION.
    Reading, Mass.:   Addison-Wesley, 1983.

    A well-documented book demonstrating how
    computers can be used in teaching reading and
    language arts.

Willis, Jerry, and Merl Miller.   COMPUTERS FOR
    EVERYBODY.   Beaverton, Ore.: Dilithium Press,
    1981.

    A paperback book introducing applications of
    the computer in today's society.

Willis, Jerry W.; D. LaMont Johnson; and Paul N.
    Dixon.   COMPUTERS, TEACHING AND LEARNING: A
    GUIDE TO USING COMPUTERS IN SCHOOLS.
    Beaverton, Ore.:   Dilithium Press, 1983.

    Outlines how computers are used in classrooms
    including sections on programming in BASIC,
    Pilot, and Logo.

Zaks, Rodnay.   DON'T! (OR HOW TO CARE FOR YOUR
    COMPUTER).   Berkeley: Sybex, 1981.

Provides practical suggestions for the care of the computer system and the computer environment.

JOURNALS FOR COMPUTERS AND EDUCATION

Byte
P.O. Box 590
Martinsville, NJ 08836

Includes many interesting but technically written articles on computer languages, equipment, and applications. A relatively sophisticated monthly publication.

Classroom Computer Learning
P.O. Box 266
Cambridge, MA 02138

A monthly publication with many practical articles on how computers are used in schools. Reviews hardware, software, and books, giving many useful ideas for teachers.

Computers Reading and Language Arts
P.O. Box 13039
Oakland, CA 94661

Provides articles on how computers are used in the teaching of reading and language arts. Also includes research in the field.

Creative Computing
P.O. Box 789-M
Morristown, NJ 07960

Offers a good selection of non-technical articles on a wide range of subjects giving many applications. Also reviews specific computer systems.

Educational Computers
P.O. Box 535
Cupertino, CA 95015

Provides educational applications of computers for schools at all grade levels. A non-technical journal published bi-monthly.

Educational Electronics
    One Lincoln Plaza
    New York, NY 10023

    Has articles about how computers can be used in
    schools as well as other articles on education
    and electronic media. This monthly publication
    has good review articles for hardware and
    software products.

Electronic Education
    P.O. Box 20221
    Tallahassee, FL 32304

    Has good articles on computers in education as
    well as electronic education in general. Is a
    non-technical journal easy for the novice to
    use, published during the academic year.

Electronic Learning
    Scholastic, Inc.
    902 Sylvan Av.
    Box 2001
    Englewood Cliffs, NJ 07632

    Has articles on electronic media in education
    including many useful ones about computers and
    their applications. This bi-monthly publication
    also gives analyses of new hardware and
    software.

Journal of Computer Based Instruction
    Association for the Development of
    Computer-Based Instructional Systems
    Computer Center, Western Washington University
    Bellingham, WA 98225

    Treats theoretical issues relating research
    reports to computers in education. Has well-
    written articles that are often technically
    oriented.

Journal of Computers in Mathematics and Science
    Teaching
    Austin, TX 78764

    Published quarterly with good articles on
    educational computing with particular emphasis
    on mathematics and science.

Mathematics and Computer Education Journal
    P.O. Box 158
    Old Bethpage, NY 11804

    Includes articles for teachers on applications
    of mathematics, programming, and the teaching
    of computer literacy.

Microcomputing
    Peterborough, NH 03458

    Offers a mix of theoretical and applied
    articles about computers. Includes articles on
    selected types of microcomputers.

Personal Computing
    50 Essex St.
    Rochelle Park, NJ 07662

    Includes articles on a wide range of subjects.
    Has regular columns of interest to a variety of
    users.

Popular Computing
    70 Main St.
    Peterborough, NH 03458

    Published monthly and includes a variety of
    types of articles written in a non-technical
    way. Offers reviews of hardware and software.

Softalk
    Softalk Publishing, Inc.
    10432 Burbank Blvd.
    North Hollywood, CA 91601

    Includes articles on a wide range of computer
    applications, including education, business,
    and home use.

Teaching and Computers
    Scholastic, Inc.
    902 Sylvan Av., Box 2001
    Englewood Cliffs, NJ 07632

    Written for the non-technical user, offering
    good applied articles on computers in
    education.

The Computing Teacher
        Department of Computers and Information Science
        University of Oregon
        Eugene, OR 97403

        Provides interesting articles on applications
        of computers to classrooms, including reviews
        of new hardware and software and books.
        Published during the academic year.

T.H.E. (Technological Horizens in Education) Journal
        Information Synergy
        P.O. Box 992
        Acton, MA 01720

        Offers articles on computers in education as
        well as other subjects. Has practically written
        articles on all types of computers and computer
        products.

The Logo and Educational Computing Journal
        Suite 219
        1320 Stony Brook Rd.
        Stony Brook, NY 11790

        Offers articles on applications of Logo to
        classrooms as well as articles on a wide range
        of subjects.

Window
        469 Pleasant St.
        Cambridge, MA 02172

        A computer magazine on disk offering articles
        on a wide range of education related subjects.
        Includes well-written software reviews.

GLOSSARY

Abacus: A calculating device developed by the Chinese five or six thousand years ago.

ACCEPT: Programming statement in Pilot letting computer treat several user inputs as being correct.

Accessories: A name for peripherals and other materials used with computers.

Acoustical Modem: See Modem.

Adaptive Firmware: A circuitry card allowing the computer to receive input and generate output by a variety of means.

Adaptive Hardware: Hardware designed for use with the handicapped.

Address: Memory locations in the main memory of the computer.

AND: A conjunction used in many computer languages.

Antistatic Mats: Electrically grounded floor mats to prevent transfer of static electricity.

Arithmetic Logic Unit: Part of the computer that carries out arithmetic operations and makes logical comparisons.

ARRAY: Programming statement in Pascal that defines a family of related variables.

ASCII Code: American Standard Code for Information Interchange. Binary code that converts numbers and letters into numbers the computer uses.

301

Assembly Language: A computer language closely related to machine language.

Base 2: A numeric system using 0's and 1's on which machine language is based.

Base 10: The numeric system using the digits 0-9 on which our counting system is based.

BASIC: Beginners' All-Purpose Symbolic Instruction Code. A programming language available for most microcomputers.

BEGIN: Programming statement in Pascal used to start a programming section.

Bidirectional Printing: Characteristic of printers that print left to right and right to left across a page.

Binary Code: A numeric code system by which computers store and represent data.

Bit: The smallest unit of information handled internally by the computer.

Boot: Process by which computers take information from magnetically stored media and load it into the computer's memory.

Brownout: Low voltage values supplied by the power company.

Bug: Errors or mistakes within a computer program.

Bulletin Board: An information service accessible from computer to computer by modem connection.

Byte: Usually comprised of 8 bits representing characters or numbers.

CAR: Lisp programming command causing the first element of a list to be printed.

Cartridge: Data storage device similar to cassette tape.

Cassette Recorder: Tape recorder used as computer input device.

Cassette Tape: Used to magnetically store
information by cassette recorders.

CDR: Lisp expression causing all but the first
element of a list to be printed.

Central Processing Unit (CPU): Acts as the brain of
the computer controlling everything it does.

COBOL: Computer language often used for business
applications.

Compiler: Translates high level languages into
machine language within the computer.

COMPUTE: Pascal statement that performs
computations and stores results.

Computer: Device able to receive information,
process it, and generate user defined output.

Computer Literacy: Being familiar with a wide
range of computer skills.

CONC: Lisp command used to join lists.

Conjunction: Programming statement used to make
logic comparisons.

CONS: Lisp command used to extend lists.

Control Key: Keyboard key used in conjunction
with other keys to perform special functions.

Control Unit: Part of CPU that translates
instructions into machine language, directs
sequences of operations to be performed, and
regulates other parts of the CPU.

CPU: See Central Processing Unit.

CRT: Means cathode ray tube. Another name for the
computer monitor.

Cursor: An indicator on the monitor screen
showing user where the next character will be
placed.

Daisywheel: Printer element producing typewriter
quality letters.

Database Management Software: Programs that store, sort, and retrieve information.

Debouncing Routine: Software used to prevent keyboards from being oversensitive to the touch.

Debug: Process of correcting errors in a computer program.

Deckwriter: Input device by which user gives input and receives output as paper copy only.

Default Values: Preassigned program values set by the manufacturer that can be changed by the user.

Descenders: Print characteristic where parts of some typed letters extend below the line of type.

Digital: Device that can perform arithmetic calculations.

Disk: Used to magnetically store information.

Disk Drive: Peripheral device used to transmit magnetically stored information.

Disk Heads: Part of disk drive that reads information from floppy disks.

Disk Operating System (DOS): Program that lets communication take place between the computer and the disk.

DIV: Pascal command giving integer quotient when one number is divided by another.

Documentation: Written materials describing how a program functions.

DOS: See Disk Operating System.

Dot Matrix Printer: Prints characters by using a series of closely spaced dots.

Double Density Disks: Have closely spaced tracks so large amounts of information can be stored.

Double Sided Disks: Disks than can store information on both sides.

Drill and Practice Software: Computer programs designed to give user practice at a task or process.

Dry Cleaners: Dry materials that clean disk heads by a rubbing action.

EBCDIC: Extended Binary Coded Decimal Interchange Code. Binary code that converts numbers and letters into numbers the computer can use.

Edit: To make changes in a computer software program.

EDVAC: Electronic Discrete Variable Automatic Computer. A first generation computer.

80-Column Text Card: Accessory that permits 80 columns of text to be displayed across the monitor screen at one time.

Electrostatic Charge: Electrical charges that can cause disruptions in the functioning of a computer.

END: Statement used in programming languages to tell the computer a section of the program has been completed.

ENIAC: Electronic Numerical Integrator and Computer. A first generation computer.

Enter Key: Depressed when user wishes to communicate with the computer. Same as RETURN Key.

Escape Key: Found on some keyboards to be used with some programs to perform special functions.

File: Collections of information treated as a unit in database management programs.

Firmware: Instructions built into the ROM memory of the computer.

First Generation Computers: Computers that used vacuum tubes for memory and to perform logic functions.

FLASH: A BASIC command used with Apple computers to highlight sections of text.

Floppy Disk: Computer disk.

FOR ... NEXT: Conditional loop used in many
   computer languages.

Formatting: Process of preparing a disk to hold
   information.

Forth: A high level computer language.

FORTRAN: Computer language often used for science
   and mathematics applications.

Friction Paper Feed: Non-perforated paper fed to
   the print head by a roller.

Game Paddles: Input device using a knob and button
   to control cursor movements.

GET: BASIC statement letting user give input during
   execution of a program.

GOTO: Unconditional statement used in many
   programming languages.

GR: Statement used with Apple computers to enter
   low resolution graphics mode.

Graphics: Dots, lines, colors, and shapes drawn
   with the computer.

Graphics Tablets: Input device letting user draw
   lines with a stylus.

Hard Copy: Paper copy produced using a printer.

Hard Disk: Information storage device able to store
   more information than a floppy disk.

Hardware: Components comprising the computer
   system.

High Level Language: Language such as COBOL whose
   instructions are first translated into machine
   language before they are executed.

HOME: Command used with Apple computers that brings
   cursor to top left position on the monitor screen.

IF ... THEN: Programming statement used in some
languages to make logical comparisons.

IF ... THEN ... ELSE: Programming statement used in
some languages to make logical comparisons.

Impact Printers: Form characters by pressing pins
or characters against inked ribbon when typed copy
is produced.

Initializing: Preparing a disk to store
information.

INPUT: BASIC programming statement used in
interactive programs.

Input: Process of providing information to the
computer.

Input Device: Peripheral device that passes
information to the computer.

Interactive Program: Software requiring user to
input information during program execution.

Interface: Connects peripheral device to computer.

INVERSE: BASIC command used with Apple computers to
reverse background color of monitor screen.

Jacks: Internal or external electrical plug on a
computer.

Joysticks: Input device consisting of a box, stick,
and one or more buttons.

JUMP: Pilot programming command causing computer to
move to another section of the program.

K: Means kilobyte and refers to the number 1024.
Used to give number of bytes of RAM memory.

Large Scale Integration (LSI): Inclusion of large
amounts of computer circuitry on a single silicon
chip.

Laser Jet Printers: Very fast printers forming
characters by spraying jets of ink.

LET: Command used in some languages to assign
   values to a variable.

Letter Quality Printer: Gives typewriter quality
   type as output.

Light Pen: Lets user input values directly on
   monitor screen.

Line Filter: Accessory that protects computer
   against power surges.

Lisp: Language used to write interactive programs.

LIST: BASIC command that lists programming
   statements.

Load: Passing of instruction from stored medium to
   internal computer memory.

Logo: Computer language often used with young
   children.

Loop: Set of programming commands that are designed
   to repeat.

Low Resolution: Graphics mode in which screen is
   divided into 40 columns and 40 rows of graphics
   blocks.

LSI: See Large Scale Integration.

Machine Language: Operational languages of
   computers written in binary code.

Mainframe Computer: The CPU of large, powerful
   computers.

MARK I: First generation computer developed by
   Howard Aiken.

MATCH: Pascal statement comparing user response to
correct ones.

Memory Buffer: Storage area used to temporarily
   hold data.

Menu: Selection of options user can choose from
   during execution of program.

Microcomputer: Computer whose CPU is a
  microprocessor.

Microprocessor: CPU of microcomputers consisting of
  one silicon chip.

Microsecond: One millionth of a second.

Millisecond: One thousandth of a second.

Minicomputer: Computer more powerful than a
  microcomputer but less powerful than mainframe
  machine.

Modem: Modulator/demodulator. Permits computer
  information to be transmitted by telephone lines.

Monitor: Visual display unit used with computers.

Monochrome Monitor: Non-color CRT providing one
  background color.

Mouse: Sophisticated input device using roller for
  input.

Mouthstick: Adaptive input deviced for some
  handicapped users.

Music Synthesizer: Peripheral using piano-like
  keyboard for computer input.

Network: One or more computers connected to main
  computer.

NEW: Programming statement used with Apple
  computers to cancel INVERSE and FLASH commands.

Numeric Keypad: Calculator-like collection of keys
  useful when performing successive mathematics
  operations.

Optical Reader: Sophisticated input device using
  typed copy for input.

Output: Receiving program results from computer.

Output Device: Peripherals that generate computer
  output.

Overscanning: All characters do not fit on monitor screen.

Pascal: An all-purpose computer language.

PEEK: Programming statement speaking directly to a computer memory address.

Peripheral Device: Accessory added to increase capabilities of computer system.

Pilot: Language designed for people who write computer assisted instruction materials.

Power Strip: Collection of closely spaced electrical outlets.

PRINT: Command used in several languages to produce computer output.

Procedure: Name given to programs written in Logo.

Programmer: Person who writes software for a computer.

Proportional Spacing: Printers allowing characters to be spaced according to width of letters (that is, according to the proportion of the letter) when printed on paper.

Puff Switch: Input device for severely physically handicapped users.

Punched Cards: Input given to card reader.

RAM: See Random Access Memory.

Random Access Memory (RAM): General purpose memory utilized when user gives instructions to the computer.

Read Only Memory (ROM): Programmed by manufacturer and unalterable by user.

Record: Defines one set of information in database management program.

REM: BASIC statement letting programmer make non-executable comments in a program.

REMARK: Statement in Pilot letting teacher make comments that are not executed when program is run.

REPEAT ... UNTIL: Logic statement in Pascal.

Resolution: Reflects number of points that can be placed on monitor screen at one time.

RETURN Key: See ENTER key.

RF Modulator: Peripheral used to connect computer to television set.

Rollover: Keyboards that temporarily store information in a memory buffer.

Roll Paper: Non-perforated paper used with friction feed type printers.

ROM: See Read Only Memory.

RUN: Command causing programming instruction to be executed.

SAVE: Command telling computer to store information on cassette tape or disk.

Second Generation Computers: Machines using transistors for logic and memory circuits.

Sector: Portion of track on computer disk.

SETQ: Statement defining functions in Lisp programs.

SHIFT: Keyboard key depressed to access upper case letters and some special characters.

Silicon Chip: Small piece of silicon containing an integrated circuit.

Simulation Software: Software depicting real life situations.

Single Density: How tracks can be structured on computer disks.

Soft Copy: Any computer output that is not paper copy.

Speech Synthesizer: Converts computer output to audible speech patterns.

SPEED: Statement used with Apple computers to set rate at which characters are displayed.

Spikes: Abnormally high electrical voltage levels.

Spread Sheet Software: Programs used to perform mathematical operations.

Surge Protectors: Prevents damage to computer equipment by electrical spikes.

Telecommunication: Communication between computers by telephone or electrical connection.

TEXT: Statement causing Apple computers to leave graphics mode.

Text Window: Portion of screen provided in some programs giving user helpful information.

Third Generation Computers: Inclusion of integrated circuits on single chips as part of computers' circuitry.

Time Sharing: Several input devices connected to central computer used on first-come first-serve basis.

Touch Sensitive Keyboard: Keyboard not requiring keys to be depressed.

Track: Electrically established concentric circle on computer disk where information is magnetically stored.

Tractor Fed Paper: Paper with tear-off perforated edges used with many printers.

Transistor: Electrical device in Second Generation Computers for logic circuits and computer memory.

Turtle: Triangular shaped cursor used in Logo.

Tutorial Software: Programs designed to help users reinforce concepts and ideas.

TYPE: Pilot statement causing text to be printed on monitor screen.

Underscanning: Monitor screen is not filled with characters.

UNIAC: Sophisticated First Generation computer.

User Friendly: Easy-to-use computer or software program.

User Groups: People using similar machines that share information.

Utility Programs: Software performing a variety of teacher related functions.

Vacuum Tubes: Used for logic and memory circuits in First Generation computers.

VAR: Statement meaning variable used in some languages like Pascal.

Wet Cleaners: Clean disk heads by rubbing action of a wetted surface.

Wet/Dry Cleaners: Accomplish cleaning by rubbing wet and dry surfaces over the disk head.

WHILE ... DO: Conditional statement used in Pascal.

Word Processing: Using software to write, edit, and print documents.

Word Wraparound: Feature of word processors that prevents broken words being left at the end of a line of text.

Write: To store information on cassette tape of disk.

WRITELN: Programming statement causing hard copy output in some computer languages.

Write Protect Tab: Plastic strip used with disks to prevent disk from being erased or written on.